'The hectic, almost MASH-like atmosphere of UNTAC is well captured by Carol Livingston in *Gecko Tails*... She has a sharp, humorous eye, and notices the good as well as the bad and ugly in the UN system... Livingston's descriptions of brave and feckless UN officials, uninformed reporters, and the relations of both with the often bewildered Cambodians, makes *Gecko Tails* a funny book and a touching one; it gives an excellent account of the day-to-day impact of a UN force on an impoverished country. Anyone interested in Cambodia should read it' *New York Review of Books*

'Urban Cambodia has the sleazy glamour of a country forced into the spotlight... Everyone has an atrocity story. Humour helps them survive and Livingston stresses that positive survival rather than buried anguish is what outsiders should expect, respect and celebrate' *Glasgow Herald*

'Funny and touching... *Gecko Tails* is a political travel book about a strange time in a strange country; it strips away some of the cliches of Cambodia, and is very good... It is a fine addition to the bookshelf of any armchair traveller and an excellent introduction to anyone who actually wants to sample the joy of Cambodia. Livingston does the country, and herself, proud' *Sunday Times*

D0167648

Carol Livingston lives in Bangkok and is the Southeast Asia columnist for the *Montreal Gazette*. Her other books include *The Wire*, a novel about Cambodia.

Gecko Tails
A Journey Through Cambodia

CAROL LIVINGSTON

PHŒNIX

A PHOENIX PAPERBACK

First published in Great Britain
by Weidenfeld & Nicolson in 1996
This paperback edition published in 1997
by Phoenix, an imprint of Orion Books Ltd,
Orion House, 5 Upper St Martin's Lane,
London WC2H 9EA

Reissued 2000

A CIP catalogue record for this book
is available from the British Library.

ISBN 0 75380 005 5

Typeset at The Spartan Press Ltd,
Lymington, Hants
Printed and bound in Great Britain by
The Guernsey Press Co. Ltd,
Guernsey, Channel Islands

Contents

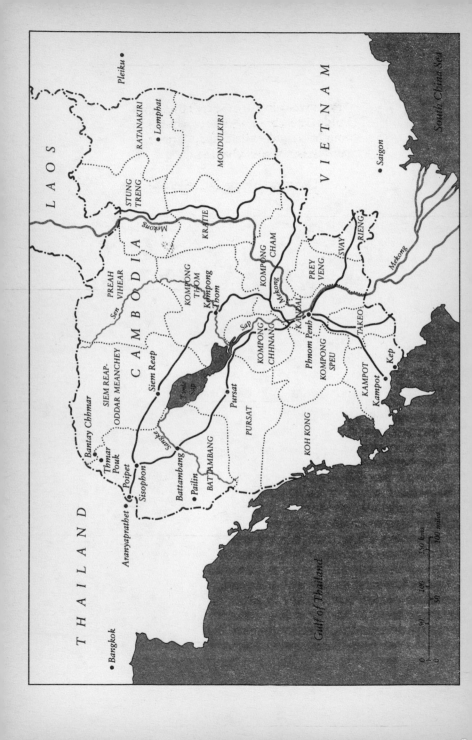

'After a week in the country I thought I could write a book. After six months I thought I could write a story. After a year I didn't know what to say.'

Unknown Rwandan relief worker

Somebody always gets there first

We were packed in a smog-surrounded tourist minivan stuck on a Bangkok flyover when the Professional Traveller started talking. A four-hour trip from the quiet Thai island of Samet had turned into six hours of Thai Traffic Hell. When Dante described the rings of Purgatory in the Inferno he forgot the Bangkok rush hour. Unfinished high-rises and skyscrapers rose in front and on left and right, heavy goods vehicles, motorcycles, and shiny Japanese cars trailed behind us indefinitely, sellers of *pad thai* and fruit peppered the pavements below.

'None of us are going anywhere quickly,' the Professional Traveller proclaimed, shaking his head as two impatient passengers, desperate for a smoke, got out to walk down the highway between the steaming cars. Looking at his diving watch, his pony-tail sticking between his back and the vinyl seat cover, the Professional Traveller figured we had another two hours caught in traffic. Meanwhile he regaled us with stories from Bangkok's last round of student riots, the Philippines during Aquino's election, Singapore when transvestites still dragged themselves down Bugis Street. At 30, the Professional Traveller had been everywhere, and held no plans to return home to Vancouver. He made enough money to live by playing music or by cooking in a restaurant a friend owned in Kuala Lumpur.

'Where are you headed next?' he asked. I had a funny feeling that wherever our destination was, the Professional Traveller had already been there.

I glanced at Amanda, my travelling partner, who was leaning against the tinted van window. She was feigning sleep beneath her Ray-Bans and a two month old issue of *Cosmopolitan*. Our

Girl Guide tour of South-east Asia had started because she was looking for a job. I was looking for something to write about.

Our only travelling pact had been that if Amanda could have a week on an island, I could have a week wherever I wanted.

Amanda chose Ko Samet, a small, white sand island shimmering idyllically off the southern Thai coast. We were both looking for romance, but we were stuck with each other. The only single man we found who was not attached to a Bangkok hooker brought specially to the island for a vacation week of sun, sex and surf was a sleazy Afghan waiter. The Mujahidin Mugger had good dope, bad come-on lines and the impeccable timing of a professional letch, leaping from behind the beach rocks just as you unhooked your bikini top. It was like being trapped in a bad Benny Hill sketch.

The next week was my choice. Once, when I was young, Jackie Kennedy had appeared in a 1967 edition of *Life* magazine stumbling across Angkor Wat's stones in the sharp jungle heat. The 1,000-year-old temples of Angkor had looked glamorous and forbidden, a place few travellers went. In the intervening two and a half decades war had stopped tourists visiting the great wat. Any place I wasn't supposed to go had sounded great to me as a kid. It still did.

I told the Professional Traveller we were headed to Cambodia.

Amanda smiled tightly. I assumed she was trying to forget that she'd started this gig. We both had been hung-over and overdrawn six weeks earlier when she plopped down on a chair in my office and announced, 'London sucks. I need a tan. Anyone want to try Club Med Kampuchea?'

As we sat in our stalled minibus, the United Nations Transitional Authority in Cambodia (UNTAC), was attempting to govern Cambodia and oversee elections in accordance with the 1991 Paris Peace Agreement, signed by the four factions which had warred throughout western Cambodia during the last decade.

Luckily for us, UNTAC's presence had caused Cambodia's lengthy visa process to be abolished several weeks before. No one knew if the fragile skin of stability the UN presence had painted across the country would break. Political violence was increasing, party workers were being assassinated and offices grenaded. If the UN-brokered settlement didn't last, this might be the only time to see the ruins for another 20 years.

The Professional Traveller, of course, had just returned from Phnom Penh, taking advantage of the UNTAC peace. We were right to go to Cambodia before it got too crowded, he concurred. The Professional Traveller had seen a tourist coach parked in front of Angkor Wat, on the abandoned site of the art deco Grand Hotel des Ruines which the Khmer Rouge had burnt in the '70s. It would be easy now for backpackers to buy a Cambodian visa on Bangkok's Khao San Road, where teenage travellers, drop-outs or skinflints stayed in cheap guest-houses. In Cambodia there was no hassle over drugs and the beaches were good. And Cambodia was as close to a war zone as most travellers would ever get.

The place had floored the Professional Traveller. 'I mean, I've been in revolutions before but, man, Cambodia was wild. There is no place like it, no place...' he said, shaking his head. 'It's not Thailand, not Thailand at all, eh?' he continued, staring out of the side window at the concrete bridge that held us 70 feet off the ground, above yet another Bangkok flyover. 'Like, I took the train from Phnom Penh to Battambang. It leaves at six in the morning and I sat on the roof. It's cheaper than the seats inside and you can take good pictures. The flatbed car in the very front, that's free,' the Professional Traveller drawled nonchalantly, 'but that's the car that hits the mines first. About an hour outside of Battambang, at this place called Moung Roussei, the train stopped. It was dusk. We sat. We sat. Then the fucking Khmer Rouge attacked! There was AK fire, there were rockets going over!'

'I don't believe a word of this...' whispered Amanda, who had pulled the *Cosmo* across her face to block the sun and was now speaking through Cindy Crawford's navel. The Professional Traveller, entranced by his own tale, talked over her.

'Man, I was lying flat with my pack on one side, thinking it was at least some protection. There's gunfire going off everywhere. And the Khmers are laughing because they've been through this all before and they're looking at me to see how the *barang* is acting. They thought I was pretty funny. They've had, what, 20 years of war? So they just lie down because there's nothing you can do except wait. And suddenly I hear this voice very politely asking, "S'vous plait, Monsieur." And I look up and it's this kid soldier. They have these soldiers travelling with the train, in case they get attacked. And he, very politely, takes my sleeping bag and says, "Merci, Monsieur." Then he sets my sleeping bag under his mortar to brace the thing, and starts firing back at the Khmer Rouge! Man, it was wild,' he said shaking his head. 'There is no place like Cambodia.'

*   *   *   *

'Cambodia. It was a place name ... accompanied in my imagination by tinkling, percussive, music,' wrote Norman Lewis 40 years ago in *A Dragon Apparent*. But now the tinkling is more likely to be drowned out by a blaring cover version of 'Woolly Bully' or a 1970s hit, still being recycled in popular South-east Asian culture 20 years later. Romantic expectations of what a traveller will find in the kingdom of Angkor are frequently at odds with Cambodian reality.

For Europeans and their cultural cousins, Cambodia has always been a fantasy. In the middle of the nineteenth century the French first saw the temples of Angkor and helped resurrect, or create, memories of the once great empire of the Khmers, the main ethnic group in Cambodia, which had ruled a thousand years earlier. Sweeping the Cambodian King Sisowath and his royal dancers to the Paris Exhibition of 1906, the belle époque colonialists revelled in a fantasy of a gentle land peopled by graceful, bejewelled, living *apsaras*, the young women depicted on Angkor's walls. In the 1950s and '60s Prince Sihanouk pretended that Cambodia was the 'Switzerland of the Orient', a well-ordered and democratic country which fell into hardship only due to American intervention in the 1970s, rather than a subsistence level oligarchy with an already unstable history.

During the 1970s, the Khmer Rouge begat the most ruthless and destructive vision of Cambodia. They wanted to eliminate all foreign influence and return Cambodia to 'Year Zero', a time in which the imagined former glories of Angkor would be restored to the Khmer people by Pol Pot's xenophobic, nationalistic foot soldiers. No one will ever know how many people died during their four-year reign. For the United Nations, the hope that Cambodia can forget its past and establish true peace and a fair rule of law after spending several billion dollars on elections may unfortunately turn out to be yet another illusion.

To individuals who travel there, Cambodia can mean many things – a different life; a mystery to be unravelled; a place in which to hide, to be excited, to cool out, or to be scared stiff. Cambodia changes constantly. Nothing stays static. It is not always possible to separate fact from rumour, or to take what you see in Cambodia at face value.

Some names in the book have been changed, especially of Cambodians, and sometimes nationalities. People in Cambodia, both Cambodians and foreigners, dislike going on record: Cambodians fear persecution and foreigners fear they will no longer be able to work easily in the country. Other people had no idea when speaking that I would write about them later, nor did I at the time; it didn't seem fair to use real names. If this were investigative journalism precise names would be important, but it is not. Stories are more important than names for my purposes.

In a country whose history has often been shaped by other nations, writing about the foreigners' impact on Cambodia, and Cambodia's impact on the foreigners during the UN stay, and what Cambodia was like after they departed, seemed a good way to examine Cambodia's history and its re-entry into the international community. It also seemed a way to see how, despite the good will and intentions, the international community *didn't* change Cambodia.

Like all books, this one can only reflect a unique and particular time. I refer to the political group which grew out of the Indo-Chinese Communist Party in Cambodia as the Khmer Rouge or KR, rather than as the soldiers of Democratic Kampuchea, because most readers will know them as the Khmer Rouge. The infamous Pol Pot, however, I refer to as Saloth Sar, his given name. The name Pol Pot is a fiction, a meaningless Khmer name designed to imbue Saloth Sar with mystery and power and hide truth. Saloth Sar doesn't deserve power and mystery.

In the end, though, my Cambodia is a fantasy too.

In the beginning

'The good news is the bathroom has a power shower. The bad news is the fuse-box is hanging next to it and someone kinda forgot to put a cover on,' Amanda announced as we looked around our Phnom Penh hotel room.

She peered at the plastic-covered hotel rules pinned to the door. 'Ummmm, number five is interesting: "ALL KINDS OF ARMS AND EXPLOSIVES ARE NOT ALLOWED IN THE HOTEL."'

The Professional Traveller had been right: for a small city Phnom Penh had more of a buzz than anywhere I had ever been. The town felt like Weston-Super-Mare meets Beirut topped with the madness of Times Square on a Saturday night. Densely packed schools of buzzing motorcycles swept down the street in the Phnom Penh rush hour, zipping past islands of white Toyota Landcruisers and pickups with 'UN' painted boldly on the doors. Cyclo drivers lethargically pedalled entire families squeezed and stacked onto a single seat, sooty burlap bags filled with charcoal, or a crewcut-sporting, shorts-wearing, burly foreign military man – maybe American, maybe Canadian, maybe German.

The foreigners, *barang* in Khmer, frequently sported a camera, either a small 'foolproof' 35 mm automatic or the latest Nikon wonder. Green and red Fuji film signs wrapped Achar Mean, Phnom Penh's main commercial drag which ran below our window, in permanent Christmas-colour decorations. Half the shops seemed to be photo developers processing the UNTACers' happy snaps or carefully posed pictures from the Western-influenced, middle-class wedding parties which paraded in the parks – men in black dinner-jackets, women in voluminous, lace-and-bow-covered Princess Di wedding dresses sewn from bright white silk. Despite the proud nuptial affluence, reminders of over 20 years of devastation and neglect were everywhere along Achar Mean. Deep, debris-filled open manholes punctuated the broken sidewalks as we wandered to the Chinese shops to buy beers and bottled water for the fridge.

Amanda was depressed as we watched the evening traffic from the sooty, skinny window balcony. She had recently finished her MA in International Relations. The MA, Amanda said, stood for 'Many Applications'. Oxfam, Save the Children, Amnesty International, International Red Cross – Amanda had been rejected by all these non-governmental organizations (NGOs). Her higher education contained no practical skill. Aid and development agencies wanted practitioners, not policy makers. Faced with continuing as London's most erudite barmaid and realizing she couldn't actually do anything, Amanda had decided she was tailor-made for the United Nations. The problem was UN jobs were coveted and usually obtained because of whom you knew.

'Look, you do have skills . . .,' I consoled Amanda as we headed to dinner and I punched the 'down' button on the brushed-steel elevator, the only Monorom renovation in 20 years.

The Monorom's room price was three times our daily accommodation budget. A sudden influx of UNTAC staff and Phnom Penh's run-down housing stock meant that any accommodation with an indoor toilet was ridiculously expensive. Until 1989 the Vietnamese-backed government which overthrew the Khmer Rouge had restricted overseas non-governmental organization and UN workers to two hotels. One of the foreigners' gulags had been the Monorom. The good-deed-doers had since left the hotel but identifying stickers were still glued to the doors – Mennonite Central Committee, United Nations High Commission for Refugees, CARE. Tape from the missing pictures and posters hung up to give the musty old hotel some feeling of home still clung to the elderly, pre-Khmer Rouge paint work, making the Monorom look like an abandoned college dorm at the end of term.

'Such as?' Amanda's tone dripped disbelief. Amanda was falling into pre-interview despair, where staying in bed and watching CNN repeats beat going out and actually looking for a job. I loyally tried to buck up her spirits.

'Such as all those things we made up on your resumé. Jesus Christ, you just got here, don't give up yet.'

We slid into our vinyl banquette seats in the hotel restaurant as the electricity flickered out in the Monorom and across the street. The only light now came from headlights careening outside along Achar Mean and from the candles the black bow-tied waiters were slipping onto each table. 'We'll find a cheaper place to live tomorrow and then you can start making the rounds. Remember, when the going gets tough . . .'

'. . . The tough hire someone else to do the work for them. Are you sure you wouldn't like to do my interviews? You're so much better at bullshitting than I am,' Amanda leant imploringly over her tablemat, giving me her yearning puppy look.

'Nonsense, look at the amount you're shovelling right now. Where's the Cambodian dishes?' I asked the waiter.

'Is dried fish. Maybe foreigner I don't think like so well. Very salty.' The waiter flipped my menu forward two pages but shook his head. He looked about 15 with a shy, full-faced smile and a deep, half-moon shrapnel scar beneath his left eye. 'Excuse me please. What nationality?'

Amanda said that although I was American, we both lived in London. Kek, the waiter, was 19 and lived with three of his sisters and one sister's husband on the airport road. His father and two brothers-in-law had been killed during the Khmer Rouge period. His mother had died from sickness the year after the Khmer Rouge fled. The shrapnel scar came when a shell had landed nearby when he was five.

Kek took English classes at six each morning, then worked to save money to go to university. Please, Kek asked, did students have to pay for university in London and the United States? Maybe he would like to be a teacher, but teachers didn't make enough money to live in Cambodia, so he would have to find another job. He didn't leave the Monorom until almost ten each night and always took a motorcycle taxi home, although he was scared at the roadblocks. Sometimes the soldiers shot at the motos. Please, Kek added breathlessly, he wanted to practise English as much as possible.

We ordered the dried fish salad, called *trei gean cheamuy*

salat, and two omelettes. Kek smiled, bowed slightly, and scooted back to the kitchen. There were only two other tables taken in the restaurant. One party included a goateed man in a safari suit pontificating about what 'these Khmers' needed. Discipline and learning to work was high on his list. With an English class at six am and working until ten at night, Kek seemed pretty disciplined to me.

'Excuse me. Can I ask question?' Kek said, bowing his head as Amanda crunched into the first bite of *trei gean* and murmured, 'Ummm, dried and salted fish . . .'

'Please, how far is North Korea from London?'

Kek seemed disappointed when we told him London to Pyongyang wasn't commuting distance, and wandered off. Three minutes later Kek was back, looking for any excuse to talk. How did we like our fish?

'Ummmmmmm, gooooood,' we lied in chorus. Kek smiled and returned to the waiting station. After conferring with a waitress dressed in a green silk *sampot*, the traditional ankle-length Khmer skirt, Kek shot back to our table.

'Please, when do you go back to your home?'

'Maybe a couple of weeks.'

'Thank you,' Kek smiled, nodding his head again, and hurried back to the waiting station. More high level waiter discussions ensued. Kek kept glancing back at our table and made a few false starts, but seemed to think he really shouldn't interrupt again. The minute our omelettes were finished, Kek rushed to take the plates.

'Please, when you return to your home, could you mail a letter to my friend in Korea? He is there studying engineering four years more,' Kek added, but his face said he expected us to say no. He burst into smiles when we agreed.

Amanda and I walked up the service stairs to our room by candlelight. Later I became accustomed to an occasional sound of gunfire in the night – Cambodians would shoot at the moon when it was full, at the skies to start the rain, and occasionally, it must be said, at each other to steal a motor-cycle. I don't know what the spurt of automatic gunfire signi-fied that first night, and cowering with Amanda behind the bathroom's concrete walls I didn't care, but at least Amanda stopped arguing about who got the bed next to the window.

I thought about Kek's friend and wondered how a Cambodian had ended up studying engineering in North Korea. As I fell asleep, the din of Achar Mean faded to a lonely buzz as an occasional Honda, having paid off the checkpoint now shaking down traffic, sputtered home.

*   *   *   *

In the morning we hopped on motorcycle taxis, often driven by students, penniless farmers or underpaid civil servants and set off for the UNTAC headquarters. Schools of bats swung in the tree branches above the UN's white pre-fab offices as Amanda attacked the personnel department and I applied for a press pass. I hoped to put together a book proposal and a few travel articles to pay for the trip. Accredited journalists could book free UN flights around the country, if there was space.

The press office seemed unimpressed by my credentials, a note from a literary agent friend supporting the book idea, but they took my application anyway. The UN had to accredit anyone who carried anything resembling a credential. Who could say that *Soybean Digest* or *Ogulambuphu Weekly Courier* didn't have the same right as *The New York Times* to UN facilities and information, except possibly *The New York Times*? Enterprising backpackers had even used fake Khao San Road press IDs to obtain a UN pass for a helicopter whirl across a recently quieted war zone. By UNTAC's end, nearly 3,000 journalist IDs had been distributed.

In half an hour the daily press briefing would start, so I waited. Two dozen journalists were scattered among the sterile conference room's white plastic chairs; they all seemed to know each other and I felt like the new girl in school. Many were Japanese. The women dressed conservatively, except for a tall blonde in baggy Vietnamese trousers, black sunglasses and stenographer's notebook. A red check *krama*, the cotton Cambodian scarf, was wrapped around her head – Lois Lane gone cosmic.

'What a pseud . . .,' I thought, sitting at the back in my teeshirt, jeans, and trainers, an elegant international style known as Haute Slob.

The press spokesman introduced a tall, white-haired British

United Nations naval observer, who had been kidnapped by the Khmer Rouge. Unlike the UN battalions which protected the UN's operations and personnel, naval or military observers (Unnos or Unmos) were by definition unarmed. All UN military personnel, however, wore a robin's egg blue beret like the Unno wore now.

'. . . I must say being shot at concentrates the mind wonderfully, especially when you've got nothing to shoot back with,' the Unno said in true Jack Hawkins stiff upper lip understatement. The naval observer and his companions had passed their captive hours by giving the Khmer Rouge guerillas English lessons.

The Unno's Khmer Rouge experience was a press officer's dream. There was drama, a happy ending and something for everyone to write about. Cambodia and UNTAC were assured of media play today. Thank god a photogenic Brit had been kidnapped and not a Bangladeshi or a Namibian. The story wouldn't have earned nearly as many column inches. Ramrod straight and firm jawed, in real life the Unno was still a public schoolboy at 50. He was a roisterous party-goer who could pass hours in dancing restaurants endlessly reciting scatological doggerel to bar girls who didn't understand English. Today, however, the Brit was an upstanding action-man hero, just the face the UN military wanted to present. The four or five hundred word news pieces filed on his adventure weren't enough to also capture his character's other facets and make him flesh, not a cartoon.

The briefing finished, the reporters scattered to file. Amanda and I crossed the traffic circle to climb the steps to Wat Phnom, a small temple on a hill around which the city was allegedly built. Several middle-aged French tourists were leaving the *wat*, leaning on the temple's doorjambs and columns as they slipped their feet into loafers and espadrilles. A boy barely school-age tried to sell a sixtyish blonde woman in a pink polo shirt maps and books about Cambodia. Looking as if she didn't know what to do, the woman kept her eyes firmly sighted on the temple and turned away, kicking at her shoe in an attempt to find it without glancing down, pretending the boy wasn't there.

According to legend, Phnom Penh was founded by a woman named Penh. Once the Sap river rose high, and Penh found floating in the flood waters a branch on which the leaves had transformed into shining golden buddhas. Rather than rush to the nearest pawn shop, Penh took the branch as a sign of good fortune and founded a temple on Wat Phnom hill. Inside the small temple, wildly coloured, blinking fluorescent clocks were mounted around a statue of Buddha. Tinsel hung everywhere.

'All it needs is lava lamps,' Amanda declared breathlessly as we exited. Vendors squatted by reed cages filled with birds that were balanced on the steps. Buddhist worshippers could buy and release a bird in order to attain good fortune or merit in the next life. Amanda, looking for job-hunting luck, pulled out some *riel*. She took a small sparrow between her palms and threw it up to the sky.

'Excuse me, madams, do you need a place to stay? I have a number one guest-house, okay? You come with me in my car. I take you there, then I take you anywhere you want to go. You can trust me. I drive everyone, I translate for everyone. I work for *The New York Times*, I work for *Herald Tribune*, BBC, everybody use Sok Sin as translator. Right now I work for *Los Angeles Times* but he goes file so he tell me to come at two. I try to find people for my guest-house. I have friends in Paris! New York! London! I know Julie Christie! Here's my card!' Sok Sin shoved a gold printed white rectangle into my hand and opened the back door to a white Toyota Corolla.

'When I came back first in '85 Sok Sin was the only cyclo driver who had business cards printed. He was always hustling. He slept in his cyclo but he had business cards,' a photographer told me later.

'Yes, we go now. I take you where you want to go, yes please. Other hotels very expensive. Sok Sin give good value. Get in please, now,' Sok Sin waved frantically at the back seat. What could we lose? I agreed and slipped in.

'Are you nuts?' Amanda whispered through the window.

'Look, we need a new place and he's got one.'

'You don't know who this guy is!'

'How dangerous can he be? He knows Julie Christie . . .'

'I know you don't believe that . . .'

'Why? You think the Khmer Rouge drive around Phnom Penh in white Toyotas trying to kidnap unsuspecting tourists with bad credit ratings?'

'My place only four dollars a night,' Sok Sin interjected.

'So what's Julie Christie like?' Amanda asked, sliding on the vinyl next to me.

As we drove off, Sok Sin pointed to a small *stupa*, a funerary monument, in front of the railway station. 'That has Buddha's finger,' Sok Sin intoned reverentially, making me wonder what sort of mutant Buddha would look like if anyone ever put all his supposed relics together.

We drove past scores of white Toyotas, Phnom Penh's favourite car model, parked on the wide grass median in front of the old colonial Le Royal Hotel, the hotel depicted in the movie *The Killing Fields*. The grass strip served as Phnom Penh's unofficial used car lot. North of the hotel graceful pre-war town houses, decrepit and filled with squatters, lined the street. Laundry flapped from any available line, tarps swayed across holes where windows once hung, and soot-blackened air conditioners which hadn't whirred since 1975 still hung uselessly in the air.

Sok Sin filled us in on his life as he drove. Apart from Khmer, Sok Sin spoke Chinese, English, French and Vietnamese. His wife had recently left him for another man, supposedly decamping with Sok Sin's savings.

'I don't think I'm a bad man,' Sok Sin shrugged the shrug of cuckolded husbands everywhere as he turned the car down a dusty street alongside the deserted pre-1975 French Embassy compound. It was to the French Embassy that many foreigners and Khmers fled when the Khmer Rouge captured Phnom Penh. The foreigners were eventually trucked to the Thai border but the Cambodians had been forced from their sanctuary, most to meet their death.

We slipped out of the car. Around us stood Sok Sin's neighbourhood – a series of bamboo, wood and cardboard squatter shacks surrounding a downed '70s fighter plane, rusting and partially cannibalized. Children ran screaming between the buildings. Sok Sin's new, two storey guesthouse looked like a jumbled lumber depot. Three tin and concrete sides surrounded a courtyard stacked full with wood. Several workers stood among the sawdust and off-cuts, staring open-mouthed as if to say, 'Look, the boss has found two live ones . . .'

'I ran out of money to fix. So I get some guests, make some money, fix some more,' Sok Sin led me up the ladder to the second-floor rooms. Amanda followed, pulling the bottom of my shirt and whispering 'No, no, no, no, no' into my lumbar vertebrae as we climbed. Plywood sheeting divided the rooms, each door was padlocked tight, and the roof was tin.

'People don't want satellite TV, people don't want hot water, own bathroom, people want cheap,' Sok Sin insisted and pointed to a scoop bath and a hole-in-the-floor toilet. 'I give them cheap!' he declared, flinging open a bedroom door to reveal two young Khmer women. On cue, one dramatically pulled down a hot pink mosquito net and posed with her arm outstretched. The other bounced enthusiastically on the bed to demonstrate the soundness of the mattress. They looked like a brace of television game show hosts displaying the grand prize.

I heard my mother's noncommittal voice going, 'Uh-huh, yes, oh, very nice . . .', but the sound seemed to be coming from my mouth. We climbed back down the ladder.

'So, you like my place?' Sok Sin inquired one last time as he dropped us at the Monorom.

'It's just that we've got a few more places to look at,' Amanda apologized.

'But we might come over in a few days,' I continued brightly. I liked Sok Sin, but I couldn't bear to tell him that even the cheapest backpacker might think twice about living in a barred building site surrounded by kindling.

'No, no. I don't think you like so much,' Sok Sin sighed shrewdly, getting back into his car. 'I don't think you come.'

As Sok Sin drove off, I felt like a prize ass. He'd just been asking for a straight answer and I'd been condescending by not giving it to him. Since I arrived in Phnom Penh I'd been viewing Cambodia as if it wasn't real, as if the people here couldn't take my measure as much as I expected to take theirs. Thinking I wasn't part of the picture simply because I was painting it was a mistake, but in Cambodia I was probably also trying to protect myself against what I expected to see. With his disjointed English and manic intensity, for some reason I hadn't thought Sok Sin could read between my words. I'd been treating Sok Sin like he was stupid, when in fact the stupid one had been me.

*   *   *   *

And then we found the Stockton Hotel, no hot water but the room had a fridge. With the tentative peace, thousands of overseas Khmers from France, Canada, the US and Australia had come home, opening shops, restaurants, and hotels. The Stockton was run by Khmer American refugees who had prospered and returned. In America the Cambodian diaspora had settled mainly in Lowell, Massachusetts and Long Beach and Stockton, California. The hotel was named after the owner's American hometown.

Thanks to satellite television in the restaurant, NGO workers and UNTACers came to the Stockton to eat, watch the BBC World Service, and gather information and rumour. Aside from weekly *Cambodia Times*, widely considered a CPP government mouthpiece, and the fortnightly *Phnom Penh Post*, non-Khmer speakers had little access to Cambodian news unless they scrounged a Bangkok paper. Thanks to UNTAC, however, the Khmer press flourished. By the elections at least 26 Khmer newspapers had opened. Many were only a few pages long, produced by amateur journalists on a weekly or fortnightly basis. Some were simply polemical tracts supporting one of the 22 registered political parties. The papers, and the parties, showed Cambodians' determination to have independent voices after years of repression by the French, Sihanouk, Lon Nol, Khmer Rouge and communist State of Cambodia governments.

In some ways, the UN overwhelmed the town. Within days we met a backpacking English television researcher who had ended up running UNTAC's radio station, an Afghan motor pool supervisor, Irish sanitation workers, Canadian schoolteachers, a Perot-voting American Air Force captain called Randy who had grown up near me, and military men of every description.

A year earlier Phnom Penh had been an early to bed place, with no traffic and nowhere to go. Since then Chinese and Cambodian restaurants with special rice crust, fried frogs' legs and cicadas, and howlingly bad English menu translations had sprung up to attract UN money. There were western bars and restaurants everywhere, too, and cases of San Miguel, Heineken, Foster and Victoria Bitter, the beloved 'VB' of Australians, were flown in to meet demand. The Gecko was favoured by journalists, the Rock Hard by the military, the Cat House by the late night pool-playing drinkers attracted by the imported Filipina bar girls sporting *faux* tiger-skin mini-dresses, the No Problem by those who fancied themselves movers and shakers. Happy Herb's catered for discerning souls who wanted marijuana instead of oregano sprinkled on their pizza. Later the Heart of Darkness would draw travellers and trendies. Hole-in-the-wall beer and bar-girl massage joints – a string of coloured electric lights blinking over a doorway, a table with a few folding chairs and folding hospital screens to provide privacy – taking advantage of Phnom Penh's new relaxed attitude to commercial social activities, dotted the side streets. Phnom Penh with the UN there was like first term of college – lots of people who didn't know anyone, whose commitments were far away, and who partied at night. Cambodians, however, were usually home by dark. The evening brought fun for the foreigners but a sense of wariness for many Cambodians, who feared *jouw*, thieves.

As usual, our social life didn't go quite the way Amanda and I expected. The Englishman disappeared, the Irish stood us up. I would shamelessly cut down side streets to avoid Randy when his loud Bermuda shorts headed in my direction. The other military were always making plays for Lee, the 24-year-old Cambodian-born Khmer American who ran the Stockton's front desk. Aside from a few close platonic male friends who took her to dinner, Lee wasn't going out. 'It's too complicated, and I'm going back to the States, anyway.'

Lee's mother, Nilda, ran the kitchen. Lee liaised with the hotel guests, and her father Eddie oversaw the books. They had returned with American passports and were all committed Christians. Since 20 years of war had left many children parentless, Eddie hired as many orphans as possible. Homeless staff who hadn't found space in a nearby *wat* slept underneath mosquito nets on the restaurant tables. Nilda was chubby, always kidding with the guests, and addicted to a hand-held Tetris game. 'My husband got so upset with me playing the game all the time he hid it!' she laughed. 'But when you're cooking all day you have to have something else to do.'

Eddie was as skinny as Nilda was round. Most afternoons Eddie could be found at the back of the restaurant, calculator steaming, managing the hotel's books. Eddie wasn't Lee's real father. 'My real father was part French and worked for the government. The Khmer Rouge killed him. I was only six. My mother walked my brothers and me all the way to Thailand to escape. We walked for two months. We didn't have anything. No money, nothing,' Lee said one night as we sat around talking after the restaurant closed down. 'My mother wanted us to go to the States but we didn't know anybody.'

I knew that Cambodians needed sponsors to get into most countries and I wondered how Nilda had done it, with two children and no means of support.

'My mother was very beautiful so she seduced men,' Lee said simply.

'She wanted to get us out of that camp and she did anything she had to. She slept us into the United States.'

It was simple

I walked all over Phnom Penh, just exploring. Cyclo and moto drivers couldn't believe anyone wanted to traipse in the sun and the heat. A farmer with trussed chickens dangling from his motorcycle handle-bars, a librarian, a Vietnamese-educated water engineer moonlighting as a motodriver, curious ten-year-olds and all sorts of people would assume I was lost and go out of their way to direct or accompany me. Eventually I pretended I had a destination rather than try to explain that the point of my walking was not to have a point.

On side streets, middle-aged men played boules or squatted in a circle slapping down cards. Children gave each other rides on the jump seats of bright pink Chinese-made Pheasant-brand bicycles. *Trei gean* sellers hung whole flattened dried fish with neon-coloured plastic clothespegs from lines strung across pushcart stalls. Shop signs flapped in the wind – giant painted teeth signifying the dentist, a bride and groom for a shop renting European and traditional Khmer wedding costumes.

Small piles of refuse often burned on the waste ground. A few donated 'Marie de Paris' garbage trucks plied the streets at dusk, but on a weekly, rather than daily, basis. Phnom Penh didn't have the money for proper trash collection, water purification, sewerage or electricity. Many people lived in squatter shacks or on the street – parks and sidewalks were their kitchens, bathrooms, living-rooms, toilets.

Technically Cambodians had an average annual income of $140 a year, half their 1960s earnings. But while country people laboured in a subsistence economy, in the cities there was a UNTAC boom. A good UN job brought a lucky Cambodian $3–400 a month; a good UN job brought a lucky foreign UNTACer a tax free salary, plus a *per diem* living allowance that once touched $160 per day.

Of the estimated 1.8 billion US dollars spent during UNTAC – the final amount varied by another billion or so, depending on who did the accounting – a large proportion either never came near, or only temporarily rested in, Cambodia. Salaries paid into Phnom Penh banks for non-Cambodian staff were quickly wired home. Almost all the trucks, cars, faxes, furniture, computers and other durable goods used by the UN were purchased in UNTAC donor countries. Even food for the UN battalions was provided by an Australian catering firm which flew meat and produce from Down Under. The capital that Cambodia needed to repair its shattered infrastructure only passed through the country, but it showed many Cambodians an enticing life far beyond their immediate means.

UNTAC had also brought inflation. The Cambodian currency, the *riel*, had shot in four years from 87 to 2500 against the dollar. Land prices had sky-rocketed. Villas were hastily renovated. Rickety bamboo scaffolding laddered the sides of houses, but most building jobs were done by hand. Labour was cheap, construction gadgets expensive. Eddie looked up from his calculator, but left his finger in place on a page of figures, when I asked how much the Stockton's owner had paid for it for in 1989.

'About 10,000 US.'

'How much is it worth now?'

'About half a million.'

Psar Thmei, the central market, resembled a leftover set from a Buck Rogers movie. Open stalls sold live chickens, herbs, rambutans, mangoes, ironmongery and new and used clothes. Fruit and vegetable purchases were wrapped in a lotus leaf and tied with the stem for easy carrying. Neon coloured dessert gelatins quivered on crushed ice, tempting shoppers who squatted on shaky white folding stools to munch snacks of skewered chicken or rice and Chinese sausage. The central nave was packed with Tetris-playing gold merchants. Cambodians didn't trust banks and kept their wealth portable in women's jewellery. Sapphires, emeralds and rubies, taken from the Pailin hills controlled by the Khmer Rouge or the north-eastern province of Ratanakiri, sparkled loose in small paper boxes or were wedged tightly into red-gold settings. If a Cambodian preferred joining the consumer boom to converting his or her wealth to jewels or gold, he or she could stroll down the market's south arm and choose a stereo, multi-system television, satellite receiver, air conditioner or fax machine.

The market summed up the Cambodian dilemma. With a little disposable income, a person could buy the latest technology. But the sewers were broken and half the children in the country couldn't go to school. A 'Médecin sans Frontières' doctor had told me that the city's hospitals were so poor the toilets were frequently blocked and unusable, the floors rarely cleaned, and bandages were washed and reused until they disintegrated. The UN had improved the quality of life for the lucky middle class, said the doctor, but it hadn't improved the infrastructure, the building blocks of society which made the difference between life and death.

Despite their poverty, I couldn't believe how nice most Cambodians were. My pathetic attempts at speaking Khmer would send cyclo drivers into fits of laughter as I ground through the unfamiliar vowel sounds. Children would follow me down the street, screaming 'Hello, hello!' and wanting to shake hands. Some days I waved more than Miss America. But I couldn't square the kindness and ready humour of most Cambodians I met with the rage and brutality which had produced the Khmer Rouge regime. Fifteen years after the Khmer Rouge had left Phnom Penh, Cambodia was still a society in which personal grievance was often redressed through bullets or grenades. Banditry, extortion and violence were rife.

And yet somewhere, sometime, in God knows whose company, I fell, if not in love at least in fascination, with the place.

*   *   *   *

Amanda and I quickly took to Phnom Penh's primary form of entertainment – talking about everybody else. We tried to tell ourselves our gossiping had a higher purpose: maybe another Stockton guest could get Amanda a job. One woman we couldn't suss. She looked like a conservative Mid-western housewife – tight and controlled, wearing sensible short-sleeved sundresses. At first Amanda and I thought the woman was a Mormon missionary. Then we changed our minds and she became the computer expert installing an embassy network. Our mystery miss read a lot, didn't have a job, yet knew a lot of people since a variety of men squired her to lunch or dinner.

Another indefatigable Afghan trapped Amanda into a date. Her attempts to blackmail or bribe me into coming along failed. I wanted a night in to read. Like most nights in, about nine o'clock I realized I now wanted a night out. Wandering downstairs to stock the fridge with our agreed upon diet food – sodas, Tiger beers, M&Ms – I noticed the mystery woman reading in a lounge chair in the wide hallway.

She was still there 15 minutes later. Curiosity overcame me, as it usually does, and I couldn't help asking, 'Look, I know this is going to sound really weird, and we should probably get a life, but my friend and I have been desperately trying to figure out what you're doing here in Cambodia. You don't act like a tourist . . .'

The mystery woman looked amused and closed her book. 'What were some of your guesses? What do you think I do?'

I decided against offering 'centre forward for the God squad' and murmured, 'Well, I heard some of the embassies were looking for a computer bod . . .'

'Computers, how boring! No, actually, I work in military intelligence.' A smile crept across her face as she waited for my reaction.

'A spook! I wondered if there were any wandering around. Want a Tiger?' Thank God for some entertainment. Rummaging in my plastic bag, I plopped into the seat next to her. I once had an older boyfriend who formerly had worked for British intelligence. Spying had ruined David, as far as I could see – other pairs of strolling lovers on Hampstead Heath would consider the flowers, the sunset, the ducks; David would point out the extraordinary number of radio antennae sprouting from the roof of the Russian Trade Delegation – but he had made me realize there were lots of supposed grown-ups out there playing hide and go seek with a straight face.

'The place is crawling with them.' Laurie didn't look like my reaction was the one she had expected, but she took a beer and introduced herself.

With no UN position, Laurie was using her vacation to see the election effort. Over the next three hours, we kibbutzed about Cambodian economics, the new political parties, why a Most Favoured Nation trading rating from the United States would help development, how Laurie's fellow intelligence workers couldn't wait to come in once the UN opened up the previously communist country, Cambodia's growing AIDS problem, and why nobody had nuked the Khmer Rouge. Laurie obviously knew her stuff.

I told her I didn't think much of 'intelligence'. The supposed secrecy was laughable; most of the game's adherents seemed to be frustrated thriller writers. Laurie couldn't agree more.

'I just try to analyze the information. Most of it you could read in the *Bangkok Post*.'

'So why aren't you in UNTAC?'

'Oh, you couldn't possibly have someone working for the UN who actually cared about the country,' Laurie winced in mock horror. 'And God forbid the boys should have a woman make policy decisions . . .'

It was Laurie who explained the byzantine nature and history of Cambodian politics to me via the example of one engineering student shivering in Pyongyang, to whom I was to mail Kek the waiter's letter. With so many countries making diplomatic capital from Cambodia's problems, and more shifting allegiances than a television soap opera, I was lost as to which faction would send a student to North Korea. Laurie offered to explain during a Cat House night out with a brush-moustached British deminer called Basil. Despite Laurie's conservative demeanour, she could drink as fast and hard as anyone. Basil had just delineated the problems of computer-mapping the country's mine fields when an oxcart was still high technology in most villages, and had retired to the pool table. Sitting on the rattan chairs watching Basil line up his shots as Laurie talked, I couldn't help feeling that there were many more sides to Laurie than she showed. If I could remember through my alcoholic haze exactly what she said, it probably would have gone like this:

For 600 years around the turn of the last millennium, the temple-building Angkorean kings ruled Cambodia from the north-western end of the great lake, the Tonle Sap. During the rainy season floods swell the lake to six times its normal size. The lake's rich mud fertilizes Cambodia's fields and brings abundant rice and fish. At its apogee the Angkor kingdom stretched west of Bangkok, north of Vientiane, and east of Saigon.

The culture of Angkor owed much to Javanese and Indian traders. To understand traditional Cambodian culture one must not look north to China, but rather west to India. Cambodia's religious and spiritual base was Hindu. Cambodians ate with spoons and fingers, not chopsticks. The *krama*, a checked scarf which could be wrapped on top of the head to provide shade and a carrying base for heavy loads, and the wearing of skirts rather than trousers by both men and women also indicated Indian, rather than Chinese, influence.

Without a mandarin culture in which a man could rise by hard work and study, a Cambodian's position at birth was usually his position for life. Although not contained by a rigid caste system like India, Angkorian society was structured so that the lower rungs of society looked to the higher for protection. Cambodian kings frequently added the Pali suffix *'varman'*, which means 'armour', to their names to emphasize their protective powers. A separate Khmer vocabulary was, and still is, used to address and describe royalty. At one point the Cambodian kingdom had 14 different categories of slaves. The Khmer word for I, *knyom*, comes from the name of one slave category, so that the very definition of self embodies subservience.

The early Angkorian kings, the *devarajas*, sought protection from the Hindu god Siva. To reinforce their identification with the gods they erected temples such as Angkor Wat. Siva represented both the rulers and the ancestors, and was deemed responsible for the rain. As Angkor's wealth was based on an extensive irrigation system of canals and reservoirs which allowed several rice harvests a year and was as impressive in construction as any temple complex, water controlled the kingdom.

In the twelfth century mendicant monks brought Theravada Buddhism to Cambodia. The sect did not require temples or wealth to maintain sacred symbols. Emphasis shifted from identifying the ruler with a god to performing good deeds, such as building roads, hospices and hospitals for the people, so the ruler and his subjects could attain merit for redemption and happiness in another life. While Buddhism heavily influenced the upper classes, it did not change the social structure. Animism continued to rule the countryside, if not the towns, for a very long time.

The borders of Cambodia have never been firmly fixed. Cambodian armies often fought off, or were defeated by, invading Thais, Vietnamese, and Chams, who fled to Cambodia when their Muslim kingdom, in what is now central Vietnam, was conquered. As Thai invasions and the collapse and destruction of the irrigation system around Angkor in the fifteenth century undermined the country's wealth, the Khmer capital moved south to Lovea and then Oudong, near Phnom Penh and the confluence of the Mekong and Sap rivers. *Okya*, relatives of the king or rich businessmen who paid for their powers, continued to govern individual provinces and collect taxes.

Vietnam captured most of lower Cambodia in the early nineteenth century. The two cultures clashed: the Vietnamese wore their hair long, Cambodians kept themselves close-cropped. The Vietnamese wore trousers, the Cambodians skirts. Even their schools of Buddhism differed. The Vietnamese longed to change Cambodia's customs, the Cambodians refused. The social, political and cultural divisions run deep to this day. A legend about the Vietnamese forcing Khmer labourers to build a 40-kilometre canal between the Gulf of Siam and the Vietnamese town of Chaudoc is still pointed to by anti-Vietnamese Cambodians as an example of the cruel Vietnamese treatment of Cambodians. According to the story, the Vietnamese so abused the Cambodians that three Khmers were buried up to their necks and their heads used as a pot rest when the Vietnamese lit a fire to brew their tea. The story, true or not, is often cited as fact.

A Thai-backed force helped install a new Cambodian king, Duang, in the late 1840s, but after a succession of Thai and

Vietnamese manoeuvres again threatened to swallow the country, Duang's successor signed a protection agreement with the French in 1863. At French urging, the new king moved from his wooden palace beneath the temples on the hill at Oudong to Phnom Penh. The French built the monarch a brick and plaster palace and supplied subsequent rulers with a steady store of opium. Colonists did not encourage Cambodian autonomy. Educated Vietnamese, skilled in French administration, were imported to work as low level colonial administrators. Many artisan jobs in colonial Phnom Penh were also filled by Vietnamese. Immigrant Chinese controlled commerce. Most Khmers stayed 'in the mud', farming rice in the countryside.

What the French did give Cambodia, and which to a large extent the Gallic colonialists created, was a belief in a glorious Cambodian past. When Henri Mouhot, a French explorer, was shown the ruins at Angkor in the mid-1800s, the massive stone complex had not been totally forgotten. The temples were known to exist; a working monastery was still sited next to Angkor Wat. But the Cambodians, it seemed, didn't particularly care.

The romantic concept of a lost temple city in the jungle, however, caught the European imagination, and a bevy of Victorian scholars cleared away debris and decoded the temple inscriptions. As a symbol of national identity for the colonized Cambodians the fallen Khmer kingdom was fitted into the nineteenth-century imperial concept of history. But concentrating on past culture presented a sharp contrast to the political realities of the Cambodian protectorate: Cambodians bore Indo-China's highest taxes, which in practice often could only be paid through corvée labour, and received practically no investment in their country. The French colonies and protectorates were administered to provide economic support for France, not vice versa. Development in Cambodia and Laos was seen as secondary to, and in support of, the more profitable Vietnamese colonial economy. The *mission civilitrice* which many French colonists had hoped would bring French culture to Cambodia never affected the daily lives of most Cambodians.

Despite a few anti-tax uprisings, the French had little

trouble controlling their protectorate in the early twentieth century. France often installed supposedly pliable boy sovereigns on Indo-Chinese thrones, so, in 1941, 20-year-old Prince Sihanouk was declared king on his grandfather's death. Sihanouk soon proved he knew his own mind. The Japanese invaded France's Indo-Chinese territory during World War II, but they let the Vichy French administration continue until Japan's defeat seemed sure. Japan then encouraged Cambodian, Vietnamese and Laotian nationalists to revolt. Sihanouk declared Cambodia independent on 13 March 1945. He also changed the country's French name from 'Cambodge' to the Khmer pronunciation 'Kampuchea'. By early 1946, however, the French had regained control of Indo-China.

As in Vietnam and Laos, Cambodia's movement toward total independence from France continued into the 1950s. Guerilla bands, known as Issaraks, operated in the countryside. The Issaraks were concentrated in the hilly north-west provinces of Battambang and Siem Reap. They enjoyed Thai support until Thailand returned parts of the Battambang and Siem Reap provinces to France in 1947. The traditionally disputed territory had been seized during World War II and was exchanged, in part, for French support for Thailand's UN membership. Issaraks were also based in the south-western seaside province of Kampot. Many Issarak forces were directed by the Indo-Chinese Communist Party.

Although Sihanouk had no political connection to the Issaraks, he waged his own idiosyncratic campaign for Cambodian autonomy. In 1953 the French ceded control, but not until the 1954 Geneva Peace Accords, which ended the First Indo-Chinese War, were the details of full Cambodian independence finalized. Unlike the Vietnamese and Laotian Communists who were accorded provisions granted territory or rights, international political legitimacy was not bestowed on the Cambodian insurgents. Several thousand Cambodian communists went into exile in North Vietnam.

To retain political control within the bounds of Cambodia's new constitution, Sihanouk renounced the throne in favour of his father in 1954, but as prime minister he retained his personal power. Not content to languish in Phnom Penh,

Sihanouk made frequent trips to the countryside and distributed bolts of cloth or other gifts to villagers, a reminder that wealth and prosperity should be seen as emanating from the person of the ruler. On these trips Sihanouk carried to rural Cambodians a twentieth-century, helicopter-supported and poster-fed version of the mystery that the *devarajas* held in Angkorean times. On the international front, Sihanouk's attendance at the 1955 conference of Asian and African states in Bandung convinced him that the policy of non-alignment with either Russia or the United States, followed by Nehru in India and Sukharno in Indonesia, would also serve Cambodia.

While democracy in Cambodia during Sihanouk's rule in the late 1950s and the 1960s was illusory – vote rigging and the persecution of political challengers to Sihanouk's own Sangkum Reastr Niyum 'socialist' party was not uncommon – the country was relatively stable. Sihanouk encouraged education, opened hospitals, and built roads. For the expatriate community life was good. Phnom Penh was often called the 'Paris of the Orient', the finest jewel among the ex-French colonial capitals. The only thing most foreigners had to fear in Phnom Penh was being trapped in a movie theatre showing one of the romantic epics Sihanouk wrote, directed, scored and occasionally starred in.

Sihanouk depicted himself as taking the traditional Buddhist middle path between his enemies, but opponents did not fare well under the former king. Political assassinations were not unknown. Rightist adversaries, nicknamed 'Khmer Blu' by Sihanouk, sought sanctuary in Thailand or South Vietnam. The left, whom Sihanouk called the 'Khmer Rouge', headed into the untamed highlands and renewed contact with Cambodian exiles in North Vietnam. Among the leftists who ran to the jungles was a communist schoolteacher and failed radio technician named Saloth Sar. He later took the name 'Pol Pot'.

Sihanouk tried to keep Cambodia neutral during the Vietnam War, but he believed that North Vietnam would win, and allowed the Viet Cong to use eastern Cambodia as a safe haven and supply line. The United States retaliated with Nixon's secret, illegal bombings. Dissatisfaction with corruption and Sihanouk's governance apparently led at least one Cambodian Army general, Lon Nol, secretly to seek assurances of support from the United States should there be a coup. No firm proof ever surfaced, however, that the United States helped to instigate the coup in which Lon Nol, a general known for crushing peasant revolts, and once – for a short time – prime minister, together with Prince Sisowath Sirak Matak, Sihanouk's cousin, ousted Sihanouk and declared the Khmer Republic in 1970. Lon Nol returned as prime minister.

'All we know about Lon Nol is that Lon Nol backwards spells Lon Nol,' ran the caption for an American political cartoon several days after Sihanouk's removal. Lon Nol was nicknamed the '*khmao*', the black one, for his dark skin which suggested peasant origins. Most of Cambodia's ruling elite was lighter skinned; darker Cambodians were sometimes looked down upon. A superstitious man with egocentric Buddhist beliefs, in Lon Nol's own eyes by deposing Sihanouk he had broken a divine Buddhist hierarchy and would pay for his usurpation. Civil war immediately followed the declaration of Lon Nol's new government, which encouraged pogroms against all Vietnamese, communist or not. Eastern Cambodia was invaded for a short time by a combined US/South Vietnamese force searching for Viet Cong troops; Ho Chi Minh's soldiers simply pushed deeper into Cambodia. Sihanouk formed an alliance in exile with the Khmer Rouge to fight Lon Nol's regime; royalists joined the communists in the jungle. Vietnamese communists, who before had rejected aid requests from the previously insignificant Khmer Rouge movement, now supported the anti-Lon Nol fight.

Whatever the United States' position before the coup, afterwards American military aid poured in. At first army volunteers rushed to defend the new Lon Nol order but corruption, and then disillusionment, was rife. Officers collected pay for phantom soldiers or simply never gave real troops their salaries. American-paid-for hardware frequently found its way to the enemy. One Battambang commander sold arms to the Khmer Rouge with the proviso they not be fired at him – how he would enforce this codicil was unclear.

Many Cambodians – teachers, medical workers, doctors,

civil servants, the university graduates with few job expectations – began to welcome the Khmer Rouge. They hoped for
stability and a respite from the greed and avarice of the
military and corrupt civil servants. After all, the logic ran, the
leaders of the Khmer Rouge were intellectuals, men and
women of rationality and vision. Many had been among the
first Khmer students to study in France. Two had served
in Sihanouk's cabinet. And soon there were propaganda
shots of Sihanouk and his wife Monique, dressed in Chinese-
manufactured army cap and pyjamas, posing with the Khmer
Rouge in front of captured Angkorean temples.

But years in the jungle fighting bombers, malaria and
madness had turned the untested theories of urban intellectuals into a psychotic political philosophy based on a totally
controlled, unmechanized, emotionless agrarian Khmer
utopia which never had existed, and never could. By 1973, the
Khmer Rouge had started deposing and eliminating royalist
allies; Khmer communists even turned against their Vietnamese supporters in some battles. By the time the Khmer
Rouge took the country their leadership accepted little dissid-
ence.

Lon Nol's government suffered massive military defeats,
opening untenably wide fronts or engaging in fights which
required lengthy supply lines. Refugees from the embattled
countryside, some of whom told stories of Khmer Rouge
brutality, tripled the Phnom Penh population. Lost in his
iconoclastic spiritualism and partially incapacitated by a
stroke, Lon Nol sought to protect the capital by having a monk
sprinkle sacred sand from an airplane circling the city's
perimeter. American aid ended. The army volunteers soon
became unwilling conscripts, students plucked from cinema
lines or any fit looking man on the street. Cities such as
Battambang became islands of the Khmer Republic within a
Khmer Rouge countryside. The towns soon became suppli-
able only by air. Finally the provincial capitals, and Phnom
Penh and the Khmer Republic, fell to the Khmer Rouge.

Within hours of entering Phnom Penh on 17 April 1975 the
new rulers began to empty the city, as they did all towns.
Urban dwellers were marched into the countryside. The
twentieth century was slowly erased, with giant bonfires of

furniture and foreign goods melting Cambodia back to the Stone Age. The Khmer Rouge were determined to enforce control. Lon Nol officials and army officers were executed. Family members were separated, the older children formed into child work brigades.

Everyone worked in strictly regulated agricultural communes. Monks were disrobed. Schools were abandoned. Private property was collectivized. *Wats* were stripped of ornamentation and abandoned or turned into factories or animal shelters. The national bank was destroyed, money abolished, records burnt. Social roles reversed: darker skinned Cambodians were treated as the true inheritors of Angkor. Minorities such as the Chinese, Vietnamese and Chams were persecuted: Kampuchea was to be for the Khmers.

It is said that in some communes the Khmer Rouge killed one member of each family to emphasize the price of disobedience to the others. Phnom Penhois were especially suspect. If you spoke a foreign language, had worked for the government or were educated, you risked execution. Only those who worked the land could be trusted by *Angka*, a Khmer word meaning organization which symbolized the new Khmer Rouge state. Angka was an amorphous, nameless higher power to whom the Khmer Rouge comrades paid fealty; Angka demanded absolute subservience and loyalty. If a Cambodian's dedication to the new revolution was doubted, Angka would wish to know. To be 'called by Angka', to 'continue education', was to vanish forever. Many people simply disappeared in the night, another murder in the killing fields.

Sihanouk, who since his ouster had posed as the public face of the anti-Lon Nol resistance, was flown into an abandoned Phnom Penh. He quickly became an imprisoned, powerless guest within his own palace, living in fear of execution. Instead, the failed technical student Saloth Sar emerged as leader of the new regime. Saloth Sar began to hide behind the name 'Pol Pot', who was listed on Khmer Rouge 'election' lists as a rubber worker from Kompong Cham. Later, after the Khmer Rouge lost control and the Khmer Rouge horrors became widely known, Saloth Sar's *nom de guerre* would be used as verbal shorthand by Cambodians for the Khmer Rouge regime. 1975–8 would be called 'the Pol Pot time'. Khmer Rouge soldiers would be referred to as 'Pol Pot's soldiers' or simply as 'Pol Pot', as if Saloth Sar had transmogrified into individual fighters. Talking with Cambodians about the past, it seemed as if that one name carried the entire responsibility for all the evil which had happened. In a country where historically the ruler was seen to hold absolute sway, 'Pol Pot' was looked on as a monstrous *devaraja*.

Under Saloth Sar even long-serving Khmer Rouge members were not trusted. Internecine schisms in the Khmer Rouge led Angka, or whichever faction Angka represented at that moment, to destroy many of the Khmer Rouge's original adherents. Bloody purges escalated within the party, especially in the eastern provinces. Thousands of Khmer Rouge cadres and others fled to Vietnam.

On Christmas Day 1978, Cambodian fighters, who had been gathered from refugees in the Vietnamese border camps, and the Vietnamese army, goaded by Khmer Rouge incursions into southern Vietnam which left many dead, invaded Cambodia. The Khmer Rouge army was pushed to the Thai border. At least one of every seven Cambodians had died through starvation, disease, war or murder. So efficient were the Khmer Rouge at eradicating potential insurgent soldiers that today Cambodia's population is estimated to be nearly 60 per cent female.

The Vietnamese had walked into their own 'Vietnam'. Geopolitics now controlled Cambodia's destiny. Vietnam was seen as Russia's client state. Since the United States hoped to improve the recently thawed US–Chinese relations, United States diplomatic decisions on Cambodia were taken in light of the Sino–Soviet split. Instead of being applauded by the international community for destroying the murderous Khmer Rouge regime, Vietnam was ostracized. Foreign aid programmes to Vietnam were reduced; China attacked along Vietnam's northern border to 'punish' Vietnam for invading Cambodia. Vietnam's fight with the Khmer Rouge was seen by global politicians as a proxy war between China and the Soviet Union.

Two weeks after Phnom Penh fell, the Thais agreed to

shelter the Khmer Rouge if China, which supported the Khmer Rouge, stopped succouring insurgent Thai communists. For many Cambodians the Vietnamese invasion stoked historical fear that Vietnam would annex Cambodia. Sihanouk appealed to the UN to condemn the Vietnamese invasion. Many Western countries, including Britain and the United States, strongly backed the Khmer Rouge as the legitimate government of Cambodia in the UN, thus currying Chinese favour. In the run-up to a US election this ingratiated the Carter administration with right-wing anti-Vietnamese Americans who had never forgiven that small country for defeating the larger one. The votes in favour of the Khmer Rouge delegation retaining the UN seat helped to set the stage so the war in Cambodia would continue.

In Phnom Penh the new government included many ex-Khmer Rouge who had defected and fled to Vietnam. Crowds of refugees, who would eventually number nearly half a million, spilled into Thailand. Many had run from the fighting. Others were the remnants of the educated Cambodian classes: doctors, lawyers, businessmen who had survived the killing fields and did not wish to remain under the new regime. Throughout the 1980s refugees continued to appear.

Small resistance armies and political groups sprang up along the Thai-Cambodian border, in France and in the United States. Most groups had a political wing, some groups had troops. No matter what side they were on, everyone had an acronym:

• The Khmer Rouge, who now fielded an army of less than 5,000 men, were referred to more and more as the 'DK', which stood for 'Democratic Kampuchea', the name with which they had christened Cambodia upon taking power. The army became the 'National Army of Democratic Kampuchea' (NADK). While Russia backed the Phnom Penh government, the Khmer Rouge continued to look to China for military support.
• Son Sann, a former Prime Minister under Sihanouk, formed the US-backed Khmer People's National Liberation Front (KPNLF) to oppose both the Vietnamese invasion and the possible return of the Khmer Rouge forces. The KPNLF's

political arm, organized to fight the 1993 elections, was called the Buddhist Liberal Democratic Party (BLDP).

• In 1981 the royalists finally stopped squabbling among themselves and formed the Front Uni National pour un Cambodge Indépendant, Neutre, Pacifique et Coopératif (Funcinpec) so they could squabble with everybody else. Their armed forces were the Armée Nationale Khmer Indépendante (ANKI) and they enjoyed French backing.

• In 1982, to stop the UN seat falling to the Phnom Penh government, the Khmer Rouge, Sihanouk's Funcinpec and Son Sann's KPNLF grumpily agreed to form the Coalition Government of Democratic Kampuchea (CGDK). Sihanouk became the titular head of the CGDK, and as coalition leader lived in Peking and Pyongyang, North Korea.

• The party representing the Communist Phnom Penh government, whose economic support by Vietnam and other Soviet-bloc countries had severely diminished with the late 1980s anti-Communist political changes in Eastern Europe, changed their name to Cambodian People's Party or CPP, in 1991. After the name change, the CPP continued to be led by the young Cambodian Prime Minister, an ex-Khmer Rouge commander named Hun Sen. The State of Cambodia's (SOC) armed forces, which for all intents and purposes were the CPP's armed forces, were called the Cambodian People's Armed Force (CPAF).

For over ten years the Phnom Penh government and Vietnamese troops fought the resistance groups based along the Thai–Cambodian border. While to some Cambodians the Vietnamese had been liberators, to others the Vietnamese were Cambodia's traditional colonists arrived again. Vietnam withdrew its forces in 1989. In October 1991 the three main factions based on the border, including the Khmer Rouge, and the State of Cambodia agreed to stop fighting and to abide by the outcome of UN supervised elections to be held in 1993. Sihanouk was to head a 'Supreme National Council', composed of representatives from the DK, BLDP, CPP and Funcinpec, which would theoretically govern Cambodia until the election. UNTAC was mandated to provide a neutral administration for the voting and the country. Three weeks after the peace settlement was signed in Paris, Sihanouk returned to Cambodia for the first time in a dozen years to an overwhelming welcome. Even though he drove from the airport alongside Hun Sen, for many Cambodians, especially in the countryside, Sihanouk was still viewed as Cambodia's rightful ruler.

For over 20 years, Cambodians had waited for the civil wars to cease. After so much waste, the world was watching to see whether Cambodia's political factions would grab the election chance to bring peace to the country, or whether Cambodia would sink back into self-destruction. As during much of Cambodia's history, other countries, now most obviously represented by UNTAC, still held control over Cambodia's future.

If the kid went to North Korea to study, Laurie probably said, his parents, if they were still alive, were aligned with Sihanouk. Ergo the kid was probably Funcinpec.

As Laurie would have said, it was simple.

Spook spottin'

I continued wandering – across town to Psar Tuol Tom Pong, otherwise known as the Russian Market, to check out the antiques, silver and silks; through the tenements behind the Pailin Hotel where the shoemakers and tinsmiths hammered all day; over to the Olympic Stadium which had never seen an Olympics; along the rutted streets of the leafy Chamcarmon residential area, where the neat green lawns and children's playswings of the Khmer American returnees transplanted southern California to Cambodia; down crowded side streets shut tight by a traditional Khmer wedding party – the groom and his best men dressed in Khmer pleated pantaloons leading a line of women in their best silk *sampots* bearing bowls of fresh fruit or meat to symbolize fertility, followed by musicians bowing the Khmer two-stringed instrument called a *throu*, who were followed by fidgeting men carrying cases of Tiger beer and Coke who just wanted to get on with the party, toward the house of the bride who would nervously wait in one of the dozen or so stiff silk Cambodian outfits tradition required that the bride wear throughout the ceremony, if her family could afford them; underneath the bright yellow cardboard 'Be a Millionaire!' Cambodia Social Welfare Lottery signs, all in English to capture UNTAC dollars, which promoted a game backed by Malaysians but overseen by Canadian accountants to allay fears that the game was fixed, even if the million was only in *riels*; by the riverside where Cambodian gamblers crowded vacant lots on Sundays to slap down wagers on makeshift games of chance and where small wooden houses stood on stilts to withstand the yearly flooding which nurtured the countryside's rice; past the mournful-looking broken bridge which had once spanned the

Tonle Sap. A Japanese aid agency was busy reconstructing the crossing 20 years after insurgent sappers had blown out the centre spans.

I wanted to read more about Cambodia. A few *barang* shops sold the odd English or French history or guide to Cambodia – you could find a reprint of Henri Mahout's posthumously printed *Travels throughout the Kingdoms of Thailand, Cambodia and Laos*, the 1860s book which had excited European imaginations with tales of the hidden temples of Angkor; an out-of-date *Lonely Planet*; a Siam Society imprint of Chinese envoy Chou Ta Kuan's memoir of thirteenth-century travels to Angkor; or an export copy of William Shawcross's *Sideshow*, which in clinical detail related the story of Nixon's secret Cambodian bombings – but there were no real bookstores. The national literary culture and educational institutions which existed in Vietnamese society had no Cambodian parallel. Individual expression in poetry and prose did not fit into the traditional Khmer cultural ethos. Cambodian writing before World War II consisted primarily of Buddhist texts and verse epics. *Nagara Vatta* ('Angkor Wat'), the first Khmer-language newspaper, and *Tonle Sap*, the first Khmer novel, were published only in the late 1930s. Until the waning years of the colonial era, reading was taught almost exclusively in the Buddhist priesthood, the *sangha*; Cambodia's first lycée opened in 1936. With education linked to religion, literacy was a male preserve.

'In the countryside the people still do not send their girls to school because they are afraid if the girls learn to read and write they will write notes to boys,' an adult literacy teacher from Pursat, a provincial capital 150 miles north-west of Phnom Penh, told me. She had been trained in Russia as a teacher to work in the communist Phnom Penh government's 1980s aggressive literacy campaigns. Despite that effort, parents' traditional concerns had not ceased. The teacher estimated that between 70 and 80 per cent of the women in her province still could not read.

The National Library was a graceful, ochre coloured, colonnaded building built in 1922. During the Khmer Rouge period, the library was turned into a pigsty. Sok, one of the few trained librarians who outlived the Khmer Rouge, let me loose among the shelves behind the front desk. International funding had been secured for the air-conditioned room needed to preserve ancient palm and mulberry leaf manuscripts, but the reference library, with titles both in Khmer and foreign languages, had little – an anthology of Haitian poetry, a Russian biography of Charlie Chaplin, a complete set of the US Congressional Record 1970–1972. Many of the other books were out-of-date Russian textbooks. Sok told me regretfully that the Cambodian National Library had virtually nothing on Cambodia.

I left the library and walked past the traffic circling Wat Phnom. Two men cruised by on a bright blue motorcycle, one balancing a beautifully crafted teak boat on his shoulder, miniature sails full as it floated above a sea of Hondas.

Passing the 51st Street school complex, I watched as parents and cyclo drivers waited for the children pouring through the gates, girls and boys in white shirts and navy blue shorts or skirts, the lucky ones slipping off to buy an ice stick or a book cover of their favourite Khmer pop star from the eager, waiting vendors.

If a Cambodian couldn't find an education through reading, he or she could certainly learn English in the many private classes that had sprung up around the city. While many older people spoke French, the young opted for the world's new lingua franca which, much to French dismay, was English. A beginner lesson cost 500 *riels* (20 US cents), the price of a meal sold by one of the women who walked the streets with a bamboo pole slung across her shoulders, a pot of curry balancing on one end and rice dangling from the other, but English was considered the key to a well-paid job. From waiters to cyclo drivers to CPP generals, everyone was taking English lessons. 'What is your nationality?', 'What is your name?', 'When will you return to your country?' were the three phrases on everyone's lips. For cyclo drivers additional sentences were included in lesson number one: 'Yes, I know' – meaning, 'I haven't got a clue where it is, but I'll just keep peddling until you catch on', and, 'No, two dollars.'

'YES!! PLEASE!! MADAM!! YOU SPEAK ENGLISH!! I THINK YES!!' I was wasting time at a poster stand, thinking how much one of the Khmer teen idols looked like Johnny

Depp, when the Shouter grabbed my arm. 'PLEASE!! YES!! YOU CAN HELP!! ME!! YOU!! CAN PRONOUNCE!! ENG-LISH!! YES!! VERY GOOD!! I THINK!! YES!! COME WITH ME!! PLEASE!! NOW!! YES!!'

The Shouter said he taught 'beginning' English. He had just finished the course himself and in the booming market had pronounced himself qualified to instruct. The Shouter's class, however, felt differently and complained about his pronun-ciation. Could I just spend 15 minutes with his class which was starting now, he asked. Or rather, 'COULD PLEASE YOU!! COME CLASS NOW!! VERY SHORT!! YES!! PLEASE!!'

Benches and long tables filled the schoolroom, dark except for the fading sunlight streaming through the large windows. Every seat was taken by men and women in their teens and early twenties. All were neatly dressed, all had notebooks out. But none of them spoke English at all – nor were they likely to anytime soon, considering the text the Shouter handed me. Jumping around like a television evangelist out to save the final sinner, the Shouter introduced me in Khmer, then abruptly nodded for me to begin. 'Please ask the bellhop to bring the tea,' I started.

I looked up from the book. Each window of the classroom was filled with students, leaning on the ledges or standing on chairs in the hall to hear me read. There were 70 or 80, quietly listening to the lesson in a foreign voice. I kept reading, taking them on an upper-middle-class jaunt from London to Brighton, through an England which only P. G. Woodhouse would recognize. If spats make a comeback these guys are set.

You had to admire the Shouter for having the gumption to teach a language he didn't know. As a student later told me, English had to be learned clandestinely during part of the 1980s, but now it was the language everyone wanted to learn. For the new independent businessmen like Sok Sin, who were looking at middle age having lost at least a decade of their most productive years to war, to the rice farmers with newly acquired, elderly Hondas trying their luck as moto drivers, to these students eagerly mouthing words they barely under-stood, but which they chanted like a magic rhyme which they hoped would take them to a better life, Cambodians yearned to catch up on lost time.

The second lesson covered sport. Its phrases were almost as useless as those in lesson one. I read through the second lesson, and then made my excuses as the Shouter hurtled forward to lead the class again.

'YES! REPEAT!!! PLEASE!!!! HE!! IS!! A!! FIRST!! CLASS!! FOOTBALLER!!'

*   *   *   *   *

The Cambodians weren't the only ones trying to come to terms with a new personal and political life. The terms of the Peace Agreement had charged the UN with administering the country's ministries, training civilian police, teaching human rights, organizing the election and overseeing the financial and legal systems. The UN needed people to register voters, investigate human rights abuses, man the computers, file reports and write newsletters. Most posts had been filled in New York or Geneva, many by permanent UN staff. Not everyone joined the UNTAC mission for the good of Cambodia; some needed a 'field' posting to climb the intricate UN salary scale. Others just wanted money, salting away their allowances. More than one incompetent paperpusher from Geneva or New York found themselves in a well-paid, relatively powerful position in Phnom Penh. Capable UN staffers, used to the UN bureaucracy, tried to work around the dead wood. On the other hand, UN volunteers often had excellent professional qualifications and experience. They lived in small villages registering voters or worked in demanding technical jobs, made less than $900 a month, and received minuscule allowances. 'I believe you have to give things back in this life. I come from a poor country, too,' said an Algerian engineer, a volunteer running part of the telephone system.

While 1970s and 80s *realpolitik* had helped to create the border camps and prolong the civil war, post-glasnost diplomatic reality informed the UN mission. Russia, which had provided the SOC government with technical and economic support, was no longer a major player. Although China provided military observers, Peking's influence held sway primarily over the Khmer Rouge and Sihanouk. Australia, which had initiated several diplomatic moves to end the civil war, provided the longest serving military commander and the telecommunications expertise. There was also a large contingent of Oz businessmen making money through imports, catering and construction. Japan had just begun to end its isolationist foreign policy with the domestically controversial secondment of military advisers to UNTAC. Americans tried to keep their profile low but still wielded enormous influence. The French helped to revamp the university, although they insisted that French-funded courses be taught in French. The French community seemed split between those who longed for a post-colonial colonial relationship and those willing to cut the old imperial ties and suppositions. After the election, university students demonstrated against French hegemony in their classes; the original language explaining the new technologies the protesting students wanted to learn was usually English. Eventually the French backed down.

Finally Amanda trawled a job interview. Searching Psar Thmei for something impressive Amanda could wear, we found Laurie among the stationery stalls quietly handing over the asking price for a book. The stall holder looked as surprised as Amanda and I. Laurie, the hardened Cambodian hand, was a terrible bargainer.

'I just can't argue about money here,' Laurie meekly admitted as we left the market, passing one of the amputees in worn-out soldiers' uniforms who held out begging caps at each entrance. Even though I haggled, I still paid more than some foreigners, and certainly more than Cambodians. Laurie's negotiating skills, however, must have made cyclo drivers think they were being offered a blank cheque by the World Bank.

I could see why Laurie was troubled by fiscal quibbling amidst poverty. A subtle form of imperialism crept into many barang–Cambodian economic relationships. An employer might balk at paying a maid $100 rather than $60 a month. The same employer might then enrol that same maid in an expensive English course, rather than pay a higher salary and let the maid decide what she could afford for lessons. In many instances the important thing for the barang was to feel they were not being taken advantage of. They were dispensing largesse and retaining control, rather than simply paying an adequate wage. In a country where even backpacking English teachers could afford, and were expected by both expats and Cambodians to have, domestic staff, the old-fashioned colonialist attitudes most *barang* would have instantly decried still existed, mutated into subtler, end-of-the-twentieth-century forms.

Returning from the market, Puth, one of the Stockton cyclo regulars ('Half of them used to be CPP security,' Laurie whispered) who lived in a shack behind the hotel, proudly showed us his newborn. Cyclo drivers were at the lowest end of the economic scale, usually renting their cyclos for several thousand *riel* a day. Some were homeless immigrants from the countryside or farmers from nearby provinces who worked in Phnom Penh only during the dry season, after harvest and before rice-planting. They often slept in their cyclo seats, massing at night in groups of 10 or 20 or 30 on the pavements around Psar Thmei, and bathed by the river in front of the palace's golden spires.

Puth handed me his naked son. Cambodian children often play without clothes and, after babysitting one *barang* friend's unhappy child squalling from diaper rash in the Cambodian heat, I understood why. Puth's family hadn't named the boy yet, a process which could take several months in Cambodia even though names served either sex. The child's family name could stem from either parent. With a mortality rate of 126 deaths for every 1,000 live births, one of the world's highest, celebrations for a child's arrival waited until the baby survived the first several days.

'God, it makes you want to adopt one, doesn't it? I always thought I'd have half a dozen kids by now.' I handed Puth's diaperless baby back. Forget about adoption, though. Cambodian authorities, worried about child traffickers, soon closed the procedure to virtually all foreigners.

'Things don't always work out the way you plan, do they?' Laurie sighed, and led us into the restaurant. We sat down and ordered. As our food arrived a good-looking, but very formal, middle-aged man stopped to say hello. Like many of Laurie's dinner dates, the man seemed to want to take care of her.

'He's one,' I nodded as he walked away.

'Go to the head of the class,' Laurie mumbled through her cheeseburger.

While most of the time Amanda, Laurie and I simply sat and gossiped, we also had developed a game entitled 'Spook Spottin'', wherein Amanda and I guessed which missionary, UN worker or traveller had once worked in an intelligence service. We were pretty accurate in our assessments, even if we never quite figured out the identifying mark, although Amanda's final thesis was, 'It's anyone who look's like they're going to ask *you* for a date.' The foreign 'spooks' in Cambodia even had their own Walter Mitty, a deluded businessman with glorious dreams, who boasted of his intelligence connections, and who kept offering the embassy information, but whom the embassy wouldn't go near. 'Unfortunately someday someone might believe him and it won't be too funny,' Laurie complained as we paid our bills.

You only had to walk into Tuol Sleng to see it wasn't funny. Tuol Sleng had once been a high school. In the Khmer Rouge time the school was transformed into a political prison, dubbed by factory workers next door as: 'The place people go into and never come out.' Despite the Khmer Rouge's supposed egalitarian stance, even the prison had a hierarchy. Several ground floor classrooms had been reserved as individual cells for important prisoners.

Everyone herded through the portals was considered a traitor to the revolution, a spy for foreign powers. There were similar provincial prisons, but Tuol Sleng was reserved for Khmer Rouge cadre, foreigners, and the highly educated. Three denouncements and you were picked up – and not just you. Your spouse, your friends, your children could all be arrested.

The Khmer Rouge were methodical wardens. They made rules. These were either written by the Khmer Rouge in English for imprisoned foreigners, or, according to the sceptics, made up by the Vietnamese to impress the tourists. I'm sure the reality wasn't much different than the one those rules depict. 'Do not try to lie with your jaw of traitor,' commanded one rule. 'Do not cry out,' demanded another.

Each prisoner was numbered and photographed – sometimes before death, sometimes after. Each wrote his or her confession; not just once, but again and again. Virtually everyone was forced to declare they had spied for the CIA. The CIA was the overwhelming, ever-present, hidden, enemy. As with other murderous regimes, the CIA's existence, real or imaginary, had been used as an excuse to unleash unspeakable terrors.

Uneducated boys from the countryside – aged 14, 15, or 16 – trained specially in torture, worked on the prisoners until the captives pleaded to whatever distorted fantasy of treason their interrogators desired. Confessions were forwarded to committees and powerful cadre hunting for any sign of enemies within. If the prisoner wasn't dead, he or she was hauled to Choung Ek, a Chinese burial ground south-west of the city which was used as a killing field. Prisoners were then bludgeoned to death to save ammunition. Of the more than 20,000 prisoners who passed through Tuol Sleng, only 7 survived.

In other countries my guide would have been called an airhead, or so I thought at first. Pholla's English wasn't so good, and she twittered a bit as we talked, but I suppose she needed a strong sense of humour in order to shepherd tourists through a torture centre each day.

Pholla came from Kompong Cham, a river city north-east of Phnom Penh. She had three brothers and two sisters. Her father had been a vet. 'He took care of chickens, snakes, foxes, geckos, horses. People had some very funny pets.'

The war started and soon Pholla's family stopped sending her to school: soldiers in Kompong Cham would take girls off the streets to serve as prostitutes. Her eldest brother went to France to study his father's trade and avoid the war. Pholla married a Lon Nol army colonel. A brother brought her to Phnom Penh for safety. She gave birth to a daughter and a son.

'People couldn't go anywhere, children didn't go to school. Pol Pot was always sending shells. When the Khmer Rouge came I was so happy, yes! I thought now the shells would stop, now we could go to the cinema again.'

The theatres didn't reopen. Instead Pholla was evacuated from Phnom Penh with her mother, her children, and two sisters. First they were marched south to Takeo, then east to

Svey Reing. Later Pholla was loaded on a boxcar and shipped west of Phnom Penh to Pursat. And Pholla, who loved the movies and pretty clothes and puffy exotic hair slides, like the one she wore now, was forced to wear only black. Everyone had to dress the same, 'except for Khmer Rouge families. They could wear printed trousers.'

One by one, Pholla lost everyone. 'First my son he die, then my mother. My daughter I thought she live but she die in Pursat. No food, no medicine, no doctor. Very bad. Sometimes I still dream, I dream about those children.' Pholla shook her head from side to side as she spoke about her lost son and daughter, closing her eyes in the middle of the dream sentence as if the past would go away when she opened them again. It didn't. We were standing inside the long middle building. Brick walls about five feet high had been built to form miniature cells, just big enough to lie down in if you weren't too tall. A leg iron was attached to the wall. Water was thrown on prisoners once a week for washing. Just the look of these cramped rooms with their crooked walls reeked of madness, of paranoid psychosis.

I didn't want to think what it must feel like to watch your children starve to death, and I didn't know what to say except that I was sorry. Pholla just shrugged. 'Thank you. I don't always talk that. Next room please?'

We passed into a hall covered with black-and-white photographs of the condemned. Whole families stared from the prints: a squad of children held still by their parents, concerned three years olds, lost grandmothers, proper young marrieds, old men who smiled simply because they always smiled in front of a camera. All had been condemned to death as enemies of the revolution.

The most telling photo on the wall was that of Hu Nim, the Khmer Rouge Minister of Information who was purged only months before the Vietnamese invaded. Hu Nim had been a boyhood companion of Solath Sar. Both had been among the several hundred lucky Cambodian children, sons and daughters of bureaucrats or the aristocracy, to enter the rudimentary education system the French installed in Cambodia in the late 1930s. Having been sent as a boy from the family farm in Kompong Thom to Phnom Penh to be looked after by a brother who was a palace courtier and an aunt who was a court dancer and a mistress of the king, Sihanouk's grandfather, Saloth Sar had qualified for a place. Later the future Pol Pot abandoned his family. His dancing aunt, then elderly, died walking on the road to Battambang in Phnom Penh's evacuation. During a meal in the communal 'dining hall' another of Saloth Sar's brothers, gathered into a Khmer Rouge commune in Kompong Thom, looked up at the portrait of the leader Pol Pot being installed on the wall. Only then did he realize what had become of his missing sibling, Saloth Sar.

In the lycée Saloth Sar had learned to play the violin, while Hu Nim took the lead in the school production of Molière's *Le bourgeois Gentilhomme*. Later, Hu Nim had been one of the few above-ground leftists operating in Sihanouk's government in the 1960s. But he, a communist member of parliament named Khieu Samphan and a Sorbonne-trained economist named Hou Youn had disappeared in 1967, joining the already renegade Saloth Sar and others in the northern jungle hills. The missing trio were nicknamed 'The Three Ghosts'. They were widely assumed to have been assassinated. Several foreign governments discounted their appearance in photos with Sihanouk and the guerillas in the jungle. As far as the French and the US were concerned, the three had died, not disappeared.

Hu Nim did not die until 1978, a victim of the revolution he helped create. His eyes in the photo tell you he knows what will happen. He would have seen the Tuol Sleng confessions sent to the central committee. Hu Nim would have known how they were obtained. His eyes see the future, and they tell you he knew the future was short and that there was nothing pleasant there. On the floor lay heaps of metal, leg irons, and two busts of Saloth Sar. I was struck by how much he resembled Sihanouk in those casts, and I said so.

'Yes, some people say he look like Sihanouk, some say he look like Mao Tsetung,' Pholla said off-handedly. That struck me as a perfect description not just for Saloth Sar but also for his political philosophy: he had mixed Sihanouk's nationalism with Mao's Marxism; which seemed more significant to Saloth Sar depended on your own point of view.

Pholla tapped a photo as we left the room. 'That's my

brother. I read his confession. In 1976 the Khmer Rouge tell all the people abroad: come back, we need you. So my brother come back. He fly into Pochentong. And they bring him here. My other brothers, since the liberation to now I ask about them. I ask everywhere. But my brothers very handsome. The Khmer Rouge, if they see beautiful they kill. They think handsome means Lon Nol officer.'

There were tears at the bottom of Pholla's eyes. Uncomfortable, I came up with yet another inadequate response, murmuring something about how hard it must be for Pholla to do this job, and suggested we try another building. We walked outside. I looked up at the central structure. The classrooms on the second floor had not been converted into cells, but Pholla said no visitors were allowed on the top floors.

A cat with a red ribbon tied around its neck ran in front of us. 'Whose is that?'

'Oh, that's the children's. The children in the neighbourhood think that is the best cat in the world,' Pholla giggled.

Pholla had remarried, and lived nearby with two new children. Her second husband was a film producer, she said proudly. 'Maybe you see his film, Yugoslav co-production, called *Cambodia: Hell Number 7?*'

But the second husband also had another wife. 'And now he doesn't give me so much money because he has two families to support and he says there is no money for films. Do men act like this in the United States?'

I asked Pholla what she thought. 'I think they act that way everywhere. Everywhere men the same!' Pholla whooped. The tears were gone and for a good while, until we reached the gate and I handed her a tip, we compared notes on an infinitely more comfortable subject.

*   *   *   *   *

'You know, the Vietnamese put that museum together,' claimed a photographer who'd been coming to Cambodia for years, 'and those torture instruments change. They're always moving those exhibits around. I've always been able to go to the second floor of the prison.'

'I didn't believe her story,' Amanda pronounced. 'It was 15 years ago and she still gets tears in her eyes. I think she made it up to get the tip.' It was funny how almost every foreigner who had come to Phnom Penh, no matter how even-keeled, sensitive or concerned they were, occasionally doubted the humble stories they heard about the Khmer Rouge time. Maybe it stopped them from imagining the same thing happening to them or people they loved. Maybe everyone's imagination faltered in sheer self-protection when presented with agony so widespread.

I didn't tell Amanda that part of me had wondered the same thing.

Six months later I visited Tuol Sleng again. Pholla didn't remember me. I had to prod her to tell me her story. The facts were the same, but the telling had changed. If Pholla's life as I heard it was a fiction, the tale was no set piece.

This time when I asked to see the upper storeys Pholla said I could but she wouldn't accompany me. Pholla said she never visited the top floors. She was afraid the ghosts were there, and that her brothers had returned as *khmoeh*, the shades of those who have committed suicide or been murdered.

In the upper classrooms manacles hung underneath the blackboard and windows; numbers had been painted on the woodwork to identify each prisoner. My moto driver, Vanna, came with me. His uncle, a teacher, had died in Tuol Sleng but Vanna had never been inside. After a brief look at the second floor Vanna wanted to leave quickly. Wire mesh covered the upper walkways so captives couldn't throw themselves from the porches.

Pholla sat on the lowest stair, chin in hand, waiting for Vanna and I to return. Maybe Pholla thought that as a veterinary student returning from France her brother would not have rated a 'private' cell downstairs. Or maybe after reading her brother's confession she knew exactly where, under which window or blackboard or number, he had been tied.

Later I would hear stories like this again. In Battambang a friend's eyes filled with tears as he said he had not seen his mother before she died because he had been sent by the Khmer Rouge to a commune ten kilometres away. One night a cyclo driver, reciting his life story, suddenly started shouting as he pedalled, 'Why did the Khmer Rouge tell me my parents would come back when they were dead? Why did the Khmer Rouge tell me my parents would come back when they had killed my mother and killed my father? Why?' His questioning yells ringing down the dark street reminded me that not everyone who had survived the Khmer Rouge physically had survived psychologically.

I did meet one Cambodian who had made up a tragic family history. He wanted a job and thought a family killed by the Khmer Rouge would elicit sympathy. But for everyone else the remembered pain was real.

I don't doubt that the founders of the Tuol Sleng museum arranged history to sell their ideas. Many confessions are missing from the archives. I doubt that one would be wrong to suggest that some would reflect badly on the Khmer Rouge who later defected, some of whom may now be in power in Cambodia. But does that change what happened?

After the Khmer Rouge had been pushed out of Phnom Penh, some observers speculated that up to three million Cambodians had been killed under their rule. The generally accepted figure is one million deaths through murder, disease and starvation. No one will ever know for sure.

The Khmer Rouge want the Tuol Sleng museum closed.

Fish legs and temples

Money was low. I had brought an Asian budget for what were European prices, but I thought I had enough material to write a book proposal. If I could flog the idea I would return for the May elections. Amanda had a job helping to repatriate the 370,000 Cambodian refugees living in Thai border camps. Laurie's vacation was almost over. She would leave at the end of the week.

But I still hadn't visited Angkor Wat, the world's largest temple, which is what I had come to see in the first place. Cambodia presented a bizarre juxtaposition of danger and vacation: travellers came to experience the temples, the politics was something they merely wandered through. Tourist buses parked in the middle of the military and election show. One minute a Ghanaian battalion in combat boots would jog by, or a white UN tank would roar up the wide tree-lined avenue named after Cambodia's first Communist Party leader, Tou Samouth. The next minute you'd see an Apsara Tours representative waving a red umbrella to shepherd a straggling gaggle of wealthy, late-middle-aged Japanese sightseers. The tourists usually wore sunglasses, golfing shorts, and a cheap straw hat with 'Apsara Tours' hand-printed in black magic-marker across the crown. They would have looked no different on an outing to Windsor Castle.

At 7 am the Kampuchea Airlines Ilyushin flight to Siem Reap, where the temples were, billowed condensed air into the cabin as we flew off. Many of the passengers were businessmen and the plane was full. One person was seated in the cockpit. Several others had been stowed on top of the luggage at the back.

Siem Reap was Cambodia's biggest potential cash cow. The United Nations had estimated that one million tourists a year might visit the Angkor temple complex. The million would need to be fed, watered, and teeshirted. At least three development plans existed for Siem Reap city; UNESCO had brought in a mapping system to plot the monuments' preservation and the town's sensitive development. A 'no building' zone had been declared along the tree-lined, mine-lined road leading from the town to Angkor Wat. Hoteliers had suggested a water sports complex along the Great Lake. Land prices had climbed as much as in Phnom Penh.

Siem Reap town was pretty. A tree-lined river in which children laughed and swam, buoyed by jet-black inner tubes, curled through the town centre. Pony carts clopped along the street. Sihanouk's villa, which he rarely visited, took prime position at the end of the park opposite the Grand Hotel. The Angkor temples lay about three miles away. In the middle of town a compound housed the French Foreign Legion contingent guarding the UN operations. The Legionnaires went nuts if you took their picture – they saw themselves as men of mystery and toughness, with their abandoned identities and secret Legionnaire songs and oaths and pseudonyms. Others saw the Legionnaires as a club for overgrown adolescents with a penchant for grievous-bodily-harm charges, but they were eventually voted 'Best UNTAC Bums' by interested parties of both sexes.

Waiting for the plane I had chatted with two Chinese-American men, cousins in their mid-twenties. Combining resources, we hired a car and a guide, Buhmi.

'Don't worry about all the mine signs,' Buhmi assured us nonchalantly as the cousins paid their entrance fee at the temple checkpoint. One cousin had pointed to the bright red, death-head squares nailed onto trees and poles. 'I'm here all the time so the soldiers will tell me if they've laid any new ones.'

Buhmi was an enthusiastic guide. Twenty-seven, tall, wrists jutting from his shirt sleeves, Buhmi wanted to study economics in Phnom Penh. His mother had convinced him to stay in Siem Reap until after the election, so Buhmi had found a retired professor who both taught economics and spoke excellent English. To pay his tutor Buhmi gave English lessons of his own and escorted tourists through the ruins. Buhmi often went alone to the temples simply to wander and look for details he had never noticed before in the stones.

'Sometimes I come out here and practise my talks for tourists by myself so I don't forget the English.' Buhmi was striding through the carved galleries of Angkor Wat. Elephants, horses, soldiers and kings charged in burnished bas-relief on the walls behind him. Buhmi whirled around with his arms outstretched. 'People look at me like I'm crazy, but I don't forget!'

By lunchtime Buhmi had marched us through Angkor Wat, steamed us across the Giants' Causeway, and deposited us at the Bayon temple in Angkor Thom, the fortified city built by Jayavarman VII, the Peter the Great of Angkor. After defeating the Chams, who then ruled central Vietnam, Jayavarman VII undertook a campaign to build roads, hospitals, reservoirs and rest houses. While retaining the grandeur of previous Hindu kings, as a devotee of Buddhism, Jayavarman VII probably believed that public works would gain him merit in the next life.

'Spooky, isn't it?' one of the cousins said as we munched a cheese and peanuts lunch beneath the hundred-plus *bodhisattva* faces which stare enigmatically from all sides of the shadowy Bayon. Around the temple walls the battles of the Khmers against their Cham neighbours are depicted in bas-relief. Unlike the carvings in the earlier Angkor temples, gods are not the stars of the Bayon's artwork. Instead ordinary people go to market, guard their children, farm and fish. The countryside around Siem Reap still looked like the Cambodia carved into the Bayon walls.

The only other sightseers in the afternoon heat were a Cambodian family who had lived the last 15 years in France. The Siem Reap temples were a readily identifiable symbol of Cambodia, a journey to Angkor a pilgrimage most Cambodians longed to make. The towers of Angkor Wat graced Cambodia's money, the flag, and teeshirts but even the great temple's image was subject to politics. CPP pictured Angkor with three towers while Funcinpec insisted on five. Many Cambodian homes prominently displayed an oil painting of Angkor Wat, but civil war had made visiting the temples difficult. The UN peace gave wealthier Cambodians a chance to make the trip. The husband, wife and two Reebok'd teenagers said they had never seen Angkor before.

On the shaded and cool temple stones the cousins and I stretched out to watch the sun cut shadows through the jungle trees. Bird songs drifted from the leafy canopy; the souvenir and charcoal rubbings salesmen were napping by their wares to avoid the heat. Siem Reap was such a small town; the serenity would be easy for developers to destroy.

Buhmi sprinted up and announced we should move quickly to see the Terrace of Elephants, a light-hearted parade of pachyderms, garudas and lions, which had once been part of the royal palace, before dusk. Then Buhmi wanted to take us to the king's bathing pool and up the Bakheng hill, the highest temple and one of the oldest, to watch night fall. 'No problem, I know where the mines are,' Buhmi's head bobbed above the weeds and shoulder-high grass as he flailed along a hidden cow-path, dragging us behind him.

A fusillade rang out. The cousins looked alarmed, and I wasn't so happy myself. We had been warned not to visit the farther temples because of Khmer Rouge. Had we wandered too far out? 'No problem, no problem,' Buhmi swung his arms and laughed. 'They shoot fish in legs.'

'The Khmer Rouge torture fish?' asked a faux-horrified cousin.

'No, no,' Buhmi was shaking his head again. 'The people they don't have net, no hooks. So they take grenade or AK to legs . . .'

'Legs?'

'Yes, yes, legs, Tonle Sap, lakes, water . . .' Buhmi flung an arm in the direction of the lake. 'Boom! Bang! Bang! Fish float to the surface and then they eat.'

Dusk was settling on the Tonle Sap as we charged to the top of the Bakheng. Located halfway between Angkor Wat and Angkor Thom, the Bakheng had been the mountain temple for Yasodharapura, Angkor's first royal city. Temple mountains such as the Bakheng, the Baphuon and the Bayon symbolized the mountain of Meru. In Buddhist mythology Meru supported the heavens. The holy mountain was surrounded by a great sea and enclosed by a high rock wall which defined the edge of the universe. The layout of both Angkor Thom and Angkor Wat, with outer moats surrounding a wall and a multi-storey inner temple, reflect this philosophical construction.

The 400-metre-high Bakheng was also one of the most strategic points for miles around. From the top a mortar could easily hit the city or the airport. A soldier cleaned his gun by a bamboo shack at the foot of a steep trail. Previously the approaches had been mined to prevent a guerilla attack from the hilltop. Angkor Tourism and UNESCO had considered this detrimental to visitors.

'It's a good thing you came this week and not last,' shouted Buhmi, pumping his way across the roots and mud. 'The UN hadn't finished demining the path then.'

'What if they missed one?' I yelled back nervously, but Buhmi laughed. Just the thought of mines and my paranoia kicked into overdrive. I tried to place my feet where Buhmi had placed his. I didn't care how stupid I looked. The cousins behind me did the same. We tiptoed up the track like an epileptic conga line.

'See that hill over there?' Buhmi pointed into the distance. 'The Khmer Rouge are there. But it's far away. Maybe ten kilometres. Khmer Rouge, no problem. *Ot panyaha*.'

'How long does it take to walk ten kilometres?' a cousin whispered.

Despite the huge radio transmitter plopped in the middle of the ruined hilltop temple, the view from the Bakheng was spectacular. Angkor Wat lay behind us. Ahead stretched the azure Tonle Sap. Green rice paddies and *thnot*, tall sugar palm trees, filled the horizon. An orange-robed monk wandered through the fallen stone lintels and porticos. He paused to consider a triangle of mortar shells neatly stacked inside a doorway.

At the bottom of the hill a tour bus stopped and the ubiquitous middle-aged French sightseers rolled out. They gamely struggled up the path, slipping and laughing. Despite the mine signs, one bearded ex-military type poked the trail's edge with a stick, as if he wanted to unearth a hidden treasure.

'Not very smart,' Buhmi shook his head. A determined little

girl, not more than ten, had followed us up the hill, hoisting an Eski thermos filled with ice and drinks as we panted our way to the top. Her drinks that had cost one dollar at the bottom were two dollars at the top of the hill. She had a selling spiel not only in English and Khmer, but also French, German, Thai and Japanese. How could we resist?

'Ask the kid if there are any mines around the edges or if those signs are just to scare us,' suggested one of the cousins as he popped open a tinned mango juice. Buhmi put the question to the girl in Khmer.

'Aiyeeee! *Mins cheran! cheran!*'.The girl made a face – there were mines everywhere. She and the other children never wandered off the paths.

At the guest-house we found another traveller, an Australian radio producer called Bill. Like every other travelling 'media person', he hoped to write some freelance pieces on Cambodia. Bill had only meant to stay in Siem Reap for two days, but watching the sun rise above the temples at dawn, swimming in the *baray*, and puttering on motos to distant temples had so relaxed Bill he found he couldn't leave after five.

'Hey, and the dope's great.' Bill stopped to buy some pre-rolled *ganga* at a night stall. Addictive drugs were against the law, but Cambodians used marijuana as a cooking herb, especially in chicken soup. An uncleaned kilo in the market cost about a dollar and a half. We tested several spliffs while walking to a restaurant and arrived ravenous from both scrambling over the temples and the marijuana munchies. *Loclac*, a beef and egg dish, and *amok*, fish wrapped in a banana leaf and steamed in coconut milk, cured that.

At dinner I suddenly felt old. The cousins were ten years younger. Although born in America they firmly embraced their Asian heritage. One sold computers in Taiwan, the other moved money in Hong Kong. They were smart, honest and interested, but they knew nothing of Cambodian history. They were amazed that many countries had tacitly supported the Khmer Rouge in the 1980s.

'The story stopped getting play,' said Bill later. 'They didn't know because Cambodia became a tiny paragraph on the "briefs" column.'

The Chinese-American cousins retired early; in the morning Buhmi was squeezing them on his moto to watch sunrise at the Bayon. Bill and I sat on the porch, surrounded by glowing, smouldering mosquito coils, and smoked. I flipped through a Thai clothing catalogue featuring trendy 'Out of Style' jeans. The country night was still except for the humming crickets, the croaking frogs, and next door's karaoke machine.

'I should really go talk to the commander and try to do a story,' said Bill. 'But it's so relaxing here . . . and I need to catch that morning flight . . .'

I'd like to come back, I thought as we lit the last joint. I could write a book, I could freelance, I could string for the wires. As a kid watching the Vietnam War close down on television, I had longed to be a 'foreign correspondent', although I wasn't crazy about their safari shirts. Despite all the moaning from friends who filed reports from exotic climes, they all agreed journalism 'beats working for a living'. Romania and what was left of Yugoslavia had been inundated with freelancers but the competition didn't seem so fierce here. Reuters, United Press International, Agence France Presse and Associated Press had offices in Phnom Penh. The wires fought to get news on the computer first so I hoped there would be at least casual work. There wasn't much in London except rain and dull office jobs. Most of my friends were in the same position. 'I can sniff out news. I can get people to talk. I've got an eye for stories coming down the road. I'd be good at it,' I thought hubristically as Bill and I said goodnight. I might as well try out a new career in Cambodia.

Back in Phnom Penh the next morning there was news. Around midnight alleged Khmer Rouge forces had attacked less than half a mile from the guest-house. The incursion was the first Khmer Rouge attack on Siem Reap since the Peace Agreement. Because UNTAC was a peace *keeping*, not a peace *enforcing*, mission, the UN soldiers could not protect the town. The Legionnaires could respond only if the UN was attacked; they had been incensed that they couldn't join the fight. The story had a lot of play.

And both Australian radio and I had snoozed through the whole thing.

*   *   *   *

'Oh, Goddddddddahhhhhhh,' Amanda cried and pulled the pillow over her head as I walked into the room and dumped my pack. 'How can you turn on that light? What time is it? How was Angkor?'

'Ten thirty. Great. Did Laurie leave?'

'No, she goes at one. Goddddddddahhhhhhh. Oh, did you miss a night last night. Carol, I can't believe you weren't here. God, there was this French guy . . .' Amanda lurched up like Frankenstein heaving to life, staggered to the fridge, grabbed a Diet Coke and pulled on the aspirin bottle.

'Laurie and I went to Ban Thai to eat and we were talking and it got heavy, I mean really heavy. Somehow we had two bottles of wine. Then they were closing and we didn't want to stop talking, so we went to the No Problem to have coffee. Except we didn't. Then these two French military guys come in wearing those stupid little shorts and knee socks the French wear and since we're two women on our own naturally they decide to do us a favour and sit with us. So Laurie gets the tall one and I get the short, fat balding one, who won't tell me what he does. All he keeps saying is, "I am a soldier of fortunnnnnnne, a soldier of fortunnnnne. I killlllllllllllll peep-ullllll . . ." But the tall one is worse! He's totally shitfaced and he won't stop talking. He keeps going on about how Cambodians want the French back. They want to be a colony again, he says. Then he starts shouting, "Dien Bien Phu was not a defeat! Dien Bien Phu was not a defeat! Dien Bien Phu was a love affairrre gone wrong!" And he won't believe what Laurie does for a living. He says no, she's a girl, she can't do that. And why does he know? Because he says he's spying for the French! But nobody knows . . . except by this time, of course, for all of the No Problem Café. Even when Laurie tells him he shouldn't be telling her all this, he still won't believe her. So then they offer us a ride home and they take us all over Phnom Penh. And I'm spending the whole time in the back seat wrestling with Baldie trying to keep him off me.'

'But, Carol, Laurie's story. Oh my god, Laurie . . . By this time Amanda had finished her Diet Coke and was head first in the fridge rummaging for another. With a sharp, fizzing tug on the second Coke's pop-tab she continued. 'Laurie was here in the '70s. She was only 18 when she arrived. She'd come as a nurse and she met this Khmer doctor. Anyway, they fell in love and got married. She went through the entire ceremony, with all those changes of clothes . . .

'They kept working at the hospital, but they waited too late and couldn't get out, so they went to the French Embassy. But because he only had a Cambodian passport the Khmer Rouge made him leave.' For years Laurie waited for any news. After the invasion everyone fled to Thailand and she was told he was dead. But she didn't know what had happened to him until she came back here the first time a couple years ago.

'Laurie was looking at the pictures on the wall at Tuol Sleng. And there he was. His picture was on the wall. No one had ever told her. And she said she just broke down and cried and cried and cried. But it's not finished, because they had a godchild, a niece. And the niece was an orphan who made it to one of the camps. Eventually Laurie found her. She wanted to adopt the girl and get her out, but because Laurie was a single woman the authorities wouldn't let Laurie have her, even though Laurie was her aunt.

'But then one of the armies came to the camp and kidnapped some girls to take back into Cambodia to be prostitutes for the soldiers. Laurie's niece and a couple of other girls escaped, but the niece stepped on a mine trying to get back across the border and lost a leg. Somehow Laurie arranged for her to be sent to a missionary school in Thailand. But the girl thought that as an amputee, no matter how pretty she was, no one would ever marry her, she'd never have a family, and she couldn't face that.

'So Laurie's niece killed herself. It sucks, doesn't it?'

*   *   *   *

Half an hour later we grabbed a last coffee with Laurie. At breakfast she had checked out the Frenchmen from No Problem. Despite the fact that UN rules insisted staff work only for the UN, and perform no duties for their individual nations, the taller Frenchman was always locking himself in his office, typing reports which no one ever saw. He was a standing joke at headquarters.

'Needless to say, the French are promoting him,' Laurie grinned.

Laurie and I walked up Achar Mean to the photo shops. We gabbled on about nothing in particular. Laurie gave a hilarious account of Amanda fending off Baldie the Backseat Masher.

I wanted to say something to Laurie about the story, but it was a sunny day, and we were laughing, and I just didn't know how to start. Laurie must have known that Amanda, a firm believer in freedom of information, would immediately blab the story to me. What Amanda had told me explained much about Laurie, the remarks about how 'things don't always turn out the way you planned', why keeping control seemed so important to her. I half think Laurie was waiting for me to say something, but I didn't. It seemed far too much to go into in the few minutes before Laurie left to catch her plane.

After that, though, Amanda's cynicism seemed to end. With Laurie there was no way Amanda could pick on cultural difference, turn Laurie into someone different from herself, as denial or protection against the story she'd been told.

I never heard Amanda doubt a Cambodian's story again.

Ming

Back in rainy, cold England I was dying to go back to rainy, warm Cambodia, but I needed to be paid something, anything, to write – I'd go broke quickly if I had to send speculative stories on Phnom Penh's six-dollar-a-minute faxes. Selling the book idea took a while. 'I just can't see who would be interested in Cambodia . . .' the rejection letters said. But one Monday my proposal sold – I had a contract for one light-hearted Cambodian travelogue aimed at the tourists who would rush into the country after the election's end.

By Friday I was on a Bangkok-bound plane that blearily connected with the morning flight to Phnom Penh. I had faxed Amanda and she was waiting at the airport, fake Ray-Bans shielding a hangover and Landcruiser keys in her hand, standing in almost exactly the same position as I'd left her three months earlier. We pulled my luggage off the jumbled pile on the hot tarmac and headed to the truck. In less than one month voting would start. Little Cambodian news had appeared in England; I needed to catch up on Cambodian politicking. But first, of course, I had to hear the gossip . . .

'And then Alain . . .' Amanda continued as she swerved the Landcruiser past a motorcyclist ferrying a pig crammed into a wicker basket on the back seat.

'Alain seems to be a major feature of this story,' I couldn't help noticing as Amanda gave a breathless rundown of her last three months.

Amanda raised her eyebrows and tried a 'don't be silly' look over the rim of her Ray-Bans. Behind her, reflections of cars and motos shooting past us shimmered on the window glass. I hadn't thought it possible, but there was more traffic in Phnom Penh than before. There were more UN Landcruisers, more motorcycles, more trucks loaded with wood or coal and carrying passengers on top, and many more Mercedes. Several were left-hand drive. Cambodians drove on the right, but Thailand's British influence had prescribed left-hand steering. Stolen cars and motorcycles from Thailand were shipped into Cambodia either via Koh Kong port or via the legal and illegal land crossings which sliced through the border.

'Carol, he's married,' Amanda spoke firmly, rammed the car into top gear, and barely missed a moto carrying a side-saddle orange-clad monk cupping his hands to light a cigarette in the wind. Thankfully Amanda decided against arguing with a large petroleum truck for possession of the centre lane. 'Lane' in Cambodia is defined thus: if there is a space into which you think your vehicle might fit, whether or not it actually can, that space is a lane.

'And, more importantly . . .' Amanda added, 'repatriation's finished. I have to find another job.' 370,000 Cambodians from Thai refugee camps had returned, she said, as the Landcruiser bumped down a potholed street between the refurbished villas of Chamcarmon, and then turned into a drive. Repatriation went well, Amanda continued, even if the last group, refuseniks who didn't want to return to Cambodia under any condition, had torn up the buses.

We dumped my bags in an upstairs bedroom of the large, seemingly deserted house where Amanda lived. The other foreign aid workers were already gone. Amanda was to close the house when the lease ended, but one of the NGOers had told his Cambodian fiancée's mother to move her family in until the contract expired.

'I don't know who they are . . .' Amanda threw her hands up as we smiled at the two women peeling vegetables in the kitchen. 'Probably some more cousins. Ma, who are these two?'

A late-middle-aged woman in a sarong stood in the doorway and waved a fan in front of her face. 'My sister and my sister's sister.'

'Your sister-in-law?' Amanda conjectured.

'Yes, my sister-in-law,' Ma sighed, as if Amanda had asked her yet another unreasonable, unfathomable question.

'I'm not being rude to her,' Amanda swore, 'but she was only supposed to bring her children and she's moved in half of Phnom Penh. The generator's going full blast, I never know what I'm going to find in the fridge, and if a TV or something disappears I'm responsible. Besides, she's practically forcing Ming to marry Edgar. When you marry a Cambodian you marry their family. It's a great bargain for Ma, she gets to be supported without having to do anything, but not such a good deal for Ming.'

Ming was Ma's eldest daughter. Bright, pretty and 27, she was to marry an NGOer she had translated for. As Amanda described him, Edgar was obnoxious and 53. He should have been marrying Ma, not Ming. Ming hadn't wanted anything to do with him, but Edgar had asked Ming's mother, who had pressured her. Ming changed completely when she was around Edgar, according to Amanda. When he wasn't around Ming was a hoot. When Edgar was there she lost all personality. To Amanda, Ma was selling her daughter.

Amanda and I sat on the porch with Ming and her mother. Some UNTACers were coming to the house tonight. One ran a division in which Amanda had applied for a job. Amanda wanted the throng to make themselves scarce for a bit. 'You'd better talk to the old bag because if I have to say another word to her I'll strangle her,' Amanda smiled. Amanda and Ming then huddled in one corner, laughing over a private joke.

'Yes, I tell my daughter she should marry him, why not?' Ma and I stood on the other end of the porch, sipping Amanda's Cokes. As far as Ma was concerned, after all she had been through, arguments with an NGO worker half her age weren't going to move her. Behind us hung the mosquito nets of family members who slept on the porch.

'I counted eleven tonight . . .' Amanda rolled her eyes as she walked by.

'Many other boys come around but Ming don't like them, she don't choose one. I tell her she should go with Mr Edgar. Why not? Mr Edgar has good job. Maybe she wait, she be too old. She don't find a husband with good job. Ming don't have a father, she should get good husband. Do you speak French?'

I admitted my French was as bad as Ma's English. Ma sighed. Even though she'd worked for the Americans for four

years, she preferred speaking French. Did I know Mr George
Goodhew of Arlington, Virginia, by any chance? From 1956
until 1961 she had worked with Mr George Goodhew at the
American Embassy. She wished she could get in touch with
him now. Maybe he could do something for her family.

'It's very hard, very hard,' said Ma. 'I have five children. My
husband engineer. We had nice house. One year after the
Khmer Rouge come they take my husband away and they kill.
I don't know how, I never want to know how. I have five
children to keep alive. Very hard for me. Very hard. Now
some work it's a little better. We have two-room apartment by
the market. Not so nice, not good house. It's much nicer here.'

The UN men, one of whom I thought had been a friend of
Laurie's, arrived. Both were friends of Edgar. Half an hour
before Ming had laughed and teased Amanda – 'Which
boyfriend visit tonight?' – but when the men appeared Ming
changed. They had news from Edgar, tasks for her to perform.
Suddenly Ming's English disappeared. The men were kind,
not rude. They joked. But Ming had fled, and a small, quiet,
Cambodian doll had appeared in her place.

*   *   *   *

In addition to the travel book, I'd returned with commissions
for several articles. Little money was involved, but the
commissions at least made me feel legitimate. One piece was
to highlight Siem Reap and Angkor Wat as a trendy, un-
spoiled tourist destination. The day after I arrived the Khmer
Rouge interrupted my career plans by invading Siem Reap,
holding the town for several hours and killing two Vietnamese
before they retreated. The tourists grabbed the first plane out.

Across the country, the guerillas were boycotting the voting
and had fielded no candidates, although several small parties
were rumoured to be Khmer Rouge fronts. Under the Paris
Peace Agreement, all four factions were to canton weapons
and soldiers and allow UN military observers into their areas.
The Khmer Rouge had stopped doing either.

Would the Khmer Rouge disrupt the election and start
fighting again? This was the question of the moment. Three
Bulgarian soldiers had been killed by Khmer Rouge in

Kompong Speu, but 'Bulgybat' was considered the least disciplined of the military battalions and the circumstances of the murders were murky. In Kompong Thom, the largest province, a young volunteer Japanese electoral worker, Atsuhito Nakata, and a Cambodian colleague were attacked and murdered by unknown assailants. Speculation frequently held the murderers were Khmer Rouge. Unlike the Bulgarians, there were no, supposedly slightly mitigating, rumours about rape or gambling to besmirch the dead young Japanese man's character.

Nippon had been riveted by its Cambodian foreign policy experiment. The head of UNTAC, Yashushi Akashi, was Japanese and Japan had twice as many news people in Cambodia as any other foreign nation. The Japanese had been the second largest contributors to UNTAC, providing the funding for all those Toyota Landcruisers. With the Nakata killing, some observers feared the Khmer Rouge were targeting Japanese to try to make Japan pull out. They also worried that if enough election workers quit, fearing for their safety, polling would have to be postponed simply from lack of staff.

The UN eventually declared Nakata had been murdered by an unsuccessful job applicant, not the Khmer Rouge. By the time the report came out, however, interest had waned. Nakata's funeral was over and the photographs of his weeping parents had already gone out. The end to the story didn't get nearly the attention an alleged Khmer Rouge attack did.

'People blame everything on the Khmer Rouge,' said an old hand who'd been coming to Cambodia since the 1960s. 'Anybody who wants to settle a score, anybody who wants to cause trouble, can do what they want and then shout, "Khmer Rouge! Khmer Rouge!" I'm not saying the Khmer Rouge are lily white, but they aren't responsible for everything.' Indeed, most of the political violence and assassinations had been attributed to Cambodia's ruling Peoples Party, not the guerillas. Despite several score killings, the UN had made few arrests.

The daily press briefings, half empty in January, now spilled into the hallway. Soon the sessions moved to a covered portico outdoors, a space which held several hundred people.

Never mind understanding the subtleties of Cambodian politics, grasping the practicalities of freelancing took long enough. I had to learn who did what and to whom they were related – since political positions in Cambodia were usually awarded on personal allegiances or enmities; find all the ministry buildings; obtain a State of Cambodia press card from the reluctant CPP-run Ministry of Information just to talk with Cambodian government officials, for CPP in practice still ran the government even if the UN was nominally in charge; deconstruct the myriad acronyms for UN agencies and non-governmental organizations; and find a place to cash a traveller's cheque or develop film, without scratching the negatives. Television crews and correspondents with good expense accounts eased their way by paying fixers, residents who knew the ropes. The fixers briefed the crews and correspondents on background, made their appointments and pointed them toward stories.

It didn't take long to realize that strings were jealously guarded. If I found the perfect *Asiaweek* story, for example, professional courtesy dictated I run the story past *Asiaweek*'s correspondent, so I didn't seem to be going behind his back to get his space, and consequently his job. It also didn't take long to realize that most publications interested in Cambodia already had stringers.

With all the tape recorders, notebooks, laptop computers and silly ink pens on a string floating around there seemed practically zip chance of getting any new work during the election. There went my money-making plans. And other freelancers were pouring into the country. The news business being perverse, if the election went wrong there would be plenty of work. Many freelancers had no firm commitment, merely a 'we'll look at what you send' arrangement with an editor somewhere. Some worked for a magazine or newspaper which didn't want to pay a writer or photographer to report the Cambodian election. The freelancer would take his or her vacation and money to cover the story, but at least they had that all important credential. They had a name card.

Cambodians don't like losing face, and unknown writers aren't much better. While others parlayed a quick discussion with a bureau chief into 'I'm working for Agence France

Presse . . .', I stuck with the story that I was writing a book. I had always thought book-writing respectable and a valid reason for being in Cambodia, until one Gecko non-believer dismissed me with 'Honey, everybody in this bar is writing a book.'

Neophyte photographers had a better chance of breaking in than writers. Writers needed sources, needed contacts and, worse, needed to know what they were writing about. Photographers just had to be where the action was, hopefully with no other photographers around, and have luck.

Being there was what Suzie and Leon, who arrived the day after I did, were counting on. Suzie and Leon had spent the last year in Japan teaching English, photographing rock concerts and saving money to cover the Cambodian elections. Leon was bearded, laconic and laid back. Suzie was outgoing, with a blonde bombshell body. As attractive to and attracted by men as Suzie was, she was determined to prove she could do without them or beat them at their own game. Some people felt she tried too hard.

Leon and Suzie were eager, they were hungry, and they were equipped. Three Nikon bodies each, every length of lens, bricks of slide and negative film (colour and black-and-white), extenders, filters, shades, Swiss army knives, compass wrist-watches so they wouldn't get lost in the jungle, combat fatigues, a MacIntosh Powerbook to log their shots, a well-stocked medicine chest with malaria pills, bandages, aspirin and Tampax, combat boots, net-backed Japanese fishing vests with multiple film-holding pockets, walkie-talkies to communicate in a firefight, and a copy of Vietnam photographer Tim Page's autobiography, *Page after Page*, which they considered the best book on war photography.

They had everything, except experience.

*   *   *   *

Suzie, Leon and I really had no idea what we were doing, so we pooled our lack of resources and knowledge. The key was to look like you had work, even if you didn't.

'The Khmer Rouge took 13 including my brother,' said

Danh as the boat rocked upon the water. The translator dutifully explained this from the Vietnamese. I scribbled in my notebook. The questions I asked Danh were obvious to someone already writing on Cambodia, but I had to start somewhere.

The day before, Leon, Suzie, another photographer called Jerry and I had waded through UN red tape, acquired all necessary signatures in duplicate, and presented ourselves at the UN Naval Observers' Phnom Penh base. We hoped to ride with the Unnos to visit ethnic Vietnamese refugees, victims of Khmer Rouge persecution, fleeing by water to the Vietnamese border. Leon and Suzie had roared off upriver. Jerry and I had boarded a bright orange Viper speedboat and bounced downstream along the Mekong to a fishing village.

'This light sucks.' Jerry was hopping from deck to deck with his manual Nikon F2, snapping an old woman on this boat, a lazing smoker on another, kids standing next to a bicycle shed on a third. His bushy iron-grey Jehovah beard mesmerized the children.

'See, I've been here a long time,' Jerry explained to me later. 'I know a lot of things. So I grew a beard, see, since the last time I was here. So this time maybe some people won't recognize me. Hey, they see the beard, so what? To a lot of Cambodians all us *barang* look alike. I've got the beard, I'm not the same person they knew the last time.'

For a moment I thought he was joking.

Jerry had freelanced in Cambodia in the '70s and had been returning ever since. During the Lon Nol war, when scores of Cambodian and foreign journalists lost their lives, Jerry had been wounded more than once. Certain subjects, like why Jerry let virtually no one see his pictures (which were said to be wonderful), or the sins of Ronald Reagan or Bill Clinton, could send Jerry into a rage. Despite an occasional temper flash to Suzie, Leon and I, who frankly didn't have a clue what we were doing, Jerry was almost always patient and helpful.

'Hey, a lot of freelancers will show up,' Jerry had said holding in his breath. He had just lit the day's first joint. The noon briefing had finished, the press corps had vanished for lunch, and Jerry and I were the only two left in the sterile white pre-fab room. 'Some will make it, some won't. I've seen it all before. You go out there, you try, you learn. Some people can't learn, so they don't make it. Some just don't get the breaks. Even if they work hard, they don't get the breaks. That's tough, but that's the way it is. If you can't hack it, you shouldn't be a freelancer. You should go home and get a safe job in Walmart.'

I guess I hadn't learned enough that day. I made the mistake of asking Jerry why he didn't use an agency to sell his shots. He angrily replied that he wasn't a 'paparazzo'. He was here for the long haul. Jerry stomped out of the room, shouting that he wanted his pictures used the right way. Hey, don't worry about it, the consensus said later, Jerry does that to us all. It doesn't mean a thing.

Everything about Jerry was intense, even his smile, which broke the ice with the Vietnamese children on the river and made them laugh. 'The light's awful. You can't do anything with it. Look at that glare. It's too fucking bright. You might as well not shoot. It's not worth developing,' Jerry grimaced, clicking away.

* * * *

'The Khmer Rouge were walking the people they had taken up the mountain and my brother escaped. The others we have never seen again,' Danh continued. Danh, the translator and I were squatting on our haunches on the boat. I was having trouble keeping my balance. The 70 or so gently swaying boats along the river's edge all belonged to Vietnamese fishing families.

The Khmer Rouge had given up many things since they ruled Cambodia. The Mao jackets had disappeared; now smart suits attired Khieu Samphan and the Khmer Rouge's UN ambassador. The guerillas had declared that they, too, were no longer communist, but capitalist. They didn't really have the details down, though. When asked what the exchange rate to the dollar would be for the paper currency the guerillas were issuing, the Khmer Rouge representative merely groaned, 'Oh, too many questions . . .'

But the one thing the Khmer Rouge had not abandoned was their xenophobic hatred of the Vietnamese. Traditionally

Cambodians fear that their country will be annexed by either Vietnam or Thailand, the 'crocodile' or the 'tiger'. The Khmer Rouge rallying cry since 1979 had been that the Vietnamese, the hated *yuon*, had taken their country. Khmer Rouge reasons for non-compliance with the peace accords usually involved the Vietnamese. The Khmer Rouge insisted that this foreign army had never really left.

After the 1978 invasion of Cambodia, several hundred thousand Vietnamese came to Cambodia seeking jobs. Many stayed. Although the Vietnamese had withdrawn their estimated 200,000 soldiers by 1989, the Khmer Rouge maintained that Vietnamese troops still hid throughout Cambodia. The Vietnamese fishermen, bricklayers and carpenters who were rebuilding Phnom Penh, even the Vietnamese bar girls – these in Khmer Rouge minds were soldiers, a reason to stay at war.

The Phnom Penh government was now headed by an ex-Khmer Rouge commander named Hun Sen, who joined with the Khmer Rouge as a teenager after Sihanouk's overthrow and lost one eye fighting the Lon Nol government. As a Khmer Rouge commander, it is doubtful that Hun Sen's moral record was unblemished. In 1977 Hun Sen refused an order to attack Vietnam and escaped to that country. He became one of four commanders who rallied troops from the Cambodian refugees camped along the Cambodia–Vietnam border and pushed the Khmer Rouge into Thailand. In the post-Khmer Rouge, Vietnamese-backed government, Hun Sen had been made Foreign Secretary at 26. At the time the unworldly farmer's son who had fought since he was 18 had to be reminded what the UN was.

Hoping people would take him more seriously, Hun Sen added two years to his official age and learned fast: at 32 Hun Sen became the world's youngest prime minister. Hun Sen proved an adept politician, even if several members of his family were allegedly totally corrupt, and blame for the murders of opposition party workers during the election run-up had been placed on the CPP under Hun Sen's leadership. But to the Khmer Rouge Hun Sen and the Phnom Penh government were only 'Vietnamese puppets'.

In March, Khmer Rouge soldiers had forced three Khmer

boatmen to sail them at gunpoint to the floating video parlour of an ethnic Vietnamese boat village in the Great Lake called Chong Kneas. The fishing families lived on their boats; the video parlour, hairdresser, radio repair shop, and other stores drifted alongside them in bamboo huts.

That night the video boat had been crowded. Shouting for the *yuon* to go home, the Khmer Rouge fired, killing 36 people. Since the Chong Kneas attack other Vietnamese had been murdered and the Vietnamese fishing community had fled. They moved in flotillas for safety. Large boats pulled the smaller boats which pulled the smallest ones. Tugs charged $200 to pull a group down river. Everything the families owned were tied onto the boats – bicycles and pots, nets and television antennae, chickens, plastic watering cans. The women cooked inside the hull and lay laundry to dry on the boats' rooftops.

Danh's brother had been abducted by the Khmer Rouge while fishing, but he escaped and the next day fled down river. Danh had waited for a convoy to bring their wives, children and boats. The twelve other ethnic Vietnamese taken with Danh's brother were not seen again. By now Danh's brother was in Vietnam.

Danh giggled when I said his brother seemed like a smart guy to me. At first when someone in Cambodia laughed, or made a joke, about disaster that had missed them, I was surprised. Then I wondered, why? Humour added balance, it meant people were getting on with their lives. I'd been looking at Cambodia only in tragic terms, but that was unfair to its people, who were as emotionally complex in their reactions to life as anyone else. Once again I chastised myself for expecting stereotypes, not subtleties.

The boats which floated here now were waiting for the UN naval observers to escort them to the border, as protection against more attacks.

'I don't have relatives in Vietnam,' Danh continued. Danh didn't think he could work there. In Cambodia the government sold fishing rights to middlemen, who then rented waters to individual fishermen. Danh assumed the fishing community in Vietnam would also have their waters apportioned and that he wouldn't be allowed to cast his nets. He didn't blame the Vietnamese in Vietnam, though. They had to make a living too.

He added that he would wait at the border until after the election, then return. Danh had wanted to vote, but when he had tried to register he was told he was not Cambodian. None of the ethnic Vietnamese he knew, Danh said, not even those who spoke Khmer, who had been born in Cambodia and whose grandparents had been born in Cambodia, had been allowed to register. For some Cambodian officials the only qualification for Cambodian voting rights was Khmer ethnicity. When I asked if he had complained to UNTAC, Danh laughed. 'I think I've got enough trouble.' He didn't think complaining to the UN would have made a difference and he didn't want to bring any attention, and possibly problems, to himself.

A British Unno and I climbed the steep riverbank to the village and talked to the assistant chief, while Jerry stayed on the muddy Mekong bank taking pictures. As we walked to the chief's house, a little girl, her chin held high to stop oversized bright pink sunglasses from slipping off her nose, held my hand. The village's several hundred people had no *wat*, school, or cement floors. The chief's house had three wooden walls and a raised wooden platform but was roofed with fronds.

'Some drunken Khmers came one night and shouted they were going to kill us all,' the chief said.

The Unno asked the chief how seriously he took the threat. The chief was quiet, watching the waters slap the bank, and then said he wasn't sure – after all, they had been drunk. He rocked on his haunches for a moment, staring at the eroded edge of the Mekong. Finally he spoke. 'It was probably just drunk men's talk.'

*   *   *   *

I saw Ming for the last time at a graduation party for her computer class. In a city with only intermittent electricity and an unsafe water supply, the going word was that a decent job required a mastery of WordPerfect, Windows and Excel. I'd just interviewed Danh and the floating refugees and wondered what the Khmer computer students thought of the Vietnamese. None of Ming's friends seemed to have anything against them.

Ming's bash started in the late afternoon so revellers could be home by dark. Ma and Ming had spent the day cooking spring rolls, chicken noodles, and *tra khoun* – flat vegetable patties. I asked Ming about her plans for the wedding. Ming refused to say whether she was looking forward to it.

About a dozen fellow students had come for the end-of-class party. Ming put on Cambodian music and everyone danced the *ramvong*. We moved in a slow circle, our hands making small graceful egg shapes in the air, 'picking the flower' Ming called it.

The music changed to a rip-off compilation tape from the market, everyone's greatest Western hits covered by unknown Thai singers. Ming wanted to dance Western, but none of the Cambodian men and boys were willing. Suddenly Sera, a Welsh backpacker who had come to Cambodia for a week and stayed a year, pulled Ming into a wild jitterbug, both of them shouting gleefully as they spun round and round and round the room.

I was upcountry when Edgar wedded Ming. Edgar had insisted the traditional ceremony be curtailed. They quickly exchanged vows and then held a reception in a riverside restaurant. Two friends of the groom had driven the couple on to their honeymoon hotel.

'Ah, hell, I don't know how it's going to work out,' said one of the friends. 'I don't really think Ming realized what she'd done. Suddenly she started shouting, "No, No, I cannot go with you! I cannot stay out late! You must take me home! You have not asked my mother!" It's a hell of a way to start a marriage.'

Ming and Edgar left for a new UN mission. Whatever his faults, Edgar did right by Ming's family, setting them up in a rented house in a nicer area of town than the market where Ma's apartment had been.

News filtered back slowly. Ming, said the reports, was miserable. Edgar was away a lot. She and Edgar shared a house with another relief worker couple, but the couple had jobs and Ming didn't. Most of the day Ming sat alone in the house. The weather was chilly, the food was different. There were no Cambodians Ming could talk to and assuage her homesickness.

The reports eventually changed. Ming had begun to adjust. Edgar had moved her to France, a place with a few Cambodians. For the first time in her life, Ming had money. She could go shopping, she could start a home of her own. Rumour said Ming no longer talked constantly about going back to Phnom Penh. Whatever Ming had thought of her mother's bargain, it was her bargain now.

Battambang

Six foot five inches, carved from stone, a half-drained can of VB grasped in one hand, the macho Australian signalman sitting at the Rock Hard bar slowly moaned. With extreme concentration, Australia's finest languidly flipped a page in *Vogue*. He eyeballed the layout, up and down. 'Aaaoooww-wwwwwwwahhhh . . .'

A startling vision of Mr Oz in a neat little Chanel number and pumps flashed through my mind before I looked over his shoulder and realized his sighs were aimed at a near-naked lingerie model, not the clothes.

The Wonderbra-loving Australian was dejected and dreading the election. 'Shit's going to go down, mate. Shit's going to fly. It's happening already. You don't know. We're in comms. We hear everything. It's not going to be happy. Not happy.'

I can't say that news did much for my mood. Every day at the press briefing I listened to reports of bridges blown in Battambang or shooty-bangs in Pursat, but I thought the election would go peacefully. I had no special information, though, and I must have been having a low day. Maybe it was long-term traveller's discombobulation but I was doubting my whole enterprise. Why had I ever come up with this freelancing idea? If I was so smart, how come I had come to a country where they shot people?

Alain and Amanda arrived and distracted me from my 'what am I doing here, I don't even like fried rice' thoughts. Despite the French name bestowed by his mother, Alain was Dutch. While the Australians took care of communications and the Italians covered traffic control, the Dutch coordinated the UN's transportation. Almost everything in UNTAC had an acronym: the Dutch were Movecon, for 'Movement Control'.

Leon and Suzie showed up late. We moto'd to the Gecko for dinner. Suzie made a triumphal entrance into the bar riding on Alain's shoulders. No one paid much attention. The restaurant was stuffy and warm inside with the dark wood Chinese furniture, so we joined a blond Englishman and a blond Californian, two freelance photographers known collectively as the Surfers, at a bamboo table on the pavement.

Across the aisle, at a large round table underneath the gaze of the blinking, red-eyed Gecko statue, sat the people with good strings, expense accounts and salaries, or at least with reputations. Jerry was already rolling joints at the far side of the big table. Suzie and Leon's icon, Tim Page, was telling Jerry a story but Suzie and Leon were too shy to introduce themselves. Tim had appeared with his usual co-conspirator, Nate Thayer, the *Far Eastern Economic Review*'s Cambodia correspondent. Nate had started as a freelancer in the border camps, learned Khmer, and now had perhaps the best string in Cambodia – a weekly which wanted serious stories. He was convinced that the Khmer Rouge would cause election trouble. His large black motorcycle, frequently shaved head and brooding Jacobean looks helped foster Nate's persona as Phnom Penh's wild boy/hard-man journalist. It was a persona some more conservative individuals encouraged, as if they wanted Nate to live out a side of their own personality they were unwilling, but longed, to act upon. Watching Nate kid the children who descended on the Cathouse selling pirate editions of maps and tourist books and, when a street urchin ran too close to the truck as Nate was parking, watching a scared-looking Nate grab the kid and shake him, shouting what an idiot the kid was to come so close and he could have been hit, you couldn't help feeling that Nate, and not a few others, went overboard on the macho stuff to hide their softer sides. Not that I would have said that to him at the time.

The more established journalists beneath the Gecko's benevolent red-eyed gaze were simply sitting with the people they already knew, but the beginners smelled elitism: they hadn't proved themselves so they weren't invited to the table. For the newcomers the Gecko caste system seemed as bad as India's.

'Oh, we are not worthy, we are not worthy,' salaamed a sarcastic Surfer in the Gecko's direction. He also dismissed Phnom Penh's version of political correctness: the knowledgeable called the Khmer Rouge the DK, for Democratic Kampuchea, rather than the passé KR for Khmer Rouge. 'Can't we just stick with MM for Mass Murderers?'

Leon, Suzie and the Surfers worried about where they should be for election week. Being photographers, they had to be where the action was when it happened. Their position was hard but clear: no one would pay them unless they had good pictures other photographers didn't. The Surfers had already lost one big scoop. The only still photographers in Siem Reap when the Khmer Rouge had attacked the week before, the Surfers had huddled in a concrete toilet with the $5-a-night guest-house owner's family while the guerillas invaded the town, then followed the retreating troops, hiding behind electricity poles and tumbling into ditches for cover, shooting film the entire time. $20,000 and a break into *Time* disappeared when a courier company left the Surfers' film in Singapore over a national holiday and they missed their deadline. 'Always hand carry' had become the Surfers' new motto.

The Surfers planned to stake out Kompong Thom. For Suzie and Leon Phnom Penh needed to be explored. Then they wanted to get to Battambang, Cambodia's second largest city, as soon as possible. Rumour had it Battambang might be in for an assault. But the UN were kicking journalists off the flights to release seats for election workers; everyone wondered how to get around. The usual Cambodian transport was a shared taxi with bad shock absorbers and as many people squeezed in as possible. Paying double or triple the going rate might buy you the passenger seat to yourself. The road to Battambang was a red dust washboard, eight hours of spine shattering bumps and the occasional security problem between Pursat and Moung Roussei.

'Bad for the cameras,' Leon mused.

'Hey, don't worry, Movecon will get you on the flight to Battambang. No problem. *Ot panyaha*,' Alain winked, and stood up to leave. Alain departed, Amanda table-hopped. Suzie talked about how badly she wanted this trip to work out.

She felt she had paid her dues. If she made some good wire sales she could then cut into magazines. Suzie had to go for every opportunity.

An elderly tourist in a *Soldier of Fortune* cap and teeshirt walked by. The upcoming election and possible fighting had not only brought out the wannabe journalists, it had also brought out the war junkies.

'You know who that is?' I winked at Leon.

'I do. Grab him, Suz.' Leon didn't have any more clue than I did.

'Who is it? Who is it?'

'It's the editor of *Soldier of Fortune* magazine! Don't you recognize him? Look, Suz, go after him! They use tonnes of pictures. You're complaining you need work – now's the time to go for it. Run after him – look! He's gone!'

Suzie stared at us blankly. Then suddenly she was off, pushing past cyclo drivers, charging into the Phnom Penh darkness screaming, 'Wait! Wait! Wait!'

The harder Leon and I tried not to laugh, the harder we did. I couldn't catch my breath. 'She's hungry. She's really hungry,' Leon kept moaning. The other table went dead quiet.

Suzie came back around the corner, panting. 'You two are such fuckheads!' Suzie flopped into her chair. The entire bar was watching her. 'That poor old man, I practically gave him a heart attack. He was all the way to the market by the time I caught up with him and he looked so scared. It was totally dark when I ran up so I flicked on my lighter so he could see who I was. And I stood there panting with my lighter flickering in the dark in the middle of the market and I just kept repeating, "What do you do? What do you do? Are you the editor of *Soldier of Fortune* magazine? Are you the editor of *Soldier of Fortune* magazine?" And he looks at me like I'm crazy and starts shouting, "No I'm not! I don't do anything! I'm not anyone at all! I'm nobody!" and he starts running and tripping. Then I'm running after him shouting, "No! No! Wait! Wait! I don't want to hurt you! I'm only a photographer! I only want some work! I don't want to hurt you! I'm only a photographer!" And then suddenly I stop and think what the fuck am I doing! I hate you two!'

Leon and I apologized. We apologized again and this time we sort of meant it. But we'd done the damage – we had revealed Suzie's newness and her desperation to get ahead and embarrassed Suzie in front of her established colleagues, the very people Suzie had most hoped to impress. No matter how hard we tried, we couldn't make her laugh for the rest of the evening.

*   *   *   *

'I just stand back and watch,' Leon said. 'Don't even bother trying to compete. Just go with it.'

The C160 transport plane made two passes over Battambang airport – the first was to scare the cows off the runway. We had barely landed when Suzie shot out of the hold and waylaid the first Dutch soldier she set eyes on. She dropped Alain's name immediately. Leon and I stood aside and considered two cattle ambling back onto the asphalt, several Cambodian ground staff napping beneath a white UN MI-26 Russian helicopter, and Australian troops filling green plastic sandbags to make a bunker.

God knows why, but suddenly I felt competitive with Suzie. I didn't have a news string for the election but with all these people in town waving expense accounts and talking bylines I suddenly felt that I should be gung-ho. I put it to Leon that maybe I should make my own arrangements – three was a bad number and we might slow each other down.

The look on Leon's face said that with Suzie in this mode it would be like trying to make my own arrangements for the Normandy invasion. Besides, I was writing, they were snapping. It was a perfect combination. What was my problem?

Within five minutes Suzie, through a heavy barrage of flirtation and badinage, had secured a ride, breakfast and a hotel courtesy of the Dutch. Breakfast was at a Thai restaurant on the airport road, the only place in Cambodia with doughnuts. By lunchtime the doughnuts tasted like bricks, a sergeant called Nol confided, but for breakfast they were not too bad.

We scrawled our names in the Hotel Khemara guest

register. Leon and Suzie picked an outside room with windows facing the market so they could photograph the Battle for Battambang from the moment it started. I picked a windowless interior room so I could sleep through it. Before I went to my cell I did a little reconnaissance with the kind, skinny 21-year-old Dutchman with ruined teeth who got the jobs the rest of Movecon didn't want. The $12 room had satellite TV and hot water. I never wanted to leave.

'Check it out! Check it out!' Suzie pulled me out of my hot shower reverie and into their room. 'Now what do you think? Nol was pretty cagey about whether they thought there'd be an attack on Battambang. We've recced the roof – it's flat, there's a ladder to it, you can see all over town but it's pretty exposed. But if there is an attack we've got this balcony. Usually they come just before dawn. It'll be dark, but if we leap we can get to the next floor, crawl down that railing and then jump to the ground. How fast do you think you can climb down? Those columns on the shop fronts should be good cover, don't you think?'

'If the Khmer Rouge attack Battambang I'm staying in bed and watching it on the World Service,' I groaned and fell back on the nubby chenille bedspread. The 4:30 am calls at Phnom Penh's military airstrip hadn't been designed for me, even if I loved rushing along the totally dark airport road before dawn, the phosphorescent street lights out along with the electricity, with only the motorcycle's single beam illuminating the knots of street-cleaning women and one lone but infamous *gitoy*, a transvestite, covered in *kramas* and long sarongs, barely able to see as they swept the pavement with twig brooms in the blackness.

Watching bullets whiz by before breakfast also seemed deeply unnecessary – I wasn't taking pictures. I could interview people later about what happened. Besides, despite my bravado, I had only accompanied Suzie and Leon to Battambang – just as the NGOs were being told to leave, at least for the election – because I couldn't think of a face-saving way out when Suzie asked. I just didn't think I knew enough to go racing off to your nearest potential battlefield. Call me chicken, I'll wear my feathers proudly. I had only been formally freelancing for two weeks and couldn't tell a DK uniform from a ANKI uniform from a CPP uniform from a KP one.

Old-fashioned girl that I am, it seemed important to be able to quickly identify which side I wanted to cower behind. Soldiers confusingly wore parts of uniforms from different factions or combined one or two armies' caps, shirts or trousers with civilian clothes – mix-and-match ensembles were definitely in for the wet season offensives. Cambodians, however, never seemed to have any trouble identifying which side a soldier was on. Still, I suddenly felt it behoved me to prove my coolness and macho credentials and drop my information.

'And,' I added, 'why don't you take the sheets from one of the beds and keep them tied together, ready to go, so you don't have to jump? You can just shimmy down. Oh, by the way, the skinny one says they think if the attack happens it will come in the next three days. The Dutch aren't supposed to have guns but evidently somebody's made "special arrangements". They think the DK will come up Route 10 from Pailin. The train station's one block behind us, the market's one block in front of us. Both have been attacked before. And there's a hole in the back wall of the staircase on the second floor, looking out toward the train station and Pailin, which should just fit a lense.'

'Great work, Carol, great.' There wasn't an inch of competitiveness in Suzie. As far as she was concerned it was all for one and one for all.

I decided this competitiveness was turning me into a churlish cow. Why was I teasing someone slightly greener than me, when I was so green myself? God knows I looked comic to more experienced reporters.

After dinner that night we came back to Suzie and Leon's room. Suzie sent Leon off to try the walkie-talkies. They'd already decided their radio call names. Because of my book Suzie offered me the handle 'Hunter S'. I nipped that one quickly – if anyone heard that in the Gecko I would never live it down. Besides, I wanted to write a serious and respected book, but the way things were going my '*Fire in the Lake*' looked more like '*Gidget Goes Gonzo*', even without the Thompson reference.

Suzie and Leon had taken a lot of trouble with their call signs, Suzie confided, snapping on the hand-held radio and heading for the balcony. As she put out her first call to Leon, Suzie said she hoped none of the military used the same ones.

'Come in, Fuzzy Bear. Can you read me, over? Do you copy?' Suzie kept repeating into the crackling set. I didn't think the military would refer to themselves as oversized stuffed animals on the radio, so I told Suzie I figured her call signs were safe.

Watching the shop-fronts lock up for the night and Suzie leaning out over the railing to see which way Leon had walked, I thought, 'Suzie doesn't think this is real yet, it's still a fantasy. She's still playing war photographer, trying out for the movie. She hasn't realized who she is yet, and she's trying to prove she has a right to be.' I probably fell into the same category.

I left Suzie on the balcony, tracking Fuzzy Bear as he wandered on his first trip through Battambang, setting up shots of an enemy who wasn't there, at least not tonight, and went to take a hot shower.

*   *   *   *

I lay in bed with MTV babbling in the background and wondered what I was doing. Was I trying to write a travelogue or was I writing about politics and the election? The truth was that I couldn't separate one from the other. Part of me was waiting for Cambodia to calm down and the other part didn't think it would. Cambodia was not a country you could cover in a single journey. There was no defining river to float down, no great train journey to take, no superhighway which crossed the country and allowed you to encapsulate a society and culture in a single trip. Circling the Tonle Sap wouldn't cover it. What had represented Cambodia for the last 30 years was not its culture or its geography, but its politics. That month Cambodia *was* the UN election: everything else in the country waited to see what would happen.

Leon and Suzie took advantage of living next door to the men who controlled the helicopter seats, and booked themselves into every military outpost they could. First they swooped in for a morning to Sok San, a small KPNLF pimple on the Thai border surrounded by Khmer Rouge territory. The areas each faction controlled were not in neat blocks. Much of the country was a giant mixed-up jigsaw puzzle, especially in the western provinces. A KPNLF village would be next to a Khmer Rouge village, which would abut onto Funcinpec territory. Some areas were mixed – the government controlled a town during the day, but the Khmer Rouge found support at night. Despite the fact that the Sok San Dutch were nominally in KPNLF territory, they were surrounded by Khmer Rouge fields they couldn't enter. The battalion had tried to alleviate its boredom and claustrophobia by building a sun-deck and planting a gnome garden. But the isolation had gotten to a couple of the Dutch, Leon said, and if you looked closely you suddenly realized that the gnomes were doing things that would make a Bangkok hooker blush.

I, meanwhile, cruised Battambang, determined to avoid the military, the election and any discussion of the Khmer Rouge for a day. The Sangke river cut deep through the middle of the city, giving Battambang a lazy air. Shallow boats plied the river's course, wooden houses on high stilts loomed over the shore, water buffalo drank from its banks, and teenagers washed their motorcycles in the shallows. Because of its proximity to, and historical and trading ties with Thailand, Battambang was more of a commercial centre than Siem Reap, but it had the same attractive air of provincial laziness.

The Muslim Chams fished the Sangke's waters. A cyclo ride along the Sangke's south bank produced a Cham village, complete with a mosque in the midst of reconstruction. Rickety scaffolding climbed the central tower. Money from the worldwide Muslim community had trickled in to help rebuild Cham mosques, and later in the year a Muslim NGO would open in Phnom Penh to provide a centre for Mohammedan activity. Two or three bearded Chams in their early twenties slept on cots behind the gates of the Phnom Penh office. The office seemed less a hotbed of Muslim fundamentalist ire and more an easy place for the organizers' friends to crash in Phnom Penh. In front of the Battambang mosque stood a Christian graveyard.

The north side of the river had the same tree-lined, lazy quality, but it was silly to think I could avoid politics, even for a morning. I went as far as the jute mill, passing a Funcinpec office which was loudly playing a taped speech by Prince Ranariddh, Sihanouk's balding son who was the leader of Funcinpec. Sihanouk had stayed out of the running and declared himself neutral for the good of the country, but some Funcinpec supporters wore teeshirts picturing a silk-screened Ranariddh sitting dutifully at Sihanouk's feet. The message was clear: vote for one, get one free. Two men sat impassively at a desk outside the Funcinpec offices. The men were confident Funcinpec would win and that Sihanouk would be returned as king. Several times a day, they said, they played Ranariddh's speeches through the loudspeakers. The neighbours probably voted CPP in revenge.

By the time I got back Suzie and Leon had returned from Sok San and were sprawled across their beds, fully dressed, crashed out in an afternoon nap. They had taken turns at sitting up throughout the night, in case the attack started.

There wasn't much to do in the evening in Battambang. After dinner in a riverside restaurant, we sat on the hotel roof and watched the stars and the rotation of the satellite TV antennae. The Dutch had rigged up a giant speaker system and blasted the sound track from *Good Morning, Vietnam* again and again toward the Pailin hills. The Khmer Rouge may not have learned democracy and human rights during the UN's stay in Cambodia, but now at least they knew all the words to Wilson Pickett's 'In the Midnight Hour'.

Leon, a translator called Seing (who had escaped the camps only to spend three years in a Bangkok jail for illegal entry), and I continued a VB-encouraged discussion of truth versus facts. I wanted to know who knew whom, how incidents fitted in with what had gone before, how to tell when an event meant one thing although it looked like another. Leon wanted his photographs to show the reality of the moment – just the facts, ma'am.

'The facts don't always tell the truth in Cambodia,' Seing said.

The next day I resisted joining Suzie and Leon's photographic tour of another Dutch outpost. Suzie and Leon were looking for a new haunt since the threat – or rumours depending on your view – of an attack on Battambang had waned. Flying in, staying an hour, and coming back out on the chopper didn't seem useful for my purposes, but when Suzie and Leon returned they had decided their election base. They would stay in Thmar Puok, a north-western market town.

'You've got all four factions there,' Suzie said excitedly. 'There's even this one armed Khmer Rouge general who lives by the market. It's cool. It could be hot.'

Instead, I cadged a lift to the UN demining school. The UN demining specialists weren't allowed to remove any mines themselves. They could only teach removal techniques to Cambodians, who would be presented with a training certificate. This credential could then be used to apply for a job at a non-governmental organization such as the Halo Trust, Mines Advisory Group or Cambodian Mines Action Centre, which actually removed mines from the ground.

'There's a black market in fake certificates,' claimed Armand, a UNTAC demining instructor. The demining teachers were proud of their mission. 'We're UNTAC's unsung heroes,' Armand grimaced. How could Cambodians ever hope for peace and prosperity with all these mines in the ground? 'But why don't the journalists write about us?'

Although a Cambodian deminer's salary was only about $160 a month, it was still attractive, and there was a family pension if a deminer was killed or injured.

'Yes, people are desperate enough for a job that they pay $80 or $100 for a fake certificate. Then they come in here and pretend they've been trained and ask for a job. They know most of the NGOs don't put them in the field right away but put their deminers through their own courses. So we take them out to the school and pretend we're going to test them. We say, right, here's a mine, get it out of the ground. They go running off pretty quick.'

Demining was a slow, tedious business. Special metal detectors could find some buried mines, but others had such a small metal content that they didn't alert the machines. Warped creativity had gone into producing weapons that would blow off arms or legs. Some mines blew up when pressure was applied, some when you took the pressure off.

Some mines sprung up to take off upper limbs, others floated. The Americans made them, the Chinese made them, the French made them, the Bulgarians made them. So did the Italians.

A German company was even working on a biodegradable, self-destructing mine. Most mines, though, could last 50 or 100 years. Usually a farmer, a child chasing the family's cattle, or a woman gathering firewood detonated the hidden destructive package, not soldiers. Many mines had been sown by the Phnom Penh government in the four years before the peace agreement. To defend towns, roads and bridges against Khmer Rouge, KPNLF and ANKI troops, the Phnom Penh soldiers had scattered mines randomly, without pattern, markings or maps. This made the mines impossible to find easily.

The majority of Cambodia's mines lay in a crescent stretching from Pursat in the south-west to Preah Vihear in the north-east, roughly the length of the Thai border. Water holes, trees under which guerillas might shelter, paths between rice paddies and the areas near army fortifications were prime mine-laying sites. Mines were still laid to protect villages or houses at night, by retreating soldiers, or to take revenge. Up to 300 Cambodians a month accidentally detonated a mine; about half died. About 1 in every 236 Cambodians was an amputee thanks to the hidden soldiers in the earth.

Squatting on the ground in red-taped aisles, the demining students patiently poked the hard soil. One student scanned the ground with a metal detector. His partner prodded for any metal the detector found with a flat stick at a 30-degree angle. The angle meant that if the deminer hit a tilt mine, which exploded if its axis changed, the pressure would not detonate the mine. Working in metre-wide lanes and depending on vegetation, soil softness, and the amount of mines or ordnance found, two deminers could cover about 100 square metres in a day.

After World War II 10,000 Polish deminers took a decade to clear large metal anti-tank mines from their country. Ninety-nine per cent of Cambodian mines are small, mainly plastic, anti-personnel mines. By the time I left there were only about 1,800 deminers working in Cambodia. Their jobs were not secure. While US $900 million was spent demining and disposing of mines and ordnance in Kuwait after the Gulf War, less than five per cent of that had been spent in Cambodia. Much of the Kuwaiti lucre went to commercial demining companies like British Royal Ordnance, paid to clear mines which they at one time had manufactured. Unlike Kuwait, Cambodia did not have the money to pay for mines twice. An estimated three billion square metres of mined Cambodian land needed to be cleared. At the current rate, demining would take 300 years.

I asked one of the students why he had chosen the work. He said he wanted to help his country. I asked if there were any other reasons.

'The money's good.'

He said he thought he wouldn't be scared as long as he concentrated, but the look on his face when I asked him about fear said that I had, yet again, asked a pretty obvious, stupid question.

Election

I left Suzie and Leon trying on helmets and flak jackets courtesy of the Dutch and returned to Phnom Penh.

The two photographers had set up camp in a half-built Chinese hotel along the river. The hotel's bottom three storeys had been finished, but scaffolding still towered overhead. Clutching the wish-list Suzie had scribbled on a page torn from her notebook, I talked the smiley desk clerk with a long hair sprouting from his chin into unlocking their room. The refrigerator's light snapped on as I pulled out film bricks to send Suzie and Leon in an emergency package marked 'Thmar Puok via the Dutch'. Before I left I wandered up the stairs. Construction workers' families, cooking-fires lit and the ever present laundry flapping, lived on the half finished, raw concrete floor above. Still, the room was cheap.

More than the photographers, I needed to do research on the election. I buried myself in translated party manifestos and UN fact sheets. The large political parties were in a last-minute orgy of campaigning, racing for the polls. Several small parties had high-profile campaigns – such as one headed by a California Khmer, a one-time king of the Long Beach doughnut industry, which featured a huge banner quoting 'Communism is Evil – Ronald Reagan' hung prominently along one side of Psar Thmei. The more visible small parties were often run by expatriate Khmers who, after seeing elections in America, Australia or France, had returned to use modern techniques like posters, flyers, stickers and teeshirts in Cambodia, where half the country hadn't even been born at the last election.

No matter how hard the smaller parties tried, however, and even with the UN-selected proportional representation electoral system, Funcinpec and CPP were expected to make the strongest showings, with the BLDP running third. The BLDP's determined election truck, a small Nissan with a giant white elephant, the Party's symbol, tied to the bed, bull-horned its way across Phnom Penh during every waking hour, playing as its theme music a nameless Mexican ditty referred to as the 'Jumping Bean Song'. Phnom Penh's favourite musical outfit, however, was the UN's Ghanaian marching band, which at sober UN ceremonies regaled po-faced politicians like the Khmer Rouge's Khieu Samphan with an out-of-sync rendition of 'Suzi Q' or 'If You're Happy and You Know It, Clap Your Hands'.

Preparations for electoral news coverage began in earnest. The television satellite link was booked out. Everyone scrambled for reliable translators and transportation. Sok Sin's Toyota could been seen screeching around corners, working flat out for somebody's *Times*. All the newspeople seemed to sport a krama eventually, judged by non-journalists as an unnecessary affectation.

'What a bunch of pseuds,' I believe was Amanda's precise description, as she tried on mine.

'We estimate there may have been as many as 800,' the UN press spokesman Eric Falt said later about the number of newspeople covering the election. Eric's relationship with the press corps was adversarial: he would have used the same phrasing to estimate the number of Khmer Rouge. The spokesman's constant complaint was that the press only wrote negative stories; the resident press's constant complaint was that the spokesman hated the press. While Falt's last name caused much comment, Cambodia had had oddly named spokesmen before: Lon Nol's press liaison person had been a general called Am Rong.

Most reporters were laid back, but some were skittish. A few thought Cambodia was Yugoslavia and showed up with Kevlar helmets and flak jackets, so that the only journalistic casualty during the election was a hack laid low by heat prostration. Many people, journalists or not, couldn't imagine the elections going smoothly: after all, the Khmer Rouge had promised trouble. There were rumours that the guerillas would mortar Phnom Penh, that they would attack on Saloth

Sar's birthday, that Khmer Rouge units were already positioned by the airport, that urban terrorism would begin momentarily. The Gecko had been named as a target and its business doubled overnight – nobody wanted to miss the story. Reuters decreed that only one of its correspondents could be in the bar at any given time so the putative survivor could cover the carnage. Armbenders joked about whether it was safer to be inside or outside when the grenade hit. Worriers stocked up on purified water, canned goods, dried foods. The UN civilian police hastily tried to form an emergency evacuation plan.

'Is ciao-ous,' Fabio, my Italian Civpol friend, declared, shaking his head.

Better-off Cambodians sent wives and children out of the country. Eddie had booked an Indonesian holiday for Lee and her young brothers. At the other end of the economic scale Puth the cyclo driver sent his wife and baby back to the Prey Veng countryside.

Total coward that I am, I caught the bug. I wasn't with any organization which would include me in an evacuation plan ('Nice knowing you,' Amanda smiled as she waved her emergency instruction sheet), so I went to the Thai Airlines office and made sure I had a ticket out. It was easy to book a flight into Phnom Penh but many Bangkok-bound flights were full.

'Informed sources', a.k.a. whoever had been sitting next to me at the Gecko the night before, had said that if things went wrong the American embassy planned to helicopter stranded nationals out of the Cambodiana Hotel car park. I went to the embassy and registered that I was staying at the Stockton. If the scaremongering Cassandras were right and things went badly wrong, I might need to rely on the embassy. Just in case, I checked my informant's information.

'The United States Embassy assumes that the situation will not deteriorate so quickly that citizens will not be able to leave Cambodia on commercial flights,' said the consular officer in a bright, official voice. 'Should anything happen to the airport, the Embassy's considered position is that, basically, we're fucked.'

So much for my team.

*   *   *   *

The night before the election was tense. Most of the shops, I couldn't help noticing, had their steel shutters down, closed tight. No moto taxis or cyclos plied the streets. Standing in the eerie dark, Amanda and I knocked on the gate of the *Phnom Penh Post* offices and headed for the roof.

A man was sprawled face down on the spare bed in the hallway. It was hard to tell whether he was alive or dead; in fact he was merely out cold. 'Say hello to Denis,' Tim Page smiled mischievously. Denis didn't, or couldn't, respond. Page seemed inordinately pleased.

'The last person you want to know is Tim Page,' a London friend had said as he listed Asiaphiles I could quiz about Cambodia. During the Vietnam war Page had been a 22-year-old, partying photographer – getting wonderful shots of movement, but avoiding emotion.

Tim had paid for his hubris when a mine blew off part of his skull and left him with a limp and occasional shakes. He had been a little over-the-edge for a decade afterward. My friend had done such a good job convincing me Page was a wreck and a wild man that I had never bothered to call him.

The loping, sometimes courtly, grey-haired 50 year old limping up the steps had cooled down considerably. Hard-working, up at dawn to catch the light, Page no longer drank, had recently remarried, and was a bit shell-shocked by impending, legitimate, fatherhood, although he hadn't totally mellowed. Page's birthday was on Wednesday but, like everything that week, even Tim's party was affected by fear that the Khmer Rouge would disrupt the polling. If they did, it might not be safe to party or, worse, Page's favourite guests might be chasing stories out of town. Jerry had already slipped off to an undisclosed destination.

Page took no chances. Election eve was as good a time for his bash as any. Tim had secured the use of the *Phnom Penh Post* rooftop via Nate, who was in bed for the thirteenth or fourteenth time with malaria, Nate couldn't remember which, and would miss most of the party. The legions had been commanded to arrive bearing their favourite potions. Tim provided his guests sustenance with a massive vat of

Cambodian chicken soup. As Page described the recipe throughout the evening it grew more and more complex. He added thyme to the story he told this person, a little white wine for that one, cloves of garlic for another, but the basic ingredients remained the same: '... five scrawny Cambodian chickens and two and a half kilos of the best marijuana in Siem Reap.'

The party was sedate. I recognized a few people from the press briefings; several long-term backpackers chatted in the corner. In total contrast to the Gecko caste system, Page had invited virtually everyone he had met in the last week. Because of security some invitees hadn't shown at all, others had left early. Amanda had borrowed a car so we wouldn't have to wander the streets looking for motorcycle taxis home. Nobody was loud, nobody was obnoxious, nobody was dancing: it must have been the chickens.

John Swain, the *Sunday Times* correspondent who usually looked as if he had been born jaded, arrived late. A gecko called in the dark. Cambodians named geckos *chincha* in imitation of their sound. Others said a gecko's cries sounded like the little lizards were shouting 'Fuck you! Fuck you!'

'Cambodians are superstitious about the gecko,' Swain explained mournfully. 'If a gecko croaks four times, someone will die.'

Page gave Swain his shifty sideways glance which I later learned meant, 'What are you babbling about now?'

We listened intently as the next gecko revved up: one fuck you ... two fuck you ... three fuck you ... four fuck you. The gecko told us off a fifth time and everyone cheered. We were safe.

At 3 am we said goodbye to Denis, still face down in the hallway. 'I think he had five bowls,' Page grinned. I'd only tried one dollop of the soup, which tasted like soggy lawn-mower clippings, but I had smoked several of Tim's joints, for which he swore he had a doctor's approval. Magnanimously, I offered everyone a ride home in Amanda's car. She hopes to return the favour some day.

On other nights sleeping hammocks hung all over Phnom Penh, under trees, on pavements, wherever the four strings which held up a mosquito net could be tied. On election eve, every street was empty. Even the shakedown checkpoint police had disappeared. The only person out was a drunken soldier weaving alone across an intersection. Ours was the only car.

'We should just let everybody out here and go straight back, Amanda. This isn't safe.' Candy, an aid worker who had been evacuated from her provincial project against her will by a wary NGO, started to freak out. I was surprised. Normally Candy was frighteningly pulled together. Caught once in a minor Khmer Rouge attack during a *dahleng,* an afternoon wander, Candy had calmly bicycled home through the barrage while the mortars were landing, much to the surprise of all the Khmers who had dived for cover.

Candy put her hand on the steering wheel. Amanda didn't have much choice but to stop in the middle of the street. She wanted to go home now, Candy repeated, and she didn't want to sit in the exposed seat next to the driver. 'I've been shelled a lot. And they shot right at my car. You don't know what it's like to be shot at. I just don't like the look of this. I don't want to sit in the front. It's not safe!'

Starting to catch Candy's escalating paranoia, I volunteered to take her place just to get the car moving again.

'No, I'll switch with her,' Swain yawned wearily, 'I want some sleep . . .'

Even though no one wanted to admit it openly we were all a little spooked except Swain, who just seemed annoyed by the interruption. Swain, who had covered Cambodia off and on for 20 years, only wanted his bed and with a disbelieving moan started issuing calming safety instructions. He turned on the overhead light, saying that way anyone out there could see *barang* were driving the car and would know we were not late-night terrorists. Someone else insisted we turn off the light, the driver couldn't see, and if there were late-night terrorists about they could, as Swain said, see who we were. Candy stayed freaked out. She insisted a totally quiet Phnom Penh was all too wild.

Amanda dropped everyone at their hotels. She left me at the Stockton. The apartment Amanda and Candy were staying in was only 100 yards down the road. I watched their fully lit car bump home over the potholes. The next week *The Economist* ran an article, written by someone who hadn't been there, about how outlandish Tim's quiet party had been. Preconceptions ruled again.

It was only when she woke the next afternoon from colourful, albeit paranoid, dreams that Candy remembered eating all those bowls of chicken soup . . .

*   *   *   *

Election day dawned quiet and peaceful – aside from the retching sound of several victims of Page's soup 'praying to the porcelain god', as one Australian cameraman put it. Final score: Khmer Rouge 0, Tim's Soup 7.

'I'm out of a job, I'm out of a job,' Nate moaned.

At the packed-out morning press briefing Falt confirmed voting was proceeding peacefully. He asked for queries from the floor. I wasn't the only one who asked stupid questions; more than one journalist who had been flown in specially for the election knew even less than I did, which was a relief. It had to be remembered, however, that they still knew more than their potential audience about Cambodia. Several of the more obvious questions were simply set-ups to get the quote or video clip the reporter wanted for their story.

The briefing finished. I was unsure about my day's plans – go back to sleep or try to look like I knew what I was doing in the hope people would fall for it – when Page cruised by and offered me an afternoon tour of polling stations that weren't 'journalist approved' by the UN. Who could be sure Falty Towers gave the whole story, Page asked. Nate was ill; there was a spare place in the car.

'*Ot panyaha*,' confirmed a relieved Cambodian election supervisor outside a Phnom Penh wat.

'No problem,' okayed the cute Jamaican volunteer with the rasta locks watching the voting in a rural schoolhouse in Kandal.

'*Nyet problemi*,' a burly Russian monitor in a too tight shirt opined on a Kompong Speu backroad.

Everywhere we went that day Cambodians were happy. Pundits had feared Cambodians would feel too threatened to vote, but 40 per cent of the country voted on the first day. In

Takmao, a riverside suburb of Phnom Penh, the polling station had been so overwhelmed the UN had run out of ballot papers.

'It's a human right to have a secret ballot. That's democracy,' a school teacher who was returning the next day proclaimed. In the end, over 90 per cent of the Cambodians UNTAC registered cast their ballots.

Food vendors and toy salesmen had opened stalls outside the fences surrounding the polling stations. People wore their best clothes to vote and they brought their children.

'I'm 88 years old. I voted the last time in the Lon Nol government. I wanted to live long enough to vote again,' declared a toothless old man who had walked to a rural polling station in Kompong Speu.

The day felt as if the entire country was on a high, save for a few miserable Khmer Rouge bastards in Pailin. For the next four days the story was the same.

Maha Gosananda, the elderly monk who was the spiritual leader of Cambodia, had led a peace march, the *Dhammay-ietra*, from Siem Reap to Phnom Penh through heavily contested parts of Kompong Thom. On one night the walkers had been mortared while sheltering in a temple. In the morning more people had defiantly joined the march, to show that they, too, wanted peace in Cambodia.

On the second day of voting Sihanouk met the marchers in front of his sunburst yellow palace. To some, Sihanouk had caused Cambodia's agonies, but Sihanouk still garnered the respect of most Cambodians. Sihanouk was foremost a nationalist, trying to keep Cambodia independent and intact. Whether or not his actions achieved this, especially his pact to let Vietnamese communists use Cambodia and his Khmer Rouge alliances, was questionable. But Sihanouk took the long view; his goal was to stay in the game. As long as he was a player, no matter how tenuous his position, Sihanouk, and in his eyes Cambodia, had not been defeated. Yet even Sihanouk greyed and aged, although giant paintings around Phnom Penh showed a vibrant, black-haired 1960s version of the monarch; at 72 it was questioned how long Sihanouk's influence would last.

Rows of monks clad in orange *sbong chep poh*, followed by

white-robed laymen known as *achars*, and finally by shaven-headed *yea chee*, the nuns, marched onto the mall in front of the royal palace. Lay people trailed behind. A young shaven-headed nun, one leg lost and struggling with crutches, recognized me from a visit to the marchers the day before and waved. Orange and white banners declaring 'Cambodian Women Want Peace' and 'End War Now', in both English and Khmer, floated above the crowd. Even the good Buddhists had press releases and knew to put their banners in English for the cameras.

Sihanouk's grey polyester-clad North Korean security guards elbowed and tackled those who came too close as Sihanouk, dressed in the traditional Khmer silk pantaloons called *chong kben*, went out to meet his people.

'This is Cambodia's last chance,' Sihanouk stressed. His soft, high-pitched voice addressed the throng in Khmer, French and English. If Cambodia disintegrated, the world would not send a second UNTAC. All Cambodians, including the Khmer Rouge, should work together to rebuild his poor, tattered country.

'It's not like the old days,' a moustached, Finnish photographer sighed as he changed film. In his prime, Sihanouk had harangued for several hours at a time; his speech to the marchers hadn't lasted one.

But most people didn't want the old days back; they wanted a new, bright beginning. A giggling Maha Gosananda stood on the bandstand in front of the palace, blessing and dousing the throng with water. Three middle-aged sisters, all widows, grabbed me and in heavily accented French said that they wanted everyone to know how happy they were that UNTAC had arrived. They had lost their husbands to the Khmer Rouge, but they had survived.

'All we want is peace for our children,' vowed the eldest.

Even one or two of Sihanouk's Cambodian security men, who tried to emulate the Korean guerillas' churlishness, had looked moved. The only aggression anyone could see came from the kids selling strings of *mles*, small white flowers used as offerings to the monks. Marchers and onlookers pulled apart their flower necklaces and tossed the petals at each other, in celebration and blessing. Jerry had reappeared and was standing on a side street, smiling and throwing *mles* over a laughing cyclo-driving friend. Several young orange monks, their arms around each other's waists, paced in step and chanted what that day was Cambodia's favourite slogan: 'Cambodians want peace now!'

*   *   *   *

Well, practically everywhere . . .

Every morning Lim had his breakfast *gwiteo* at a window table in the ground floor restaurant on a busy Achar Mean street corner. Lim didn't have any particular political allegiance. He'd gone to the United States from the Thai camps, worked in a factory, started a business, then been hired by Chinese entrepreneurs to return to Phnom Penh and run their small firm. His family had stayed in the United States.

The restaurant was always packed with the Phnom Penh business community making early morning deals, swapping information. Like many businessmen which brought in materials via the Sihanoukville port, Lim had dealings with the military. Occasionally Lim spent a night in a dancing restaurant drinking Hennessey with high-ranking officers, friends from before his exile.

'The CPP generals aren't happy.' Lim was stirring chilli into his soup. Each day votes were tabulated and totals placed on the giant tally sheets, like ten-pin bowling scorecards, at UNTAC headquarters and in front of Sihanouk's palace. The results were broadcast on radio and television. Funcinpec had a small lead over CPP, but the CPP army was five times that of Funcinpec and KPNLF combined. If Funcinpec won that meant the present government officials and army would be expected to relinquish some of their power and lucrative side deals. Lim didn't think the transfer would be easy. He named a well known CPP official and recited a current rumour: 'He was so angry when he saw Funcinpec was ahead he shot the television.'

Despite the UN's euphoria, Lim wasn't advising his bosses to put more money into Phnom Penh yet. As far as Lim was concerned it was one thing to win an election and another thing actually to take charge of the country.

'We'll have to wait and see what happens.'

                    *   *   *   *

What with all this peace, freelancers who weren't on a day rate took a financial bath.

'I stood in the middle of Angkor Wat and shouted, "Shoot at me! Will someone please shoot at me! I've got to file by three o'clock!"' confessed an English tabloid stringer; it may not have been true, but the story sounded good. Suzie and Leon ferried back rolls and rolls of film from Thmar Puok, but since nothing awful happened few of their pictures made the wire. The several hundred dollars Suzie and Leon earned didn't match the seven thousand they had spent on their dream. They left several weeks later, broke and returning to a six tatami mat Japanese apartment and English teaching, but talking bravely of trying again in South Africa or Mozambique.

I had already submitted my commissions, but then a hacked-up version of one article appeared in Cambodia. A sophomoric sub-editor on *The European* had changed 'Hun Sen' to 'Gun Sen' throughout the piece, added a bad joke about mines and the entire country 'limping' toward the future, attached a 'comic' sketch of an amputee and put my name in bold letters across the top.

'That's bad, that's really bad . . .' judged the Gecko's front tables. Incensed, I was ready to moto to the military market and buy a 50-cent grenade to lob back to Fleet Street. There went my reputation before I even had one. Wise heads counselled me against buying every copy of *The European* in Phnom Penh at its price of $6 a whack, imported newspapers costing 12 times the grenade. Nobody read *The European*, the heads said. Now if it had been something everyone paid attention to, like the *Sunday Sport* or the *National Inquirer*, then I'd really have been in trouble . . .

The UN opened up flights to journalists again, but this didn't improve the freelancers' lot. Several television crews and correspondents had pulled out to spend their budgets somewhere more dramatic. Once the election was deemed peaceful, breaking news simply wasn't happening; people were desperate for anything colourful to write about or photograph.

A Bangkok-based photographer known as The Animal was sighted in Thmar Puok market approaching two armed men dressed in partial Chinese uniforms. They were probably searching for the latest trendy upcountry gear, fake Ray-Ban sunglasses worn with the manufacturer's sticker left on the lenses.

Sticking out his hand, The Animal introduced himself with 'Hi, I'm an American. You must be the Khmer Rouge . . .' The Animal spent the rest of the morning buying the Khmer Rouge rip-off Adidas tennis shoes instead of letting them steal his gear.

'Ah, they couldn't have worked the cameras anyway. I can't work them. Do you think I should put my picture from Tiananmen Square on the cover or on the back of my book, whaddya think?' The Animal asked me later.

So, with nothing else exciting happening, in the true spirit of hard-hitting journalistic inquiry I accepted when Page suggested we try the opium den. When Page had first been in Phnom Penh 25 or so years ago, opium had been easy to acquire. He longed for a hazy evening of nostalgia. It was Page's real birthday; he'd been working hard and felt he deserved a treat.

Hey, I was game. What better represented the romance of the Orient than an opium den – silk curtains gently swaying; wafts of perfumed white smoke melting into the dark; ancient, wizened wise men lost in reverie lounging on richly embroidered day beds; jade and silver pipes resting languidly on bloodless red lips? It would be perfect for my book.

Alas, the Khmer Rouge and 15 years of communism had wrecked the Phnom Penh drug scene. Friends in low places could name only one opium purveyor: Papa.

Our friends' van dropped us off on a darkened street corner. First shack on the right, the friends said, and sped off into the night.

When Norman Lewis had written *A Dragon Apparent* about 1950s Cambodia, Phnom Penh's leading opium palace had been Madame Shum's. 'In these romantic surroundings the raffish elite of Phnom Penh meet together at night over the sociable sucking of opium pipes,' Lewis had penned.

Papa's didn't quite fit that description. Phnom Penh's top-rated, okay, well, only-rated, fumerie was one room walled with slapped-together rough boards, a concrete floor, a wooden table carved from a tree trunk, and children's drawings of Angkor Wat and Khmer pop stars taped to the walls. Papa's family, which consisted of several daughters, grandchildren, uncles and cousins, snored beneath mosquito nets hidden by a curtain three feet behind us. Our sole companion was a petroleum salesman who had just graduated from Birmingham University and was trying to grow a Trevor Howard moustache.

'But I want a pipe! I want a bed! I know there are pipes and beds here!' Tim was desperate. What are birthdays for except to have what you want?

No beds, no pipes, said Mama, who was minding the place in Papa's absence. She flashed a gold toothed smile. No beds, no pipes, she repeated to the disappointed Page, but she did have some opium she could sell us. And she could run out and get us a couple of warm beers, if we wanted. Cambodians didn't smoke, only *barang*, Mama said.

Tim bought a small, cellophane-wrapped chunk of taxi girl black. He mushed the sticky brownish gunge into a cigarette and we puffed, but to little effect. It wasn't like the good old days. Cambodia's election had been a kind of homecoming for Tim. Many of Tim's journalist mates from his Vietnam days were covering the story, trying to see an end to what had begun so long ago. The general, penny-analyst consensus was that the Cambodian election almost marked the final chapter of the Vietnam war. Once the United States lifted their economic embargo on Vietnam, hostilities would finally have ceased.

Page loved the congeniality of his Vietnam press corps friends. 'I mean, the closeness you develop when you go through something like that together, they're closer than any wife,' he reflected, Marlboro Light smoke drifting across his face. I got the dismissive sideways glance when I suggested maybe that's why he'd been married three times.

In a way Tim had never really left Vietnam, although he had

led several lives since then. Twenty-year-old Tim in Vietnam had created a persona the older Page couldn't live down. At times he didn't want to; most times, though, I think he would have given anything to have been somewhere else then, even if that persona helped sell his pictures and books now. Whenever an involuntary shudder went through Tim, a neurological memento from his Vietnam wounding, it was a salutary reminder not to get too carried away by the supposed glamour of this journalism gig; in the end it was just a job.

'At that age you don't know you're born yet,' Tim had sighed earlier as he watched a downy backpacker, maybe 20 or 21, in stylish, trendy traveller all-black with a *krama* tied round his head, negotiate a wad of unfamiliar washed-out red *riel* from his jeans. 'I was too young to be there.'

Our conversation drifted. Mama yawned and watched from a corner. The Birmingham petrol pusher said his company was in Cambodia for good. His outfit felt they were well positioned to take advantage of Cambodia's post-voting economic renaissance. The company was now supplying the UN, but it had already started signing contracts to sell petroleum products to commercial buyers once the UN departed. Now that polling had finished peacefully, the gasman claimed, any week we would see a surge of foreign investors bringing capital into the country.

Tim wasn't so sure Cambodia would take off quickly, unless the new government invested heavily in wells and new roads in the countryside. Cambodia was not just Phnom Penh. 'They can't govern places they can't get to.' Whatever happened, Tim continued, Cambodia had better move quickly, because once the embargo was lifted on Vietnam this place was going to be an economic sideshow, just as the Cambodian war had been a sideshow to Vietnam.

By 10:30 Mama was yawning continuously and the Birmingham salesman had left. We followed soon after. So much for Tim's nostalgia and my timeless oriental encounter.

'Well, at least the election's gone well and these people can get on with their lives.' Tim stamped out a cigarette butt as I climbed into a cyclo. His birthday was over, and Tim loped off across the darkened park, past the waterless fountain and the tank with a hammock tied between the turret and a tree, back to his room at the *Post* offices, the BBC on satellite TV, and a cup of English tea.

Movie time

Funcinpec won the election. CPP came second. Communism in Cambodia was officially over.

The businessman Lim had been right. Certain CPP followers, who were accustomed to power and who, more importantly, controlled the largest army, weren't happy. CPP contested the election results. The UN dithered, then Sihanouk pre-empted everyone and declared a draw. There were a few dance steps left in the wily ex-king yet. Sihanouk announced he would be prime minister and that Ranariddh and Hun Sen would share the deputy prime ministership until a constitution was drawn. 'Western analysts' thought the interim government was a blueprint for the future Cambodian government, with Sihanouk returning as monarch, but they scoffed at having two prime ministers. 'Why not?' retorted Hun Sen, fixing an inquisitor with his one good eye. 'Cambodia is unique.'

At least Sihanouk's plan didn't leave the winners voiceless in government, as a coup would have. The unstable peace continued. Those who complained that Sihanouk had no legal power to form a government were labelled spoilsports; the UN wanted to leave. The job was declared finished. Foreign UNTAC staff began to volunteer for other missions. Cambodian UNTAC employees, however, had no place to go. The UNTAC economic bubble, which had supported many the purchase of a new motorcycle, had begun to burst. Trying to get off the cheap hotel circuit, I moved into a shared flat. There I could hear and see the rhythms of daily Cambodian life – the eerie clopping of the noodle soup seller's wood block in the dead of night; Khmer music wafting from a tinny radio at dawn over the hacking sounds of wood being chopped for the day's first fire; motos coughing on tanks freshly topped up by two litres of watery orange petrol poured from scuffed Fanta bottles at the makeshift stations run by a woman with a battered wooden chair and several petrol filled plastic soda containers – sodas which weren't found in Cambodia and whose discarded plastic flasks must have been imported from Thailand; geckos sneaking across a flaking, painted wall; the noodle shop selling the day's first breakfast *gwiteo* to a group of men in their late twenties, at least one of whom would be in uniform or carrying a mobile phone; a monk carrying a silver begging bowl followed by a boy, the *kohn seik*, the parrot child who handled the offerings from women or money, both deemed unclean, which the *bonzes* couldn't touch; the tottering ox carts piled high with a house-storey's worth of hay, ochre-brown clay pots strapped to the sides, the driver selling pottery he had hand thrown and fired in Kompong Chhnang – a two-hour drive and three-day ox cart ride away – where according to time-honoured custom, a village either made the pots or lids but never both, a choir of frogs honking loudly after a rain; the quiet from eleven until two as most of the town slept through the burning-hot, midday hours; a few shots of gunfire in the night for no reason; rickety ancient men or young teenage boys on rickety ancient bicycles shouting '*nam pan*' and selling bread from tarp-covered rattan baskets tied behind the seat; the shock of an early cold water shower; vendors pushing sweet ices and cakes, or fried noodles, the woks sizzling as each new ingredient was tossed on; the electricity going off just when you needed it; a woman placing cards on a *krama* spread across the ground in front of a school in a seven-card monte game, with six and seven year olds handing her crumpled, dirty green 100 *riel* notes, betting on the next card, just like everybody else.

As a colonel my landlord, Chhoun, made $50 a month. Divided into two flats for foreigners the house grossed $1500. Most landlords with apartments and houses to rent, including Chhoun, had connections to the CPP. They had received their property, appropriate to their status in the communist party and the state, during the 1980s. Chhoun's family squeezed into the former servants' quarters, four little rooms with a small Buddhist altar in each, connected to the main house by a walkway at the back.

'My uncle lost his wife and my auntie lost her husband in the Khmer Rouge, so they married,' Monita, Chhoun's studious niece, told me. The extended family Chhoun supported now consisted not only of his own wife and three children but his wife's sister-in-law, her children, and several other, occasionally resident, relatives and passers-through who camped outside on headboardless wooden beds spread with straw mats. Monita was studying to enter Phnom Penh's university; matriculation could cost as much as $2,000 in bribes. On the other hand, Chhoun's 18-year-old nephew Chea was good hearted and funny, if a little feckless, and happy sitting on the front step with his *krama* wrapped around his waist, smoking cigarettes with his friends. Chea seemed pleasantly skilled at avoiding his uncle Chhoun's questions about what Chea would do now that he had left school.

Sometimes suppliant relatives arrived looking for work. Opening the gate for me late one night, candle flickering in the dark, Chhoun rolled his eyes at the new guard, sprawled on a hammock underneath his mosquito net, transistor radio blaring, head lolling, mouth wide open in a snore. The sleeping guard couldn't hear the dogs barking, a motorcycle roaring off, me shaking the iron gates and yelling to be let in, or Chhoun and I laughing. '*Cousine*,' Chhoun clucked his tongue as if there was nothing to be done, and shook his head. Chhoun had power, so he felt obliged to find his snoozing second cousin a job.

It was obvious to me that if I wanted to understand the place at all I would be in Cambodia longer than I, or my publisher's advance and budget, had intended. The market for articles looked saturated for the moment, so even I went hunting for a temporary job. Several other freelancers relied on English lessons, but an office in the United States Embassy wanted someone to teach their staff word processing. I interviewed.

'Ah'm lookin' for someone ah can just throw into the deep end and they'll swim, no matter whut comes up,' drawled the first interviewer, a bear-like, middled-aged bearded man with military carriage and a country accent. He squinted, paused a minute, then continued. 'Now ah'm lookin' at you, and ah think you can swim. Ah think you can swim good . . .' he nodded knowingly, and added that he had an import-export sideline and good, inside information. 'Ah hear a lot about what goes on up country, a lot of things people down here don't know. Stuff goes on, you wouldn't believe. Maybe you could help me put a couple *Soldier of Fortune* articles together . . .'

The second job interview, with the bearded interviewer's boss, didn't go much differently. The air conditioning in the boss's office was almost arctic; the embassy had its own, independent, power supply. Perhaps it was the safari shirt and the unconfirmed hint of hair dye that put me off, although the boss, like the first interviewer, was perfectly amiable.

'Now, I don't think it's any secret that there's a side we support in this election,' the boss confided, leaning back confidently in his stately leather chair, 'and they might be assholes, but at least they're *our* assholes . . .'

Maybe the two men had seen too many *Rambo* movies, but after the interviews it seemed to me more than one person was using Cambodia to live out some private fantasy. I thought I'd stick to my own, thanks. Besides, if I worked for the embassy, and people thought the embassy supported one faction, openly or otherwise, whether or not it actually did, they might think I supported it, too. There would go my reputation for journalistic neutrality, even if I didn't have one yet. I decided to pass on the job and prayed I sold more articles quickly.

Alain was driving a Landcruiser to Sihanoukville, on the coast, so Amanda and I tagged along. Route 4 to the Sihanoukville port was the best road in the country, built in the early 1960s with American money before Sihanouk severed relations with the United States. The Landcruiser sailed through the checkpoints, a few ill-clad soldiers standing beside bridges or swinging on hammocks underneath trees. Aside from hitting potholes, the only jarring incidents on the four-hour journey occurred when Alain would shout 'Jesus Christ! It's the Bulgarians!' and swerve to avoid a hurtling UN truck.

The checkpoints were not only a product of greed. The CPP government was almost broke; salaries had not been paid. Armed free enterprise was seen as the soldiers' way of surviving. Vehicles carrying only Cambodians and no foreigners often were stopped, especially in the afternoon if the soldiers had been drinking. Cambodians' trunks were sometimes rifled, their drivers asked for money. The foreigners appeared magically protected. 'Don't touch the *barang*, it's not worth it,' seemed to be the sentiment.

While the government nominally held the roads, south of Kompong Speu town and as far as Sihanoukville the state shared suzerainty with bandits and the Khmer Rouge. All three groups had interests in logging the dry hills which gave way to scrub brush and the pepper plants that looked like grape vines along the roadside. Small sawmills and desperately poor woodcutting villages hugged the highway as it cut through the badlands of Kompong Speu and Koh Kong provinces. Since the road led to Cambodia's ports, almost all the foreign goods supplied to Phnom Penh came up the highway. To keep their trucks on the road haulage firms paid thousands of dollars each month in bribes – to enterprising government soldiers, the Khmer Rouge, simple bandits, or any combination of the above.

Graced with clear blue water and white sand beaches, Sihanoukville had become the UN's playground. Real estate speculation was rife. A dozen new hotels had risen around the town; there was talk of developing an island casino. Thai, Malaysian and Chinese investors denoted ownership by erecting high walls around empty acres. Technically only Cambodians could own land, but street wisdom said that for a back-handed $1,000 any Asian-looking individual could buy a Cambodian passport. Half of Sihanoukville, or Kompong Som as it was also known, seemed to be fences surrounding nothing except a down payment on the owner's commercial dreams.

As we lay on the beach, Amanda was uncharacteristically moody, staring absent-mindedly into the waves. Even the joys of Sihanoukville couldn't change the fact that Alain was married, which as far as Amanda was concerned meant she was sharing a room with me, once again. Amanda and Alain kept their relationship platonic, but it seemed to everyone that if Alain had been single romance would have followed. The extra-marital affair, divorce and broken relationship rate was high among the UN staffers. Some had come to Cambodia as an excuse to change, looking for something different in their lives even though they weren't sure what that difference should be. For others, living rootlessly among the poverty and the effects of 20 years of war had transformed them more than most had ever anticipated.

That night the sea breeze was cool and clear. Opposite the Rendezvous the Soriya Hotel had opened a top-floor discothèque. Amanda, four Dutch and I took a table away from the strobe-lit dance floor. Cambodian couples or single-sex groups of Sihanoukville's unmarrieds peopled the centre tables. A beautiful girl with waist-long black hair danced with one of her girlfriends. At the back of the room sat a row of prostitutes, less prosperous looking than the girls in the front.

I sat next to Alain, with Amanda at the opposite end of the table. We tried to order several times. Waiters eventually brought large bottles of Angkor, Cambodia's only domestic beer. The band played both Khmer and Western tunes. Whichever they played, it was loud. I had to keep my head next to Alain's to hear anything he said. The band, named Angkor Rexum, was quickly renamed Angkor Rectum by the soldiers.

Alain hadn't seen his wife or child for six months. His wife was beautiful, he shouted at my ear, with long black hair she'd been growing since she was a child. Every day Alain's little girl drew him a picture and mailed it to her daddy. One day Alain's daughter would outline and colour a cow or a tree, the next day the TV, the next day what she thought her daddy looked like on a helicopter in Cambodia. He had all the pictures taped to his hotel wall.

The music grew louder. We mulled around, switched seats. I went to find the toilet. The prostitutes stood in front of the mirrors and relined their lipstick or straightened their hair with bright plastic combs. Then they went out to stand against the wall again and go back to work.

When I returned Alain and Amanda were sitting next to each other, talking seriously. Bored, I tried to convince the newly arrived quartermaster to try the *ramvong*, but he said he never danced. A bespectacled captain leaned over and shouted, 'He just got divorced. He's still shy.'

Suddenly Alain stood up and surveyed the room. He walked to the dance floor and took the hand of the beautiful girl with the long black hair. As Alain led the girl to the middle of the floor, the music changed to a slow number. Most of the Cambodian couples danced formally beneath the throbbing strobe lights, slightly stiff and apart. Alain held the girl close to him, his arms clasped around her back, her head just reaching his shoulders. Her long black hair swayed back and forth across his hands as the music slowly moved them around the floor.

Amanda, with her back to the band and the dancers, chattered with the new quartermaster for a bit. Then she went to fix her make-up, and didn't come out for a while.

*   *   *   *

Back in Phnom Penh, I started to make plans to leave the capital, but history, and my innate cowardice, conspired against me. Barely two weeks after the election Cambodia's politics turned into a family drama and took on the quality of a Shakespearean tragedy or a soap opera episode, depending on your cultural reference.

After six wives, several at the same time, and numerous liaisons, Sihanouk had produced more than a dozen children; five had been killed by the Khmer Rouge, as had eleven grandchildren. Two sons, Ranariddh and Chakrapong, now were players in Cambodian politics. Ranariddh was a one-time law professor in France who headed the Funcinpec party. As a child Ranariddh, the son of a royal ballet dancer, had never commanded much of Sihanouk's attention, but when the son Sihanouk had chosen as successor demurred, Ranariddh became the anointed heir. Now Ranariddh looked and sounded like his father's younger double, down to identical bald spots, but he lacked Sihanouk's political nous and creativity.

Chakrapong, whose mother was not only Sihanouk's wife but also Sihanouk's aunt, had started his own resistance army on the Thai border after the Khmer Rouge's fall. Chakrapong was also rumoured to be the favourite of Monique, Sihanouk's last wife, whose own sons preferred ballet to politics. It was said others in the royal family disliked Monique and her sway over Sihanouk.

Ranariddh looked down on Chakrapong and Chakrapong's bullying, deadly businessman's ways. Even though Ranariddh's blood was not as blue as Chakrapong's, it was the sleek, sometimes witty Ranariddh who represented the old royal elite. Chakrapong was the brash, militarized yuppie South-east Asia – if you weren't a general you drank with one, mixing power, politics, brute force and money in whatever was the most potent combination at the time. With no love lost between the brothers, Chakrapong had broken with the Funcinpec royalists and joined CPP a year before the election.

'How can I work with Chakrapong who has no other aim except my death?' asked Ranariddh, who didn't want to share his premiership with CPP. During the election Ranariddh had been painted as the bright hope of liberal democracy, but he was also accused by some of braggadocio and bullying.

The voting didn't bring the two brothers closer together. Ten days after the election, Chakrapong and Co. declared a breakaway state made up of seven eastern provinces to be called the 'Samdech Euv Autonomous Zone', roughly translated as 'if Ranariddh gets a country I want one, too.' No one was surprised that Chakrapong was among the conspirators.

*   *   *   *

'I'm a lieutenant!' Chea, dressed in brand new officer's fatigues, announced proudly on my doorstep the first day of the secession. The prospect of civil war meant that even Chea had to find a job.

Chakrapong's secessionist movement lasted all of a week, but it solidified CPP's position within the coalition government. The personal allegiances of some of the other CPP conspirators, however, led many to think the secession represented deepening schisms within the CPP. Loyalty was rewarded: the week after the coup ended my landlord Chhoun, a fervent Hun Sen supporter who had joined Hun Sen's anti-Khmer Rouge army from a Vietnamese refugee camp in 1978, appeared with a new uniform and his first general's star.

I never learned how Chhoun had spent the 1970s; he evaded questions. Chhoun would only say, 'I wanted to go to university, but my parents were too poor.' For someone I shared a house with, I did a remarkably bad job of learning Chhoun's story. In his late teens and early twenties then, Chhoun could have been conscripted by either the Khmer Rouge or the Lon Nol governments if he hadn't picked a side. Many middle-aged Cambodians had made political choices in their youth which they regretted now. Caught between the corruption and deadly ineffectiveness of the Lon Nol government and the mad fantasies of the Khmer Rouge with whom the royalists had made a devil's alliance, neither choice would have been right.

Like many of the 'young turks' in the CPAF army, colonels and generals who had once been soldiers recruited from the Vietnamese refugee camps in 1978, Chhoun identified with and firmly supported Hun Sen. Hun Sen had been a farmer's son, like many of them; Hun Sen had had to make the same decisions, at least as Chhoun saw things. I never knew if Chhoun had been Khmer Rouge or if he simply preferred not to discuss the past, especially in front of his niece and nephew, whose policeman father had been killed by the Khmer Rouge. Chhoun's major concern was always his family.

'I'd have been Khmer Rouge – you would have, too,' said a French UN worker, hunched over an outside café table one night in the shadow of the jagged, red-stone Independence Monument. 'I would have seen the corruption, I would have seen the Vietnam war coming into Cambodia. I was young then, I would have gone to the jungle.' The 'I would probably have been Khmer Rouge' sentiment came from many *barang* after a few drinks. From abroad, Cambodia's good guys and bad guys were easily identified. In Phnom Penh perceptions changed. To have been young in the late 1960s or early '70s, especially if you were poor and unemployed, before the Khmer Rouge took the countryside and reports began to filter into Phnom Penh about their increasingly brutal governance, before the killing fields were sown and the madness became clear, to be forced by war to make a choice – I was glad it hadn't been me. How could youthful idealists have known what would follow? Royalists loyal to Sihanouk had joined the anti-Lon Nol forces as much as democratic leftists. The Frenchman, however, was right. Had I been Cambodian when Sihanouk was overthrown and the B-52 bombings started, I probably would not have been totally immune to the original Khmer Rouge message.

Waiting to make sure the situation was calm, I waited another week, meanwhile dutifully interviewing whomever I came across: a forestry expert, the polyester-shirt-wearing Jehovah's Witness missionary who hadn't made a single convert in his entire year in Phnom Penh, a real estate fixer who had made so much money finding UN personnel houses that he, who couldn't afford a motorcycle two years before, now wanted my advice on what long-term, five figure, dollar Certificate of Deposits to buy. But the more people I talked to, the more I realized Cambodia was full of contradictory tales. Take the issue of American servicemen still considered 'missing in action' in Indo-China.

'Ah, you hear so many MIA stories, in the end usually it's just Cambodians wanting money,' an officer from the American MIA team in Cambodia told me at the fortnightly Australian Embassy booze-up. The MIA teams had a hard job – trying to figure out current stories was hard, trying to discern what happened 20 years ago was close to impossible. Many of the MIA 'sightings' in Vietnam in the 1980s had turned out to be foreign aid workers. In Cambodia, the MIA team's grim task was simply to recover remains.

The MIA officers' position was reasonable. Politicians took advantage of the MIA families' misery, why wouldn't unscrupulous Cambodians? But the MIA task force didn't get rave reviews from everyone. I talked to someone who had offered tips to the MIA office in Thailand.

'I tried to give the MIA office in Bangkok information from the camps, but they just said, "The Khmer always lie." But the Khmer don't lie. You know their big MIA find here, that camera crew? I knew where they were for years. The Khmers told me, but the MIA office didn't want to know,' said a disgusted one-time border camp worker. 'The MIA office just said, "Don't go bringing any bones in here." '

I finally flew back to Siem Reap with Andrea, the *Phnom Penh Post*'s journalist intern. In the same post-graduate job trap as Amanda, Andrea was finishing a master's degree and gaining professional journalism experience by writing for the *Post*. Andrea's $400 a month salary didn't even pay her living expenses. We found a guest-house for $3 a night, complete with hot and cold running rodents given testimony to by teeth marks on the soap the next morning. Aside from another tourist and party-loving Stef, a twenty-something Englishman with Hugh Grant hair who ran the UN's Battambang fuel operation – with whom we shot arrows at piles of Tiger beer cans in the lounge of the Grand Hotel with toy bows bought at Angkor, much to the nervous management's dismay – we were the town's only sightseers. According to the rumours, Siem Reap was supposed to be attacked again.

But it wasn't. The pink sandstone temples of Banteay Srei, some 20 kilometres away, had Khmer Rouge nearby, as usual, but we could still moto to the Roulos group – crumbling red brick temples on the other side of town – and chat with the monks about the rich yellow marigolds they were growing from the hard orange earth. After lunch the heat defeated Andrea and she fell into a dead sleep in our airless, rough board room. I went off with Rity, my moto driver, and shot pool on a shaky table with torn pockets at the back of the market, between the basket stalls and the hanging chicken carcasses. A woman shooting pool, much less a foreign woman, nonplussed the local hustlers – five or six boys and some moto drivers – but they didn't give an inch and I lost embarrassingly.

Rity looked confused when I asked to see what he thought was important in Siem Reap. He took me to his parents, who sold soap, dried noodles and fishing nets from a small stall along the river, and to the *wat* where he had gone to school. A small ruin stood behind the *wat*. Lines of tinsel and coloured paper clung to the walls, reminders of the last festival. Another head monk, Rity said, had been killed earlier in the year by the Khmer Rouge for being too outspoken, but Rity wanted to introduce me to the new one.

The new head monk was ecstatic to see me. At last a foreigner from the UN to talk about fixing the road. I tried to explain I wasn't from the UN, I was only a lowly freelancer. This didn't seem to matter. Waving his hand for Rity and me to follow, the monk led us to a rutted path beside the *wat* which led back through the paddies.

'Look,' the head monk said, 'the villages back among the paddies need this road to get to market. The road's too rutted for ox carts or bicycles. All the UN has to do is take a road grader . . .'

I tried to say again that I wasn't from the UN. The monk just kept on talking. He was sure if the UN knew about the road they'd come to fix it. The repairs wouldn't take much. Now if I could just talk to my bosses . . . This went on for half an hour – the monk, as civic head of the local community, explaining again and again how important the road was and his faith that the UN would fix it, me protesting I'd like to help them but I couldn't. The monk remonstrated – he was sure I had some pull.

Finally I gave in. I made a few vague promises. I would talk to my non-existent bosses, I would see what I could do. The monk's determination showed the problem the UN's presence had created: people knew it would only take a road grader or what to a big organization like the UN was a small amount of money to fix their problems, to provide a road or a school or a well. Expectations were high, and when problems weren't solved by the UN, or the Cambodian government soon afterward, disappointment was strong.

Driving back, Rity and I stopped to watch a strongman who'd gathered a 100-strong crowd by the river. Loudspeakers attached to a battery on the back of the strongman's remorque hung from the trees. A young teenage girl put a tape in the boom box. Like Anthony Quinn in Fellini's *La Strada*, the strongman, telling jokes before each feat, bent iron bars and broke bottles over his head to prove the potency of the small green bottle of elixir he sold when his performance finished. The magic potion tasted like glue. The strongman laughed when I asked if the girl was his daughter. He made his living by travelling the Siem Reap countryside and selling patent medicine wherever he could. The checkpoints didn't bother him much – he gave them free samples. Then he listed all the little villages where he'd be playing in the next three days if I wanted to catch his act again. Oh, and I should bring some friends.

It was just before dusk when Rity dropped me at Angkor Wat. He putted off to find petrol. Women in long-sleeved shirts, broad sun hats and ankle-length cotton sampots were cleaning the stones with stiff brushes and a green liquid. The French said the Indians, who were restoring Angkor Wat, had ruined the walls by using abrasive cleaners. The Indians said the French didn't know what they were talking about. UNESCO tried to coordinate efforts to preserve the ruins, except they couldn't. The World Monuments Fund let everyone else argue and went off and worked on their own temple, Preah Khan. Some days the Cambodian ministry in charge of the ruins wanted them all to leave.

When the Khmer Rouge had invaded Siem Reap earlier that month they had torched a row of houses. Some of the homeless now dragged loaded bicycles and children along the main avenue into the sanctuary between the balustrades carved in the shape of a *naga*, the fanheaded serpent which protected Buddha in legend.

Cows wandered across the walkways and families washed and gathered water in plastic buckets from a hand pump near the stone lions guarding the steps leading to the inner galleries. The galleries on the north side of the temple depicted scenes from the *Ream Ker*, the Cambodian version of the Hindu myth the *Ramayana*, in which the god Rama, riding the half-human half-bird *garuda*, commenced the Battle of Lanka to defeat the army of giants led by Ravana, seducer of Rama's wife Sita. The eastern side of the temple portrayed the Churning of the Sea of Milk, in which demons and gods flail the sea with a snake's body in order to raise a flask containing the elixir of everlasting life from the sea bed.

The displaced occupants now lived in one of two small 'library' buildings or in the main temple's southern gallery, where scaffolding held up the corner lintels. The refugees had spread out their mats, belongings and children below the bas-relief carving depicting a battle scene from another Hindu epic, the *Mahabarata*. In the carvings infantrymen fight beneath elephant-riding officers and royalty, protected from the sun by multi-tiered umbrellas, *klaw*. The same type of umbrella had shielded Sihanouk, a thousand years after the walls had been carved, when he had left his palace to greet the peace marchers. Smoke from the flames beneath a blackened aluminium cooking pot wafted toward the temple roof.

I climbed to the highest steps and watched the sun go down, streaks of orange and yellow cutting against the blue behind the palm trees. There was not another *barang* or tourist to be seen. At a shrine on top of the *wat* monks began to chant. I sat quietly, surrounded by several soda-selling kids and the still stones, watching the tiny, silent forms of wood-gatherers with their precariously piled heaps of branches and twigs bicycle home on the paths around the wat, and listened to the rhythm of the monks' chants as the jungle swallowed the sun. The minute the Khmer Rouge scares ended the tourists would pour in, I thought. I would probably be one of the last travellers to have the great temple to myself.

I knew more philosophically minded individuals would take the moment to meditate, reflect on the grandeur of Angkor and the folly of man, examine their life and the reasons they passed the years as they did, but all I could think was this: someday, someone will find a determined, elderly bonze in the middle of Siem Reap province, sitting in the lotus position for years on end and patiently waiting not for perfect karma, but for a Caterpillar road grader and a 7–11.

* * * *

Back in Phnom Penh, the 'I'm a freelancer and I really should be doing something but oh god it's rainy season look at that lake where the street used to be is anything in the fridge' sorority called an all-day session. Nothing was really happening; there was no news and it was too wet, we told ourselves, to chase features. Shel, the blonde New Zealand freelancer with a *krama* wrapped around her head whom I had thought was such a pseud during my first UN press briefing, busied herself trying to work the video as did Anne, a preppily dressed stringer who filled the role of everybody's tomboyish younger sister. Shel was enormously self-confident and one of the few foreign journalists relatively fluent in Khmer. By contrast, Anne, only a year younger, worried about being taken seriously and tried to get as much advice as possible about her chosen profession. But Anne said Shel drove her nuts on occasion trying to tell her what to do. Just like a younger sister.

A journalist nicknamed Fester arrived as the show started; Fester saw himself as the *éminence grise* of the foreign journalist community, the man who dispensed wisdom, resolved ethical questions and offered sound practical advice; Anne frequently looked to Fester for guidance. We were glad of the company. Any hopes of a weekend walk to Wat Phnom park, surveying the kids riding the merry-go-round of miniature MIG fighters and the vendors touting balloons or masks of rabbits and gods, or a stroll along the river to watch families picnicking and the rental boats filled with Sunday rubbernecks floating down the Mekong, had been washed away. Outside the house kids played the toss-the-flip-flop game, a plasticised version of horseshoes, in the rain. Cyclo drivers huddled in their passenger seats under plastic sheeting to avoid the water, while the sorority's afternoon plenum watched videos of Sihanouk's movies in the name of research.

Sihanouk was extremely proud of his directorial abilities, so much so that in the late '60s he held the Phnom Penh Film Festival and awarded his film the solid gold statue for best picture. After the movie the sorority dwindled to three members. Fester, who had a penchant for secrecy, cried off to a mysterious destination and, in her 'I have to forget Alain' mode, Amanda abandoned us for a date with a Uruguayan UNTAC accountant. Renowned for patrolling Phnom Penh on his UN motorcycle in search of unattached females, the Uruguayan had hit on every single one of us in the past month. A man who made silk shirts look synthetic, the number cruncher had, through careful back-to-front combing, skilfully styled his natural hair to resemble a cheap toupée.

'Save me,' Amanda mouthed silently as the Uruguayan dragged her away to a hotel happy hour.

Anne declared she wanted to try opium; she longed to be deep and mysterious but her image was cookies and milk. An emissary was duly dispatched to Papa's and returned with a gooey chunk of his finest Laotian. Once again, we lacked the paraphernalia the drug required.

'Hmmmm, opium on Pringles,' Anne crunched down tentatively on a brown smeared potato chip. 'Yeucchhhh!'

'Absolutely the best, mate. They're so sweet,' Shel continued on about the wonders of Asian lovers. There wasn't much else we could talk about, because Shel on a roll was virtually impossible to stop. In the two years since she had left for a three-month vacation from Sheep Island, as Shel referred to New Zealand, she had gone through the same mid-twenties romantic phases her friends at home had, but Shel's boyfriends reflected her itinerary. There had been the Burmese Karen rebel, who thought a penis covered with chewed tobacco was the height of eroticism, a Vietnamese fisherman who penned Shel delicately mournful love poetry, and a Cambodian businessman permanently welded to his mobile phone.

'Finished,' Shel pronounced and admired her handiwork. She stoked the pipe. Once again nobody felt much of a buzz – maybe it was the ignominy of smoking opium through a toilet roll. We were doomed as opium smokers: Papa's little brown square sat in the freezer for the next two months until the maid thought the package was chocolate gone bad and threw it out.

'I need a big story,' Shel mused, blowing rings at the ceiling. Anne glanced up. If Shel received inspiration from the ceiling, Anne didn't want to miss it. Freelancing in a foreign country sounded exotic, every day should present a new story idea, but all the talk in Phnom Penh was now of development. The government would stabilize, said the analysts. The Khmer Rouge would be defeated, investment would pour into Cambodia as part of the new Asian boom. At the moment there wasn't much eye-catching news to write about. Internationally, editors were interested in Cambodia if the story covered a foreigner doing something weird/wonderful/wacky or provided new information about the Khmer Rouge, i.e., they wanted 'people like us' or war-related stories. Otherwise a freelancer's markets were the local *Phnom Penh Post* or the Bangkok papers, with an occasional sale to Singapore or Hong Kong. The going rate was 10 cents a word for the *Post* or the Bangkok papers, with the wires offering $50 a story, which barely covered expenses. The hardest part was selling yourself all the time, putting your ego on the line for fifty to a couple hundred bucks, paid after publication, probably three months down the line. And no matter how good the piece, you had to have a market and hit it at the right time. Cambodia had its moment in the sun during the election; now interest had completely waned.

We decided the cure to our problem was travel. Ratanakiri, the north-eastern province peopled by hill tribes who didn't speak Khmer, was the sorority's favoured destination. Ratanakiri, which means 'jewel mountains' in Pali, had gold mines, smugglers, the Ho Chi Minh Trail, exotic wildlife, and numerous hill tribes – surely there would be something to sell.

'Nah, been there. Too many of us after the same stories, mate, too much competition.' Shel shook her head. On her Ratanakiri trip Shel had found an excellent hill tribe translator, a Jarai who had worked for the Americans during the Vietnam war. She needed to go back before he went wandering off into the forest, she said, but not with all of us. 'How about Kep? Let's go to Kep! Nobody goes to Kep . . .'

I had the funny feeling Shel was trying to change the subject . . .

'Yes! One hour and 13 minutes! A new bad date world record!' Anne shouted as Amanda collapsed through the door and onto the couch.

'Oh Godddddd! He's so terrible! No wonder he's an accountant, he's so cheap! He brought his own soft drinks to happy hour and he argued with the waiter about it with all these people I know staring at us! Then karaoke starts – and Ebenezer Scrooge decides to get up and sing. At least he called it singing. He grabs the mike, gets down on one knee in front of the Filipino band and starts doing it straight to me . . .' Amanda threw her arms out and wailed like a Castillian-Uruguayan Neil Diamond, ' "Feelin-tha! Nothing-gah more dhan Feelin-tha!" And as I'm leaving the manager, who I know, comes up and whispers in my ear "Feelin-tha!" and starts laughing – I am never going to live this down!

'And then,' Amanda grabbed the toilet-roll pipe, inhaled deeply, and concluded without any air, 'he takes me to the cheapest Chinese restaurant in town and tells me that he's married!'

'Okay, well, that finished that one. Now ...', satisfied with Amanda's spiel, Shel closed her eyes, leant back, crooked one arm behind her head, and took a drag from a Heineken can. 'Did I ever tell you about the Khmer Rouge virgin ...?'

Hun Sen's favourite volleyball player

The Malaysian battalion was jogging around the Olympic stadium as Shel kicked the tyres on a rental taxi, checked the tape player, negotiated a price for the entire weekend, and we hit the road to Kep.

'I am Hun Sen's favourite volleyball player,' our driver told us proudly. Alas, Hun Sen's favourite volleyball player didn't really approve of us. None of us spoke Khmer well enough for him. We were three women travelling alone, and we weren't married.

'He wants to know why you don't have a husband. He says at your age all Cambodians are married,' Shel translated the volleyball player's questions from the front seat. Anne was busy rummaging in her pack for a new cassette to replace the driver's favourite melodies from '50s Phnom Penh in the iffy tape player, which had been stuck on the same song for half an hour.

'Has he been hired by my mother?' Cambodians often asked whether or not you were married and how many children you had, but the volleyball player's disapproving voice got on my nerves. 'Ask him why, if he's Hun Sen's favourite volleyball player, he's driving a taxi.'

'I don't think he'll like that question.' Shel looked at the window as we crossed a newly built concrete bridge with a green kangaroo painted on one side, signifying that Australian aid money had built the bridge. A thousand years from now archaeologists will probably use those green stencils to prove that Skippy once hopped freely among the sugar palms. Several confused Cambodians had already asked why the Australians painted green chickens on everything they built.

Lining both sides of the bridge were old people, young

children, and amputees with arms outstretched wanting alms from the passing traffic. Some held baskets for carrying dirt, or hoes, to show that they had been filling in the potholes and thus deserved payment for this socially worthwhile activity. Loudspeakers blared chants and old men or young women raised silver bowls asking for donations to restore the local wat. The volleyball player sped past them all.

Despite the havoc the rainy season wreaks upon Cambodia's mostly red dirt-roads, this was the time when the Cambodian countryside was most beautiful. Rainfall brought lines of farming families bending over the fields, broadcasting seed in shimmering white falling arcs or transplanting rice. The paddies became verdant, a crazy-quilt of brilliant green. Pairs of women stood on paddy walls and swung buckets back and forth between a water-filled field and its dry neighbour, scooping water in a basic irrigation system. In one paddy stood one of the abandoned, hand-built clay dikes which the Khmer Rouge had hoped would increase Cambodia's rice production fourfold. The untutored dam designers did not understand basic engineering and the dams had proven almost useless, but costly in human lives.

We stopped for *gwiteo* in Kampot, the provincial capital nestled along a river about 20 miles north of Kep. Here, in the 1930s the Cambodian arm of the Indo-Chinese Communist Party was founded among Chinese and Vietnamese workers, supposedly by an itinerant Vietnamese tailor, a disguise Ho Chi Minh reputedly used when travelling through the French colonies and protectorate.

With access to the sea, Kampot had always been a thriving commercial town. Half a millennium ago the Cambodian kingdom extended into the Mekong delta; Saigon had started as a *kampuchea krom*, lowland Khmer, village called Prey Nokor. Kampot's location meant the town had always been swayed by outside influences, especially Vietnamese. Southern Vietnam, only 40 kilometres away, is still home to hundreds of thousands of *kampuchea krom*. They follow Cambodian religious rites and are considered Cambodian by the Vietnamese, Vietnamese by the Cambodians. True to form, the Khmer Rouge considered the delta Cambodian and wanted it back.

By the end of the day, it was plain that the volleyball player hated us. He didn't approve of the noodle stand we chose, he favoured another. We asked to drive to the top of Bokor Mountain, the site of a former casino resort, he said there were too many Khmer Rouge. We wanted to go to the waterfall locals bragged about, he showed us some minuscule rapids. After inspecting the Kampot market, filled with a line of women in broad hats squatting before baskets loaded with oranges, species of fish you didn't even see in Phnom Penh still flapping in buckets, and bright yellow and orange palm sugars being sold from paint drums, the volleyball player announced he wanted to pack the trunk full of foul-smelling but expensive durian fruit to sell in Phnom Penh and move our bags into the back seat where Anne and I sat. We firmly said we were renting the car from him, not vice versa.

Grumbling, the volleyball player drove us to the Kep promenade, past the ocean-side salt flats where women collected and dried the salt used to preserve the fish harvested from the Great Lake and rivers. The asphalt road was rotten and potholed. Elderly, faded Shell signs swung above abandoned petrol stations like rusting, long-necked swans' heads.

As we rounded a hill the highway swept down to Kep's beach-front promenade. Burnt-out, deserted villa walls and foundations dotted the slopes above the shore. In 1917 Kep had been founded as a colonial resort. The small seaside village had been Cambodia's most exclusive seaside getaway, the Khmer Antibes or Martha's Vineyard. Pol Pot's troops had completely destroyed this symbol of bourgeois comfort. Now only three or four carloads of holiday-makers from Phnom Penh and Kampot were using the beach. Most Phnom Penhois had not seen the sea. 'I'd like to take my family to Sihanoukville, but it's too dangerous,' said a Cambodian friend. The fear of checkpoints along the highways and the Khmer Rouge, unfounded or not, kept many people from travelling.

On the beach Anne, Shel and I struggled into our bathing suits underneath our sarongs; the few Cambodian women who went into the water did so fully clothed. We lazed on the sand and played with the kids who crowded around. Picking up a little boy Shel ran to dump him in the surf. The boy screamed with delight and fear. Shel was one of the few expat women who dived fully into Cambodian life. She didn't mind being known as a 'long-haired dictionary', the Cambodian slang for a Western girl who dated Khmer men and improved their French or English. Shel needed a 'short-haired dictionary' herself.

Soon the rain came. We left the beach to eat shrimp and chicken barbecued over charcoal braziers at waterside huts. The chicken cooks told us there were no hotels or guesthouses anywhere in Kep; in fact, there were virtually no habitable houses there at all. We thought we would have to return to Kampot, but a UN civil administrator munching prawns suggested the Unnos down the road had spare beds. On weekends, and for a small fee, the Unnos gave UN personnel lifts in their bright orange speed boats to the beaches of a deserted island just off Kep.

I didn't want to impose on the Unnos and said we should rent a room in Kampot. Shel gave me her squint-eyed, eyebrows-raised look, said, 'They like journalists, usually, and it'll be free. You've got to take advantage of what you can here,' and insisted we visit the Unnos immediately.

'Shouldn't be a problem for you, girls. It just so happens three of the boys are away,' said a greying, bushy-bearded, middle-aged British sailor named Morris from the steps of the Unno house in Kep. In his tight pink spandex bicycle shorts and white plastic flip-flops, Morris' outfit would have made Admiral Nelson wish for a patch over both eyes.

'Club Kep', as the Unnos' house was called, was a cavernous rough-plank barn on stilts inside an oceanside compound. Like Noah's Ark, everything in Club Kep came in twos. A new wooden jetty, with two bright orange Viper speedboats and what looked like an old fishing rig tied to the pilings, jutted into the sea. Two dozen Filipino marines assigned to guard the Unnos, whom Morris labelled 'the flip-flops', bivouacked in tents behind the house. Two cooks fed the sailors. Two maids cleaned and, evidently, provided other services.

'They can't keep their hands off us,' Morris confided with a dirty laugh and a conspiratorial wink as one of the maids, named Mi, walked by. Morris reached out, grabbed Mi by the waist and started tickling her. 'Gotchaaaaa!'

'Ayieee! *Ach choi! Ach choi!*' Mi started beating Morris to push him away, telling Morris to fuck off in Khmer. Dressed in a long sarong and a ruffled white blouse, Mi had greased back black hair and dark skin. Her face was covered in heavy white face powder and bright red lipstick to hide her complexion. 'Englishman no good! No good!' Mi glowered dramatically as she ran down the wooden stairs.

Morris had just brought in the final boat-load of suntanned, sandy UN holiday-makers from the island. By 6 pm the compound was shut tight. The road and environs between Kampot and Kep was considered unsafe toward dusk and the beach seekers wanted to be on the road early.

Anne, Shel and I sat on the porch discussing the Khmer Rouge situation in Kep with another Unno, Flicker. With its proximity to Vietnam and the support provided by the Viet Cong, in the 1970s the Kep region had been one of the earliest areas to fall to the Khmer Rouge. Flicker said there was still strong Khmer Rouge support in nearby villages. 'Until about a month before the election the Khmer Rouge, the police and the government soldiers had a sort of unspoken understanding.'

The Unnos hadn't visited the Khmer Rouge villages since before the voting, but Flicker delineated the previous working arrangements. The Khmer Rouge camped on Phnom Vol mountain would visit their families in the villages on the flat fields near the sea at dusk. They would return to their base at dawn. Since the voting, however, there had been problems and the police and army had tried to keep the Khmer Rouge away.

'Yeah, everything fell to pieces during the election when some fuckwit government soldier put out a mine on a bridge, just like he did every night, then forgot he'd put it out and stepped on it himself. He was too embarrassed to say, "Hey, I'm a stupid asshole – I just blew off my own foot," so he blamed the Khmer Rouge.'

Morris, holding his toiletry kit, had wandered onto the porch to deliver his political commentary. He snapped his towel at Mi, who screamed and called him several names in Khmer, then he flip-flopped down to the showers.

'I really want to write about the new DK,' announced Shel emphatically.

Flicker stayed quiet as Shel launched into her spiel. Suddenly it was clear why Shel had been so nonchalantly keen on the Kep trip. She hadn't been trying to keep Ratanakiri to herself, but she was looking for back-up while she scouted her next subject. Even the intrepid Shel thought it was bad idea to chase after the Khmer Rouge on her own. Her thesis was that while the old Saloth Sar-Khieu Samphan guard was still in power and did terrible things, there were Khmer Rouge villages in which life wasn't so bad. Everyone painted them as almost mythic monsters; Shel wanted to write an article to show the Khmer Rouge as mortals. She wanted to spend time living in a Khmer Rouge village. Any of the ones nearby would do, Shel continued innocently.

Flicker didn't look convinced, but took us inside to look at a local map. He pointed out the Khmer Rouge hamlets a few kilometres away and, reading Shel's mind, suggested we not go racing off there.

'God, I've just fulfilled my life's dream – sex in a shower with a nymphomaniac. Now I can die a happy man.' Morris had returned and stood in the doorway, herbal shampoo in one hand, VB in the other. 'She can't get enough – the way she was clawing at me . . . It's not as good as the orgies, though. Yeah, you see, we take the money we get from the lard-butts on the boats, then go out and get a couple new girls, you know, for variety. No, you can't have a good orgy without variety. Then we just go at it – threesies, foursies. They'll do anything you want, anything. Of course, I've been in the navy 20 years so I'm used to it.'

Morris exited, chuckling and dripping, stage right. I tried to give Flicker a 'Is this guy for real?' look, but he was studying the map intently. In the embarrassed silence that followed none of the Unnos in the room denied the story. Finally a blond Unno called Henry looked up from the letter he was writing and shook his head; he seemed the most conservative Unno, the most formal, the least integrated into the group.

If there's a nutter or a drunk on the subway, somehow he always ends up sitting next to me. True to form, I got stuck with Morris that evening. His bloodshot eyes not focusing on anything, at least he stopped talking about sex and changed his subject to the medical runs the Unnos and the Filipinos made to the villages and a school the Unnos were helping to rebuild. He said they made this job worthwhile.

On the first sane note I'd heard from him all day, I left Morris on the porch and trundled along to bed. The Unnos had promised to take us to the island in the morning, but a fine drizzle was pouring on Kep when I woke.

Downstairs the giggling, grey-haired cooks were all standing in a line between the charcoal braziers and a guard's hammock. Mi was teaching them disco hustle. It looked like a saronged ladies' night at the local pub circa 1976, but when I passed Mi suddenly turned off the tape player, as if I wouldn't approve. Only when I rhumba'd to the shower and the cooks laughed did Mi stop looking at me like I was a member of the anti-fun police. I couldn't figure out what I'd done.

The rain never stopped. The day went by lazily – chatting with Henry about navy budget cuts and how he might not obtain a further commission, reading old magazines and talking to the interpreters. Heng, the head translator, had huge, twinkling, mischievous eyes and habitually beat the sailors at poker. After spending the Khmer Rouge years in a commune not far from Kampot, Heng had come to Phnom Penh and pedalled a bicycle taxi to support himself while he went to the country's only high school. The Khmer Rouge had destroyed most of the motos and all the cyclos.

Eighteen-year-old Heng had a wide choice of deserted shop-front flats, French and upper-class Khmer villas, or Chinese tenements in which to live. The echoing rooms of the old villas hadn't appealed. Heng didn't know whether people had died in the houses and Heng was afraid of ghosts. He took some rooms by the Olympic market. Like the other city dwellers drifting back Heng raided the empty villas for wooden furniture to use as fuel. With the loss of all title records, old rights of ownership no longer applied. Possession was the only law. Many people didn't want their former homes, which held memories of parents, children and friends who had disappeared. In 1989, the government decreed anyone occupying a house on a certain day owned that house, and not the state. Heng had been studying in Vietnam and was left homeless.

By dusk the Club Kep gates were shut tight. The Unnos were cut off, and at night they were bored. There were only so many new versions of darts you could invent, so many variations on poker you could play, so many paperbacks you could read, so many beers you could drink. That evening Heng and Mi decided to teach Shel, Anne and I new Khmer phrases. Morris joined in, even though he said all he knew was that *ach choi* meant he was in trouble. Mi spoke almost no English.

'But you can still communicate, can't you?' Morris gave Mi a deep, bushy-eyebrowed look.

'English *ot la'aw*,' Mi sniffed. English no good.

Morris and two of the other Unnos had found 'girlfriends' at the Soriya dancing restaurant in Sihanoukville and brought them back to Kep. Mi hadn't been working at the Soriya very long, Morris said. Being very dark-skinned and at 23 older than most of the other girls, Mi had decided she couldn't wait for men to approach her. She had cannily positioned herself by the men's toilet so virtually every man in the place had to pass her way.

The Unnos had paid off the girl's pimp. The other two sailors had even gone through mini 'marriage' ceremonies with the girls' families, involving yet more cash.

'I'm not having any of that marriage stuff.' Morris was firm. Morris already had a wife and children at home. He thought the fake marriage ceremonies, and the inability of the other men to tell their girls that they couldn't come to England were not meant to be mean, but that they raised painful false hopes. Morris had simply paid Mi's 'owner' and made it clear that he already had a family. 'Mi even asked for a picture of my kids. Wants to the see new ones before I do.'

Mi had not been the only girlfriend in Cambodia to want a family snap from her foreign lover. A European military man, married to a dark Asian woman, had lost a favourite portrait of his wife and three kids sitting in their house's neat northern European backyard. One Sunday the European wangled the day off. A large group of friends was going boating on the Great Lake. The military men brought their girlfriends – several were professionals. The European's girlfriend walked up the plank to the boat dressed in her best: silk *sampot*, lace blouse, and the wide-brimmed felt hat adorned with a silk flower that the girl never went anywhere without.

In the middle of the lake the hat flew off, not into the water but into the boat. The girlfriend had kept important papers and money in the brim for safety; the papers fell onto the wooden deck. The European retrieved the hat. He picked up a paper and started shouting at the girl; what was she doing with his lost picture? Maybe he'd been abroad too long – he kept shouting, asking what voodoo she was trying to place on his family with the stolen photo. The girl cried, the other girls tried to explain, but he said he was finished with her. The European was leaving soon, maybe he was looking for an excuse. Whatever the reason, he couldn't accept the answer. The picture was an icon for the girl. Here was an Asian wife – her own, expensive European house, healthy kids, a life outside dirt and poverty and prostitution, a passport from a safe country – everything the girlfriend wanted and would probably never have. The family and the photograph were something to aspire to, not something to destroy. But the European never truly, I think, believed that.

Heng translated Morris' account of their meeting to Mi. She rattled off several quick Khmer sentences back to Heng.

'What's she saying, Mr Heng?' Morris asked.

'Mi – she wants you to take her back to England.'

'You know I can't. We've been through this. This is why I didn't do any of that marriage stuff.' Morris was firm.

'*Bon slang, bon slang te,*' Mi pointed to her own chest, then to Morris'.

'Ooooooh,' Heng was shaking his head, but his eyes were twinkling. 'Do you know what she says, Morris?'

'No, but I'm sure it means I'm in trouble. What's she saying, then?'

'She says, "I love you, but you love another," ' Heng answered.

'You do,' Morris looked straight back at Mi and posed the question as a statement.

'*Bon slang, bon slang te,*' Mi nodded again. Everyone was silent for a minute.

'Gotcha!' Morris screamed, and lunged to tickle Mi.

'*Ach choi! Ach choi!* Asshole! English no good!' Mi screamed, and started hitting Morris to get away from his tickling. She backed toward the door and they raced down the stairs, scrunching the gravel as they sped into the night, Mi's yells of 'Ach choi! Ach choi!' becoming softer in the distance, until suddenly she stopped, and we didn't see them again for a while.

*   *   *   *

Just after midnight, Flicker, Morris, Shel and I finished our beers as rain splatted across the porch. Anne had gone to bed. The boys looked like they wanted to say something. When they finally did they kept finishing each other's sentences.

'Listen, if you want to come back . . .'

'We've only got two motorcycles, so there can only be two of you . . .'

'But we want to go back when we've got both the bikes working . . .'

'So if you come again we can take you to those Khmer Rouge villages.'

'I'm there,' Shel and I said simultaneously as soon as Flicker aspirated his last 's'. We felt a little guilty Anne was left out, but that was the breaks.

First thing in the morning the volleyball player drove us back to Phnom Penh at twice the speed he drove down. Rice stacks standing like hay houses lined the road, as did beehive-shaped mud kilns which incinerated local logs – the black charcoal remains would be hauled into towns to be sold as cooking fuel. A toddler led a line of massive, placid water-buffalo along the road. The tiny child next to the enormous buffalo would have made a lovely shot, at least for someone with her maternal instinct in overdrive, but I was afraid if I stopped to take a picture I would spook the animals.

North of Kampot, the checkpoints were already waiting in the hot morning sun. On some stretches a man with a gun stood every 100 yards or so. Sweating in what must have been 100-degree Fahrenheit heat, one checkpoint fashion victim sported Ray-Bans topped with a large Russian fur hat with the flaps pulled up, tiestrings bouncing as he waved our car through. Again I thought about stopping to take a picture, but then I considered his carefully chosen AK-47 accessories and tried to decide exactly how crazy you would have to be to stand in 100-degree heat in a Russian fur hat. Pass.

We crested a hill to see another Ray-Banned man, his face wrapped from crown to jaw with a krama, squatting in the middle of the road behind an ancient machine gun. The volleyball player stopped completely. When the machine-gunner saw *barang* he passed us on.

'What are you doing in the middle of the road?' Shel called out.

The soldier kept his machine-gun sights firmly on the hill behind as the volleyball player started to accelerate, but after a second he shouted, 'I'm just trying to make a living . . .'

Bat massacre

Shel and I now felt extremely cocky – the UN had been banned from Khmer Rouge villages and here we were about to be escorted straight in. Between press briefings, interviews and any outing that involved free food, Shel sat on my couch, waved her cigarette with one hand and Pepsi with the other, and explained all the reasons why she thought it would be safe to stay overnight with the Khmer Rouge.

Gulp. Thank God I couldn't get a word in edgeways when Shel was talking because then I didn't have to own up to the fact that, personally, Our Lady of Perpetual Paranoia here was only buying a day ticket. I didn't understand much about Cambodia, and I questioned what I thought I knew, but I did know that, even under the UN truce, bunking with the Khmer Rouge contradicted every single one of my personal safety requirements. I knew I kept on blathering about how I'd like to be an intrepid foreign correspondent but, really, I'd be sooooooooo much happier in the YWCA . . .

Meanwhile we watched the beginnings of the 'resurrection' of Cambodia. Once the election was over the new government was determined to modernize the country. Roads, bridges, schools, sewers, a national phone system, hospitals – there was much to be done, but little money and few people qualified to do it. Many educated Cambodian professionals had fled or been killed during the Khmer Rouge period. Others had gone from the Thai refugee camps to the United States, France or any country which would take them. Foreign experts flew in to help write the constitution or advise on the environment, health, education and the military.

'Cambodia no good.' Puth the cyclo driver complained he didn't have the $200 bribe he needed to become a police officer, one of the many jobs available only after paying the appropriate backhander. Puth had expected it from CPP, he said, but the man he had to pay now was Funcinpec. The corruption associated with the old regime showed no sign of ending. Kickbacks simply went into new pockets. Like many others, Puth wanted to leave Cambodia. The country was an entity beyond the would-be émigrés, aimed at defeating its own population, not something of which they were a willing part. After the voting the immigration queues at foreign embassies were just as eager.

But after the election other Cambodians came back. Many of the new Funcinpec and BLDP appointees in the government had spent the last 20 years abroad. Men and women who left as teenagers returned nearing 40. Their spoken Khmer was rusty, their writing skills limited. For many French was their first language, the one in which they had been educated in Phnom Penh's private lycées before the fall. The most important thing Funcinpec and BLDP could offer Cambodia that CPP couldn't, one theory went, was supporters with up-to-date technical and managerial skills.

'I can never get the respect in France I get here,' said one returnee. Simply by coming back to Cambodia, the new elite gained positions far more elevated than the day-to-day jobs they held in France or Australia. The returnee had been a computer systems manager abroad. In Cambodia he was in the diplomatic corps. Some returnees left behind families and spouses holding down jobs and mortgages while the returnees tried to make a life in their former country. They were dedicated, they would sacrifice, but they wouldn't be silly.

'What passport do you have?' I asked one friend, who was talking about how determined he was to stay and help Cambodia.

'French,' he smiled. 'I will always have a French passport.'

The other part of that one theory said that most CPP supporters had never left Cambodia, and had no other place they could go. The CPP would eventually gain control of Cambodia, that theory went, because Cambodia was all they had.

Despite the pessimism of some cyclo drivers, investors were still bullish. Phnom Penh continued to erupt in new hotel signs and soon sported a Foreign Correspondents' Club. Even if there were fewer than a dozen foreign correspondents in Cambodia the owners were not deterred. They gambled that Phnom Penh businessmen, like their Bangkok or Hongkong contemporaries, would pay big membership bucks to drink alongside journalists complaining about their modems. The club was a high-raftered ochre room romantically overlooking the river, but construction had finished behind schedule. By opening day the owners still hadn't dislodged the bat colony swinging from the roof. Several swooped down to join the club's inaugural party, which featured free food and booze to tempt you into joining. Unfortunately, the winged rodents hadn't noticed the ceiling fans and ended up as an impromptu chopped garnish on the potential members' hors-d'œuvres.

With the proliferation of satellite dishes, faxes, and private clubs, the rush to join the modern world and the chauvinistic need to define and protect what was 'Khmer' sometimes collided. 'Khmer' art, as produced by most Phnom Penh sculptors and painters, was repetitive paintings of Angkor Wat and *apsaras* or carvings of a Bayon head. The School of Fine Arts sought to protect indigenous crafts, but seemed to promote the philosophy that the only Cambodia worth depicting was the myth-bound past. Artists representing daily life were few. The classical Cambodian dancers, with their gold-encrusted costumes and intricate, what looked like finger-breaking, gestures rarely performed inside the country. The art had virtually died when many dancers were killed by the Khmer Rouge. Now the national dance troupe was nurtured in a small village on the far side of the river in Phnom Penh, supported by a British oil company whose manager was an amateur actor.

Even before the Khmer Rouge, the dancers and the shadow-puppet theatre had lost the majority of their audiences to movies and television. Perhaps the real Cambodian arts were now the populist ones – the comics performing with a portable microphone in the park below Wat Phnom each morning, the high-voiced female singers wailing teenage love songs, or the endless soap operas that played each afternoon on Khmer television, the comic character always wearing a black Charlie Chaplin moustache. At the 'up-market' end of the scale, Cambodia had an entry at the 1994 Cannes Film Festival. *The People of the Rice Fields* had one showing in Phnom Penh, then it was back to Indian musicals.

Much to the dismay of nationalistic Cambodians, imported culture ruled – Hong Kong Chinese Kung Fu movies, Thai television, Western-style rock. While the invited and uninvited members of the press stuffed their faces with free horsd'œuvres at the opening of Phnom Penh's first Englishlanguage movie theatre, someone mentioned the Khmer rock music videos produced by Long Beach entrepreneurs.

Khieu Kanharith, a Cambodian journalist who once languished under house arrest for displeasing the SOC government but who had metamorphosed into a bon viveur CPP press spokesman, didn't approve. The videos were not truly Khmer, Kanharith said with an uncharacteristically stern face. Cambodia needed Khmer arts.

Someone asked Kanharith what movie he wanted to see next.

'Jurassic Park,' Kanharith promptly replied.

But the people who had done the most to destroy traditional Khmer art forms were to be given a second chance. Sihanouk declared that Funcinpec should make peace with CPP and that everyone should accept the Khmer Rouge. 'National reconciliation' became the Phnom Penh buzz-word. Analysts posited that Funcinpec had done a pre-election deal with the Khmer Rouge to prevent violence in exchange for cabinet positions, which they hadn't received. CPP, filled with politicians who had been Khmer Rouge 20 years before, had a far more belligerent stance toward the guerillas than Funcinpec. Perhaps because we hadn't witnessed what Cambodians had, foreigners were often surprised at how many Cambodians were willing to forgive the Khmer Rouge, at least legally. 'If it means an end to more then it's good. Khmer Rouge are Cambodian people, too. I do not care,' said one friend. 'No more killing. That is what's important. No more.'

'Highly placed sources' felt the Khmer Rouge had made a fatal mistake when they boycotted the elections. Once the new Cambodian army combining the Anki, KPNLF and CPAF forces was in place, with a combined strength of between 5 and 25 times the Khmer Rouge force, depending on which official unofficial troop estimate you believed, the Khmer Rouge would be reduced to the status of the Thai communists, a few lonely survivors in the border hills.

Khieu Samphan, the Khmer Rouge president, arrived in Phnom Penh for talks aimed at including the Khmer Rouge in the new government. It was his first post-election visit. A French-educated communist, in the 1950s and 1960s Khieu Samphan had been a newspaper editor and a popular member of Sihanouk's assembly noted for incorruptibility, shunning the traditional politician's Mercedes to tootle around Phnom Penh in a Volkswagen Beetle. Sihanouk had for a short time appointed him a cabinet minister, but in 1967 Khieu Samphan joined the guerillas in the jungle.

Khieu had been a leading member of the Khmer Rouge inner circle for nearly 40 years. When Khieu first returned to Phnom Penh after the peace agreement was signed, 12 years after the Khmer Rouge abandoned the city, the CPP government, which hated him, had ordered demonstrations and orchestrated rioters to storm the Khmer Rouge headquarters. In the commotion Khieu was bashed on the head. Photos flashed on the wires of the Khmer Rouge president stemming the blood running down his face with a pair of men's briefs. Reports said Hun Sen had calmly watched the protesters attack the compound, claiming there was nothing he could do.

When Khieu arrived at Pochentong airport this time the only rampaging hordes were 30 journalists scrambling in a 'cluster fuck', crowding around his Mercedes like a rugby scrum, practically knocking the cold-faced, white-haired 60 year old over in the hope of a quote. The Khmer Rouge president managed to squeeze into his car without saying a word or being decapitated by the two-foot-long fluffy pink boom-mike a Japanese television crew kept swinging at his head. As usual when Khieu Samphan arrived in town, that evening government television broadcast *The Killing Fields*.

Kor Bun Heng, a Khmer Rouge functionary, waited on the tarmac for his boss. In a short-sleeved, striped cotton shirt and gold-rimmed aviator glasses, Kor Bun Heng looked like a small-town economics professor.

'I think everyone is aware that we support the plan for

national reconciliation.' He chatted diplomatically with Kevin Barrington, a fast-talking cynical Irishman who was soon the Agence France Presse correspondent, and me, neglecting to mention the fact that the Khmer Rouge had attacked and taken Preah Vihear temple on the Thai border, second only to Angkor in its sacredness, two days before. 'I hear you now have a Foreign Correspondents' Club . . .'

I had a momentary fantasy in which Kor Bun Heng asked Kevin and I to support his membership application. Disappointingly, the guerilla in the slip-on loafers only wanted the details of the bat massacre and to ask whether or not we had electricity. I dutifully wrote down every word.

Maybe if I could get my mind around discussing how chopped bats became canapé decorations at Cambodia's first private members' club with the representative of a murderous ex-Maoist political sect this country would begin to make sense . . .

For unto you is
born this day in the city
of David a Savior,
which is Christ the Lord.
And this shall be a
sign unto you;
Ye shall find the babe
wrapped in swaddling
clothes, lying in a manger.
LUKE 2:10

...EHOLD,
...ING YOU
...INGS OF GREAT
...OY, WHICH SHALL
BE TO ALL PEOPLE.

Mi

Back in Kep, I was suffering from severe confusion.

'Don't talk to the rabbit when you can talk to the water-buffalo,' Morris winked, and tapped the side of his nose twice with his index finger.

'Yeah, I always say that . . .' Shel nodded sagely.

I was glad Shel knew what Morris meant, because I didn't have a clue. Neither did Shel actually, because the next thing she said in her strong Sheep Island accent was, 'Morris, what the fuck are you talking about?'

What Morris was talking about was Mi. Mi was now forbidden by the powers that be in Phnom Penh to live with Morris.

'That's why George has gone to Phnom Penh to try to sort this all out. Go to the top. Oh, hell, I just made all that stuff up about sex in the showers and orgies to throw you three. I didn't know you were all right. You could have been a couple more lard-butts for all I knew.'

Flicker had left and George, on leave on our last visit, had taken over as the Kep Unnos' commander. Fifteen years younger than Morris, George looked every inch the proper British officer, but as long as the work was done George saw no reason to stop partying. Like Morris, George had found friendship at the Soriya dancing restaurant.

The Unnos didn't really mind providing a water-taxi service to the beaches for the UN's civilian staff, said Morris. He and the other Unnos always hit the administrators for a contribution toward their village medical runs and the two schools the Unnos were building. But one or two shocked spoilsports had complained that the Unnos had women living on the base. Mi and the other two girls were forced to move. That had happened our first weekend at Kep, and explained why Mi would go quiet when Shel and I were around. After that, Morris worked hard at shocking the lard-butts.

Following her expulsion from Kep, George had taken his girlfriend to Takeo and given her money to start a dress stall. The first week or two George had visited her, Morris said, but the last time George had merely watched the girl from the market's edge. George wanted to make sure she was okay, but he also wanted her to forget him.

Only Mi had stayed at Kep, renting a room in the local strongman's bright blue house 100 yards down the road. Despite their radically different cultures, Mi and Morris were much alike. Coming from what some would see as the lower rungs of the British class system himself, Morris sympathized with Mi's position. He hadn't started life with many advantages and neither had Mi. Mi stayed on the Kep payroll as maid. Each day she came to sweep the fraternity house. Morris had taken to spending the occasional night off base. He was already on final warning for wearing shorts on duty and other minor rule infringements. The powers that be in Phnom Penh wanted to make an example of Kep.

As we went to sleep that night, in the absent Unnos' bunks underneath the mosquito nets, Shel reiterated that an article about life in Khmer Rouge villages was her idea. I should only use the material I found for the book.

'Funnily enough, I know it's your idea.' I didn't intend to steal Shel's article and I was narked that Shel thought she had to bring it up. If the thing I liked least about freelancing was the competitiveness, the second least was the paranoia. Besides, although I was convinced Shel's idea might be dangerous, I wasn't convinced that Khmer Rouge village life was sweetness and light. But Shel's comment brought home the depressing fact that I hadn't sold any new pieces in the last month.

The next morning the rain fell in clear sheets. A sole dinghy braved the sea. The fisherman, covered in an oily blue plastic slicker, rowed in giant butterfly strokes against the green-grey waves. The fraternity house was empty except for the straight and narrow Henry, bent over blue airmail stationery, busy scribbling letters back home. I wandered to the translators' room and gabbed with Heng. He showed me a snapshot of his wife and child.

During the Khmer Rouge time, rather than admit her son was a student, Heng's mother had insisted he was a farmer. His mother told the soldiers the 14-year-old Heng was backward. 'Every day I have to hear my mother say how stupid I was. It was very hard to hear my mother say every day I am stupid so I complain. I say, "Mother, how come you always say I'm stupid? I'm not stupid." Then she say if I don't understand why she tell them I am stupid then I really am stupid.'

Heng had been 14 when the Khmer Rouge took over, and 18 when the Vietnamese invaded. His teenage years were not carefree. 'I didn't care if I died then, no. I just prayed, please, God, do not let them kill me by hitting me over the head. Anything except being hit over the head. Otherwise I did not care. And I wanted to die. Even after the Khmer Rouge left, I wanted to die for a long time.'

Now, Heng said, he never thought like that – he had two children, life was different. He had a house now, and was saving to buy a car – 'I want my children to have the best life I can give them.'

After the Khmer Rouge era, when many women temporarily lost their menses due to malnutrition, Cambodia had experienced a population boom. More than 50 per cent of the population was now under 15. No figure could be precise since no census had ever been taken. 'I think children are more precious to Cambodians after the Khmer Rouge. My auntie and uncle and mother want me to have what they didn't,' Monita, my landlord Chhoun's niece, had told me one day as I helped her with her English lesson.

You could tell Mi would have been a good mother, Morris said that evening after dinner, by the way she entertained the cooks' children.

'She hasn't had an easy time. You haven't had very good luck, have you, eh?' Morris gave Mi another of his deep looks. 'You don't like to talk about it, do you?'

'English no good, fuck you,' Mi exaggeratedly mirrored his frown.

Shel asked what we were both thinking: what would Mi would do after Morris was gone?

'Sell oranges.'

'You won't go back to the Soriya?'

'Maybe I won't make enough from the oranges.' Mi didn't look entirely comfortable with the questioning, but she didn't deny she might return to her dance floor perch by the men's loo. And Mi was very quiet and serious during the conversation that followed: yes, she knew this thing called *Sida*, the Khmer word for AIDS taken from the French. The foreign men usually wanted to use condoms and she did, too. But the Khmer men frequently said no. Mi said she had seen in the market a medicine which could cure AIDS.

'That medicine is no good, it's a lie. They sell that medicine just to take your money. Nothing can cure AIDS,' Shel was cutting the air with the sides of her palm in short, fast jabs to make the point. It was an important one. A year later the HIV-positive rate among prostitutes in Sihanoukville, where Mi had worked, was 40 per cent. Some experts reckoned that 60–70 per cent of Phnom Penh's prostitutes were HIV positive.

Mi was quiet. Shel asked Mi if she understood. 'I don't want to die,' Mi soberly announced. She worried, though, that some days the orange business would be bad.

Conversation faltered. Mi was realistic about the economics of orange selling. What could we say? We all knew that Mi might not have much choice. The chat drifted into English. Mi, looking bored, announced she was going home. Morris said he would follow later.

Not so long ago Mi had been married, Morris said after he was sure Mi had clumped down the stairs. While pregnant with her second child Mi's husband left. With more women than men in Cambodia some men felt there was always another wife to be had; polygamy, after all, had not so long ago been common in Cambodia. To support her baby Mi had worked in the salt flats. She miscarried. Mi didn't earn enough to feed and take care of the other child and the baby died. Mi had been too poor to have pictures taken of her child.

Alone, Mi turned to her only relative, a brother who lived somewhere near Takeo, for help. Mi's helpful brother sold her to the Soriya's pimp. Like many prostitutes, Mi was working off a 'family debt', the money the pimp had paid her brother.

The amount wouldn't have been much. With the onslaught of AIDS virgins were highly sought after. The girls were sometimes kidnapped and sometimes sold or used as collateral for a loan by relatives. They fetched about $400 for their families. Mi's debt would have been less.

'She doesn't like to talk about the children. Poor thing cries. She doesn't like to remember that.' Morris, the old softie, was not looking too dry himself. 'She won't do things now, you know. When we were first together she'd do anything. She was just a whore and whores did these things. But now she won't. She says good Cambodian women don't do these things. This is like being married for Mi. She's a good girl.' Morris suddenly stood up to retrieve some sodas from the fridge, marking them on the slate by the window. 'Mi's smart, you know. She can't read, she can't write, but she's smart. Give her money, she knows where every penny is. And she doesn't really want money, doesn't trust it. She wants gold. She knows if something goes wrong you can always sell gold.'

What would sell seemed to have been the theme of my day. Earlier in the afternoon, as the sky had cleared, Morris had packed Shel, a bald, barrel-shaped British Unno called Rafe, Heng and I into a Landcruiser and offered us the tourists' tour of Kep.

As usual, I had my camera along. I didn't plan to push photographs; it was just much simpler to take pictures than scribble notes immediately for description. But you never knew: Shel's comment about Kep being 'her' story, and the fact that I hadn't sold anything new since the election, niggled. Besides, I had a half-decent camera and Shel didn't – no competition.

The tourist itinerary didn't have many stops: a *wat* that was being refurbished, the school the Unnos were rebuilding, the hotel the military had taken over, a few small villages like Chang Aeu, a crossroads marketplace. Chang Aeu could have been any countryside town, but a moto driver told us he thought the government had Khmer Rouge bandits trapped near a coconut grove.

Since Morris and Rafe's job was to monitor military activity, we drove toward the grove. Every 50 yards a group of three or four soldiers stood before the straight rows of coconut trees, behind grenade launchers, AK-47s or stationary machine guns. Here was a sure-fire sale: the newly integrated Cambodian army readying to battle with the Khmer Rouge, who only months before had been allies of Funcinpec and the KPNLF. I'd only make $50 a shot from Associated Press or Reuters, but more importantly I needed to sell something to appease my insecure ego.

Morris had just braked and I had barely raised the camera to my eye when through the viewfinder I saw the 35mm-framed troop commander screaming and charging toward the truck. The commander started to pull open my door and grab for my camera, but Morris and Heng frantically assured him no film had been shot. Rafe threw his arm across the seat to stop the commander and Morris plied him with tobacco, telling him to calm down.

The commander lit the cigarette Morris gave him, took a couple of deep, angry drags, then said the guerillas had just attacked a train on the rail line behind the coconut grove. The freight included two cart-loads of new motorcycles which the Khmer Rouge wanted. There had been a firefight not half an hour ago. Now the commander's troops were trying to stop the Khmer Rouge from going to their villages on the flat, seaward side of Route 16.

We drove a few hundred yards further along the road before we turned back to Kep. The soldiers were tense and the Landcruiser, looming above the brush, was a perfect target. I was still shaken by the commander's attempt to come after the camera and/or me, and that I'd been so stupid as to try to take a photo, but everyone else said the soldiers usually had no problem with pictures. I'd just unfortunately come across someone who was really, *really* on the edge.

Later we paid our respects to a local CPAF officer, who, with his soldiers hanging out on the blue-painted ruined staircase of his office quietly smoking cigarettes, was not part of the anti-Khmer Rouge attack. He said the troops that day had been specially brought in from the A3 unit, trained in Vietnam and East Germany in counter-insurgency tactics. The A3 wasn't even supposed to exist, much less be photographed by a money-grabbing freelancer who didn't know what she was snapping, only that there was something to snap.

The young monks at the *wat* the next morning, however, all crowded together to get into the frame. We had danced the pothole polka with the motorcycles down Route 16, past the coconut grove. The A3 soldiers were still positioned in ones and twos every 100 yards or so. We then slid onto a side-road off a side-road off a side-road. The trail stopped at a *wat* covered in scaffolding. Beyond that it faded into a paddy-track.

Half a dozen teenage monks from Battambang were helping to restore the *wat*. After a brief *sampeah*, hands pressed together in front of their chests, the orange-wrapped novices surrounded the motorcycles and began the traditional Cambodian religious ritual, The Adoration of the Gas Engine.

Other monks had more serious matters to discuss. They complained of banditry, with the attackers dressed at least partially in government uniforms. Rafe asked if the monks had been similarly troubled by the Khmer Rouge.

'No, we like the Khmer Rouge,' one monk smiled. 'Three Khmer Rouge sleep here at night. They come to protect us from the bandits. Sometimes the Khmer Rouge pray with us.'

None of us had expected that answer, or at least I hadn't. The Khmer Rouge were the bad guys. They weren't supposed to protect monks from government soldiers, much less bend in prayer. But where virtue suited their purpose, the Khmer Rouge offered protection which the government didn't. The Khmer Rouge had followed a selective hearts and minds strategy 30 years before and they were doing so now. In other hamlets the Khmer Rouge ruthlessly murdered and kidnapped to get their way.

Morris explained that we wanted to talk to the Khmer Rouge about what had happened since the election, and especially to Khmer Rouge families. Did the monk know any in the area? '*Ot panyaha*,' there were enough around. The monk pointed down the track. 'Past the rice mill, first hut on the right. They're Khmer Rouge.'

We revved off and stopped in front of two women weeding a sweet potato field. They wore ankle-length sarongs, long-sleeved print blouses in a different pattern and *kramas* wrapped around their heads in turban fashion to keep off the sun. I remembered Pholla, the giggly Tuol Sleng museum guide, and her fashion tips – you could tell Vietnamese women from Khmer women because Khmers wore two prints at the same time. The Vietnamese always wore plain trousers or a plain top.

Morris explained that we just wanted to talk about the elections. We were ceremoniously offered seats on a shaded sleeping platform. An old man with spiky white hair sent two boys clambering up a coconut tree to collect drinks. A woman handed the green orbs around, then tried to control her unruly four-year-old son who screamed whenever Rafe held out a hard candy. She pulled her son onto her lap. An older grey-haired woman, with a mouth stained red from beetlenut chewing, sat beside them, patting the boy's legs in a silent admonition to be a good kid, stop trying to get all the attention and shut up. Then it was time to talk.

His village, the old man said, had overwhelmingly voted for Funcinpec. No one belonged to the Khmer Rouge, he continued, but since the election the government soldiers, who were still under control of the CPP, had come to the village and threatened Funcinpec voters.

The old woman waved her hand again as if to say, 'Oh bullshit,' and started heckling from the back; the old man purposefully continued to ignore her. They were probably that way every night over the rice bowl.

Morris said he was sorry that the soldiers had harassed the villagers. He promised the UN would do what they could; it might not be much. As Heng translated this to the old man, the wife loudly burst in again. Heng couldn't finish. Once or twice the old man opened his mouth to speak, like a fish gasping for water. His wife's counterblast cut him off at each attempt. A truce was called and they both fell silent.

'The people have asked me to tell you the truth,' the old man said finally, with great seriousness. I suppose 'the people have asked me' sounded better to him than 'my wife's making life hell . . .'

'We're all Khmer Rouge,' he started. His son had joined three weeks earlier. The old man himself had retired from the guerillas ten years before. The Khmer Rouge did not have new uniforms or a weapon to give his son, but the son already had a gun.

I asked the old man how often the guerillas came to recruit.

'We go to them,' the old man continued. It was the threats of violence and robbery by the government soldiers which had caused the join-up.

'Last week when I was talking with Khieu Samphan ...' Shel made an Oscar-winning bid for Best Name Dropping in a Bamboo Hut in the Middle of a Rice Paddy, which to her credit she later admitted she deserved. Shouting a question didn't really qualify as cocktail conversation, but the farmers didn't know that. They nodded sagely as Shel launched into her analysis of the situation in the countryside.

There were better villages to talk to than his, the old man offered, and sketched in the dirt a map of some DK villages across the paddies. We left.

*   *   *   *

'No, nobody here's Khmer Rouge,' said a squat man who wouldn't stop shaking Morris' hand in the next village. Up and down up and down maybe up and down up and down over up and down there ...

We bounced on across the paddy walls, Rafe and I accidentally taking a short-cut through someone's lean-to kitchen. No matter where we stopped however, the Khmer Rouge seemed elusive. The villagers in the next hamlet also said, 'No, it's not us, maybe in the next ...' but a very tall woman with gold-capped teeth didn't see any reason to pretend.

'CPAF came here and took the village chief's cows because they thought the village belonged to the Khmer Rouge. The chief knew my brother and husband were in the Khmer Rouge, so he took my cows and left.' Mrs Goldteeth was *pissed off*.

The village contained both Khmer Rouge and CPAF families and both Funcinpec and CPP voters. Many of the men who had joined the Khmer Rouge had done so in the mid-eighties to eject the Vietnamese, Mrs Goldteeth insisted. And whoever had told us the Khmer Rouge hadn't come across the highway was lying, she said proudly. They'd been here for days and were so now.

Morris asked how many men had joined the Khmer Rouge

from this village. A middle-aged man in a battered trilby hat squatted on the ground next to Morris with the other village elders. He took some time counting, but after consultation with Mrs Goldteeth said that since the election 16 men from the surrounding villages had signed up. Morris asked if we could meet the local Khmer Rouge leader. Mr Trilby conferred again, then parlayed with three young men wearing only *kramas* wrapped around their waists who had quietly slipped in at the crowd's edge.

The young men, happily perusing the motorcycles, didn't want to set off to find the local Khmer Rouge commander. 'Instead he has sent the two girls to find the Spy,' Heng announced seriously, as two seven or eight year olds ran off behind the houses. *Chhlops*, watchers who reported on villagers, had always been part of the Khmer Rouge structure. Children were especially favoured for the work. Angka was said to have had the 'eyes of a pineapple', watchers everywhere. If people at times seemed paranoid in Cambodia, they had good historical reason.

While we waited for the Spy, Shel walked off with Mrs Goldteeth to find the sanitary facilities, masquerading as the ditch behind some palm trees. When Shel came back she whispered that she had made a bid to return to Mrs Goldteeth, who said she would have to check before Shel could make a hammock reservation.

Meanwhile, the villagers complained that the local school had closed – teachers thought the hamlet too remote and insecure. And there was no medical care nearby. To reach Kampot hospital meant passing over 20 police or military checkpoints which cost about 400 riels apiece, money the villagers didn't have.

'We see the Red Cross truck on Route 16 but they never come to us,' complained Mrs Goldteeth as she and Shel returned. The explanation that the Red Cross truck could not negotiate the paddies did not placate Mrs Goldteeth. Several people asked for malaria medicine. Morris promised that he would bring the Filipino medic.

'The Spy is coming!' Heng shouted and pointed toward coconut trees leading to the paddies.

Through the trees a dozen children ran and laughed on the

path ahead of the Khmer Rouge's answer to James Bond, a grey-haired, late-middle-aged woman. She squatted beside us and settled an unhappy three year old on her knee.

'When the Khmer Rouge are here we do not have trouble with bandits.' The Spy unwrapped a piece of hard candy Rafe had handed her, trying to distract her crying child. Shifting the boy's weight, she confirmed the local Khmer Rouge leader was about 500 yards away, among the trees. He and a dozen guerillas had been in the village for the past several days. Today, however, was not a good meeting day.

'Come back another day,' the Spy said. Shel controlled a smile – at least she could make one more trip. Morris agreed to return three days later with a medic.

The entire time we had been talking, the bare-chested *sampot* trio and several other local lads had performed the ritual Examination of the Motorcycles.

'How'd you like to drive an ox cart?' a man asked Morris in what to a cynic might have seemed a desperate gambit aimed at a Yamaha test drive.

Morris quickly encouraged the oxen into fifth gear, but he never quite found reverse and he couldn't stop. Everyone ran to watch Morris pound through the coconut copse. The last thing the Khmer Rouge soldiers concealed there must have expected was an out of control UN ox cart invading their hideout, racing back and forth from one edge of the grove to the other, the driver unable to make the animals go back the way they had come.

The adult villagers were collapsing with laughter. Morris was in his element, making a fool of himself so the villagers would trust him, and hopefully give him the information he wanted. He loved performing and, in truth, he loved Cambodia. The day before, Morris had shown us the schools the Unnos were building. Morris was determined to finish the windowless shells before the Unnos left. The pride, concern and wonderment in his face as he described teaching the local children to play soccer made you feel he could barely control the strength of his feelings. All these kids, he said, deserved a chance and it didn't take much to give them one. It wasn't until that night, lying underneath my mosquito net listening to the rain drip through the leaky fraternity house roof, that I realized that Morris' seemingly uncontrolled ox-cart ride was also a very good way to see who and what was in the grove. Going into the villages zipping across the paddies which were technically forbidden territory for both journalists and the UN military, seemed like motorcycle rallying on the edge of danger. But at the moment the devils, at least for the foreigners, were relatively tame ones.

Morris finally executed a right turn and returned. The ox-cart owner was white and shaken. He declined Morris' offer of a whirl on the Yamaha.

'You must leave soon, by three.' While we were watching Morris' act the Spy had sidled up to Heng. The police and government soldiers might give us trouble if we left later, the Spy said.

Half an hour afterwards we slithered across the gravel and potholes of Route 16. One checkpoint soldier sat in the shade by the road next to his AK and smilingly waved us away with a bright red flower. He looked more like a stoned hippy than an extortionist.

Shel and I waited for the return trip, improving our darts and poker skills with the Unnos. I think they liked having us around – someone different to joke with and play jokes on, someone simply female who could complete a whole sentence in a language they spoke – but over the next few days things went wrong. George returned. Instead of bearing good news, though, he had been relieved of command. Mi was banned from the base. I lost my place on the motorcycle to the doctor and missed the Unnos' medical run. My competitive urge returned although I didn't argue – I knew it meant more to Shel than me to visit the villages. I even lent Shel my shoes so she wouldn't lose her flip-flops in the mud, but I somehow felt I wasn't working hard enough if I didn't get a big Khmer Rouge meeting out of this trip.

Shel and Morris zoomed back to the villages. I went to Kampot and spent the day in the rain trying to convince the French military to take me to a Khmer Rouge rendezvous on Bokor mountain, near the ruins of the destroyed casino resort. No dice. The French Unmo said he was sorry but the French, alone among the battalions, had their own press officer in Sihanoukville who had to clear my visit first. Although I returned soaked and quoteless, Shel returned ecstatic: 20 Khmer Rouge had appeared in uniform, including one of the well-built motorcycle admirers, and the villagers had agreed to a subsequent visit by Shel.

I retired to my bunk for a spot of non-competitive teeth-gnashing.

Morris dutifully filed a full report and estimated the Khmer Rouge strength in the area to be at least 100. The UN military in Kampot, especially the French, Morris later said, dismissed his figures. That many Khmer Rouge in the area simply couldn't exist.

My last morning in Kep I went with a Filipino Unno, nicknamed 'Zorro' by the others, to visit the dozen government soldiers living in Sihanouk's father's gutted World War I villa across the road. Beaux-arts cornicing still graced the bullet-pocked façade. According to the other Unnos, Zorro had been a renegade '60s student radical who had worked clandestinely for the Marcos government. Zorro, said my sources, later had a United States holiday for anti-insurgency training and was reputed to possess many useful, and several nasty, intelligence skills. The Unnos thought Zorro did a great job with the local soldiers, administrators, traders and crooks, gossiping and drinking beers, returning with new and usually accurate information. Zorro took a fancy to me and poured out the compliments – I was there and unattached so why not try for a legover? The others, however, had told me about Zorro's wife and the girlfriend at the local dancing restaurant.

'I have no girlfriend! I have no wife!' Zorro declared, looking deep into my eyes. Just what I needed – a married, spook-trained sociopath. Zorro took defeat gracefully.

The government soldiers were courteous and friendly – communicating in a fractured mélange of French, English and Khmer, setting up another soldier to look foolish in a photograph. For the last three months the soldiers had not received their salaries. Even when the soldiers were paid a foot soldier only earned 38,300 *riel* a month, less than an UNTAC staffer's *per diem* for each hour of an eight-hour day. Like the villagers, the government soldiers asked for anti-malaria medicine. Fighting kept both sides similarly disadvantaged.

Zorro and I stayed at the crumbling villa only an hour, if that. By the time we returned, Morris was gone, taken to Phnom Penh to be shipped home. Morris had stayed up all night drinking, missed a roll call, and his nemesis, the ever-proper Henry, had reported him. Henry, who had been worried about climbing the military ladder, had been given temporary command. When Zorro and I entered the subdued fraternity house the straight and narrow Henry was standing in front of the radio set handing out orders, reminding everyone that life at Kep would now be strictly by the book. Henry looked determined, but he also looked like he knew his unpopularity.

In the late afternoon George and I sat on the porch, watching the drizzle. Morris had been whisked away so quickly he hadn't even had time to say goodby to Mi, he said. George and Heng had visited the blue house to break the news and give Mi $200 from Morris, all the money Morris had with him. I couldn't help thinking that with only $200 Mi would be forced back on the game if orange-selling failed her.

'I think Morris partially did it on purpose,' George mused. Not only had Mi been banned, but the UN naval authorities had banned any more medical runs to the villagers. Higher powers were worried that the Unnos might be perceived to favour one faction over another. The things Morris loved in Cambodia had been taken from him all at once. Why stay?

'Nobody meant this to happen,' George continued. He hadn't been prepared for the loneliness of Kep. 'If you'd told me six months ago I'd cheat on my wife with a prostitute I would have laughed. I know you're not going to believe this, but I didn't sleep with her more than two or three times. It wasn't about sex. She was someone to talk to, have a laugh with. This place changed completely with the girls here.'

'But Morris and Mi,' he added, 'well, in another time and another place, who knows?'

Looking across the muddy compound, we saw Mi standing by the front gate. George moaned and stood up. 'I'm not looking forward to this.'

By the time I had found my flip-flops and reached the guard-house George was deep into his stiff-upper-lip officer's spiel. 'Please tell her,' George instructed Heng, 'that those of us who knew Mi will never forget her good humour and the happiness she brought to us all, and especially the happiness she brought to Morris. Go ahead, tell her, Mr Heng.'

Heng hesitated, then rabbitted on nervously in translation. He was adding far more than George had said. George stared into the distance while Heng spoke. Mi bit her lip as she listened intensely first to George, then Heng. While Heng talked Mi's made-up white face was still, but as she quietly replied Mi looked as if she was lost in a world we couldn't even see.

'She says she looks at the pictures we took of all of us and of Morris and she doesn't know what to do. She says she looks at the pictures and sometimes she laughs and sometimes she cry. Sometimes she thinks maybe she is going crazy. She doesn't know what she feels,' Heng translated.

From the dark grey sky the drizzle had started. Suddenly all Mi could do was cry. We were standing by the guard house, watched by an embarrassed Filipino guard who liked Mi but had been told he shouldn't let her in. I put my arms around her.

After an uncomfortable moment George murmured a stiff goodbye and sloped off – trying, he said later when I walked into the fraternity house making chicken noises, to look like a commanding officer but feeling like a total shit. Eventually Mi's tears slowed. Shel joined us, and we dealt with Mi's practical problems. Mi clutched the $200 which Morris had left for her. She had zipped the money in a small plastic shoe on a key-ring. But Mi was frightened of taking the key-ring and the little gold jewellery she had to Sihanoukville. Mi thought that if people saw the jewellery and knew she was on her own they would steal from her. I looked at her heart-shaped locket on a slender gold chain, small ruby ring and little gold earrings. Altogether they couldn't be worth more than the $200 Morris had left her.

For the last few minutes Zorro had been standing behind us, watching. He offered help. Some of the Filipinos were transferring to Sihanoukville in a few days. Mi could ride with them. And Zorro would arrange for someone to keep Mi's money until she found a safe place to live.

Mi only looked back at the base a few times as she walked

down the road to her room at the blue house. I had given her my address at Chhoun's apartment; she couldn't read it.

The next morning Shel and I left Kep. We met Morris in Phnom Penh. 'She got to me, she really got to me. I didn't expect her to.' Morris sat on my couch, VB in hand to take the edge off the morning, shuffling through my Kep photos. Here was the one of bulky Rafe modelling orange monk's robes and carrying a furled umbrella, looking like a cross between a Hari Krishna convert and a London stockbroker; another close-up showed a manically leering Morris with his cheek against the dartboard, moving a feathered shaft to the bull's-eye to cheat on our score; Mi's stark white made-up face stared straight into the camera above her heart-printed babydoll pyjamas; there were Morris, Shel and Heng, squeezed on the Yamaha balanced on a paddy wall, smiling and squinting into the sun, on the day we invaded the villages.

'I had time to see Mi,' Morris confessed, 'but I couldn't have said goodbye. Couldn't have done it. Didn't have the courage. I would have broken right up. She really got to me.' For a moment Morris was quiet, then his pluck returned. 'Awwww, she'll be all right. Mi's a good girl,' he said, but it was without much conviction and he quickly went on to other things.

I'm a coward, too. I didn't have the heart to lambast that middle-aged little boy, holding the photos between his knobbly knees and rummaging through the images yet another time, for only leaving Mi 200 bucks, just about what he made every day from the UN. One day's work to Morris was several months' living to Mi, but I don't think that had really sunk in to me yet. Looking at Morris I knew he would crumple if I started in on him. Morris had divided his life into two worlds and they were coming dangerously close together. Mi was a life he was leaving behind. Looking back on it, I should have.

A week after we left Kep, the non-existent Khmer Rouge successfully attacked the train as the carriages passed the Chang Aeu coconut grove. Grenades were thrown through the passenger cars' open windows. At least a dozen people were killed and 40 wounded. 'It was not a pretty sight,' said an Unmo who arrived shortly afterwards. The bandits, later identified by passengers as Khmer Rouge, forced survivors to carry the motorcycles and stolen goods toward the northern hill, Phnom Vol.

Shel returned to the village several times. Once or twice she asked me to accompany her; I didn't want to take risks when I wasn't sure I would ever use the material. Shel found the stories the villagers told her changed. The school they had told us was closed because teachers thought the village too remote was actually closed because the Khmer Rouge didn't want a school in the village. Mr Trilby turned out to be the village Khmer Rouge liaison, much more important than the Spy. Oh, and the kitchen Rafe and I had driven through had belonged to the Khmer Rouge commander we had been trying to meet.

After five or six trips, Shel was marched into the paddies by four Khmer Rouge soldiers and robbed of everything. She never knew if the robbery had been sanctioned by the local Khmer Rouge leaders or whether her assailants were simply thieves. A sympathetic villager hid Shel in his cousin's house near the main road that night. He collected money from the villagers so Shel could take a motorcycle to Kampot and then a shared taxi to Phnom Penh. Unable at the beginning to abandon so much work, Shel talked of returning for weeks afterwards. Friends, especially Heng, counselled against this. The Khmer Rouge had no way of knowing, Heng said, that Shel would not be returning to take revenge, to identify and turn the robbers over to the government. Many Khmers would expect Shel to want revenge. In the end Shel felt she had been lucky, the robbery a warning of other things to come.

I had expected that I would go to Sihanoukville soon and intended to find Mi, but instead left Cambodia and didn't return for a while. Before I left, I heard that Mi was working as a hooker again at the Soriya. The unsubstantiated grapevine also said Zorro, who felt Morris badly wronged, had taken advantage of Cambodia's depressed criminal economy and put a contract in the high two figures on Henry's life, a hit which George, during a very long Cat House drinking session which left him nursing an even longer hangover, eventually talked Zorro into withdrawing, albeit reluctantly.

Several months later I looked for Mi in Sihanoukville. Driving to the beach or wandering near the hotel, I expected to see Mi walking along the road swinging her reed shopping basket or squatting on what passed for the curb selling oranges. Trying to trace her, I dragged a friend to the dancing restaurant. By then the UN men were all long gone. The dance floor had become the haunt of young middle-class Khmer couples. A fire-eating midget dressed in a red spangled harem costume performed between the band's sets. Professional girls who sat on folding chairs in neat rows at the back were overseen by madam in a dark red business suit with hefty shoulders. The girls looked like budding MBAs. Mi, with her garish white make-up and frilly, market bargain dress sense, would have been out of place. Neither the madam nor any of the girls had heard of Mi. The new, efficient, Chinese *maître d'* shook his head: the management had changed. As we left a Khmer yuppie gingerly held his mobile phone away from his body while he chucked down the red carpeting on the staircase.

Early the next morning I combed the market. Foolishly, I suppose because I wanted an easy, happy ending, I hadn't brought Mi's photo with me to Sihanoukville. I queried all the orange sellers, asking for a dark faced orange seller named Mi, who had lived at Kep and wore white make-up, but I had no picture to show them. I walked all the way to the trash heap at the back where the scavenger children picked through the refuse, irrationally fearing I would suddenly see her there. But Mi had disappeared.

The white rhino

Shel's Kampot pushiness had convinced me I had to be more aggressive. Anne, another freelancer called Louise and I decided to go for an airborne *dahleng*. We would hop on a UN plane and see where we ended up. In my new, aggressive mode I worked the tarmac before the plane took off. Waylaying James, an English Border Control Officer I had never met before, I inveigled an invitation to James's Ratanakiri jungle outpost on the Ho Chi Minh trail. Or at least I pushed James into a position where he couldn't say no.

'Yes, well, I'm not sure we have enough beds, but you can come if you want. The Uruguayans will certainly be excited when I get off the helicopter with three women,' James demurred hesitantly.

'Oh, don't worry, we cun sleep innnywhere,' Louise's Missouri drawl poured over the Japanese fan she waved before her face. Louise, with her Southern belle accent and curly, Botticelli-like hair, was coming in for the kill. My Midwestern slur also surfaced around Louise; together we sounded like drag-queen finalists in a Tammy Wynette imitators' contest.

'There's unfortunately not much to do in Ratanakiri,' James started to backtrack apologetically.

'Don't worry,' Louise flapped as the engines started, 'we don't uuusually dewwww much.'

In Stung Treng, a muddy Mekong market town, we had to wait for a helicopter in the morning. The rolling brown river swept down from the Tibetan highlands, through China and Laos to divide the wooded hills of Stung Treng province. When the Khmer Rouge took Phnom Penh, Cambodia had ceased to be a member of the Mekong Commission, the regional body representing the countries which the river touched. The development of the Mekong had to be carefully planned; hydro-electric dams upstream could reduce water levels; logging deforestation could cause flooding. Since the rains and the rivers watered the ricefields and supported the schools of fish which fed most Cambodians, the newly elected government quickly asked to be readmitted.

Three Western women in Stung Treng caused a stir: the Dutch at the airport, who alone among the Dutch were renowned for being unhelpful, immediately offered us hot showers and home-cooked dinner. We stood in respectful silence before large plastic barrels as the Dutch proudly showed off the tiny UN water-purification works, which cleansed the mud-brown Mekong water which gushed from the tap. The Irish catering manager stopped by for a drink while the Dutch cooked, then alerted the Russian pilots. When Louise, Anne and I returned to our room, the ex-Soviets were waiting with a military bow, the words 'Good Evenink. We are Russin pilots. Small, small problem. Need small, small girl.' Good for malaria!', and the demand that we come for a drink, for medicinal purposes only, and a second supper they had cooked on their hotplate. Thankfully the Russians had already finished the 'helicopter vodka', orangeade mixed with grain alcohol. In the morning the Irish and the Russians fake-fought across the runway for the honour of carrying our luggage to the helicopter.

James hadn't even found dinner.

As we flew closer to the Vietnam border more and more perfectly round B-52 craters, left by the American bombings which began in Cambodia as they had ended in Vietnam, dotted the landscape. The Nixon administration had initially tried to hide its computerized Cambodian onslaught with 'dual reporting'. Under dual reporting, bomber pilots were given targets inside neutral Cambodia, where some of the American military thought a giant, Pentagon-like Viet Cong headquarters, acronymed COSVN, was located. Destroying COSVN had obsessed some of the American military, but even Richard Nixon considered it a major *faux pas* to be caught bombing a neutral country. Officers were ordered to record false coordinates which indicated the targets had been inside war-torn Vietnam. The attempt to find out if a United States State Department official had leaked the truth about 'dual reporting' lead to 'Watergate' and Nixon's resignation from the presidency. Nobody ever successfully defined the difference between dual reporting and lying.

Wind from the whirling UN chopper blades bent the trees crowding the field where we touched down. Ragged children, two boys carrying bows and arrows, lined the jungle's edge, squinting in the airwash to watch the landing. While James had been away a new Indian military observer, Rajiv, had arrived. James tried to be a good host, but every time he made a suggestion Rajiv was there first. James told us to drop our bags in one room, Rajiv started moving his clothing and insisted we should have his. When James suggested darts, Rajiv declared himself a darts' rules expert. James mentioned food. Rajiv scattered pre-cooked, tinned army MRE rations ('Meals Ready to Eat', more commonly called 'Meals Rejected by Ethiopians') across the table.

Ashe, the Australian radio operator sitting in the shade shooting arrows at a tin can with a hand-carved tribal crossbow, opted out of the Revenge of the Raj competition. Anne and I needed 'the facilities', there was nothing at hand except a makeshift shower fashioned from a dangling plastic water container punched with holes. Ashe stood up, laconically handed us a shovel and nodded toward the forest.

'Watch out for the wild boars and snakes and don't go too far because there's a minefield. Cheers.'

In that forest lay hidden the villages of the Jarai, Tapoun, and other tribes whom the lowland Khmers called *khmer loeu*, highland Khmer. The tribes were renowned for their ferocity in battle and imbued with an air of mystery. In Cambodian folk-tales evil came from the forest, as did the tribes. Animism, not Buddhism, ruled the tribespeople's inner lives. Ritual buffalo sacrifice was common; witches led the religious life in some villages. The tribes fed themselves through hunting and slash-and-burn agriculture, moving their villages every 15 years or so to let the fields lie fallow. Wandering between Cambodia and Vietnam, to the tribes the concept of nation states was unimportant compared to their fields.

But in Ratanakiri local businessmen and military officers

had staked claims to the lands which the tribes farmed but to which they held no formal legal title. Almost all title records had been destroyed by the Khmer Rouge. Land disputes simmered around the country, with people whose families had farmed certain fields before the Khmer Rouge demanding back their land, frequently unsuccessfully. Because of the tribes' rotation farming, the issue of who farmed and had rights to which plots was even more complicated in hill-tribe areas. In the 1960s Sihanouk had tried to develop Ratanakiri, importing lowland Khmers and establishing a rubber plantation, but the highlanders had not been happy. When the Khmer Rouge fled to Ratanakiri in the late 1960s they played on this resentment to recruit hill-tribe supporters, who became among their most loyal and fierce adherents. The Khmer Rouge valued the highlanders' tribal lifestyle no more than lowland Khmer traditions, however. Tribespeople had been made to abandon their traditional silver-making, rice-planting techniques and their costumes in order to serve Angka or perish.

Also hidden in the Cambodian jungles were a few Montagnards, Vietnamese hill-tribe people who fought the colonial French, then were co-opted by the Americans to fight the North Vietnamese. Called by the French name Front Unifié pour la Lutte des Races Oprimés (FULRO) as far as the international community was concerned, as the Vietnam War ended the FULRO fighters fled to Cambodia, waiting for the return of their leader who had gone to Phnom Penh to seek assistance. They stayed for nearly 20 years. Although sorely out of touch with the modern world, the Montagnards had not been completely forgotten. Since the majority of FULRO were born-again Christians, Baptist missionaries in the Philippines still broadcast religiously to them by shortwave in the Montagnards' own language.

Of course there had been reports of FULRO hiding in the Cambodian jungle, and the year before, Nate had talked someone into setting him down, alone, into the middle of the jungle to try to make contact.

'I stood there and thought I'd really gotten myself into it this time,' Nate said later about looking around the lonely jungle, where no one would find him if something happened, and thinking that may be he had taken this intrepid journalist thing just a *little* far. Luckily, some FULRO appeared from the forest. They did not know their leader had been singled out in 1975 for expulsion from the French embassy and executed by the Khmer Rouge. On hearing of their leader's death 17 years before, the FULRO group reluctantly admitted their struggle was over and took asylum in North Carolina.

With no lights for miles except from our camp, the stars shone clear in the sky that night. There was silence and peace in the forest except for geckos, ducks, crickets, and those sodding cattle with the bells on. The nearest village let their herd graze in the jungle. The cattle thought the rough wood barracks made perfect scratching posts. Wooden bells around their necks clanged all night, the hollow jangling only periodically broken by Ashe stumbling down the steps, chucking stones and cursing the bovine sleep-killers in finest Australian. By morning everyone was tired and grumpy, which almost explained James's testiness with Rajiv, but not all of it. Take, for example, the first medical run . . .

'It's not.'

'It's measles.'

'It's not.'

'I know it very well, very well. Children have measles all the time. That is what this child has.'

James looked up from his copy of *Where There Is No Doctor*, a paperback medical guide often used by NGO workers who were asked for medical assistance even though they had no qualifications. Closing his eyes briefly, James composed himself. He turned to Rajiv and handed him the book.

'Okay, handle it.'

'I do not mean to offend, but I have seen these spots before and I know very well it is measles.'

'No, no, go on, go on.'

James stalked off, hands on his hips and studying the ground as he tried to keep his temper. The Jarai villagers, especially the children, crowded around Rajiv, the medical book, and the metal chest of drugs open in the back of the truck. Occasionally a loin-clothed old man ventured outside a hut to watch the commotion. The elderly had distended earlobes, with large holes in the middle and sometimes a round wooden plug filling the empty space.

Aside from the medicine and the natural curiosity of children, there wasn't much interest in our visit. Until the UN electoral workers had arrived most tribespeople had never seen a foreigner. They didn't seem too impressed. Women carrying firewood in intricately woven baskets strapped to their backs, wearing only waist-high sarongs and occasionally smoking a home-made cheroot, would stop and watch from a distance, then continue on. The houses were built on stilts, and two or three miniature huts, slightly away from the larger dwellings, dotted the inner ring of houses. The little huts were hideaways for pubescent girls, given their own nests where they could meet boyfriends until they found a mate. Louise and I agreed that kind of forward-thinking real-estate deal would have improved our adolescences enormously.

'Sometimes I think we travel to see ourselves rather than what we've supposedly come to see,' Louise would say later, sitting beneath a bright pink mosquito net in an ex-bordello turned guest-house in Ban Loung, a dusty backwater that was the provincial capital. The Vietnamese Friendship Monument gracing the town's one roundabout also served as a goat-grazing lawn.

Louise had already worked on magazines for a dozen years, but she had only recently started freelancing. 'I worry about getting it right. Sometimes I think I stop myself from doing more because I worry if I'm up to the responsibility.'

As Louise and I continued the discussion later, sipping sodas at a wooden table on what had once been the bordello's dance floor, you could see Anne quietly making mental notes of what *not* to do in the next ten years. She had no intention of being a struggling freelancer later on, still worrying about getting the story right.

But why we chose that particular responsibility was also a puzzle. What was this gap in us, Louise wondered, that this travelling was supposed to fill? Here we were, two girls from the staid American Mid-west, a land of flat cornfields, flat vowels and what had seemed as kids to be even flatter horizons, chasing hill tribes and goldminers and guerillas through the Asian jungle half a world away. Ostensibly we searched for fascinating people, places and events to write

about, but we were obviously searching for something more
than stories.

At the moment, though, writing some stories would do.
Louise, Anne and I were subjectless, even though we all
snapped pictures and took notes. Anne was especially dili-
gent, scribbling in her notebook as soon as we came back from
each adventure. For all her girl-next-door innocence Anne
was aggressive and determined to prove herself. Still in her
early twenties while we were in our thirties, Anne had a
slightly superior air of confidence as she listened to Louise and
I try to figure out our true best course. Anne was convinced
her fantasies would become reality: she knew her career
would be successful, she would eventually work in the Middle
East, where she would marry a slightly older journalist. Anne
was, in some ways, mesmerized by the male reporters twice
her age, and their tales and advice on pursuing her career.
Sometimes you couldn't help but wonder if Anne was looking
to replace the distant father she had lost in her teens. Oh, well,
give her ten years. In the meantime we all needed to find
something to write about. While Louise and I sat under the
disused silver disco ball, sipping sodas at a wooden table on
what had once been a dance floor, plotting how to get around
the highlands, Anne decided to leave us early, to make sure
she returned home in time for the *Phnom Penh Post's* first
anniversary party, where she could schmooze.

Louise and I didn't find anything that would make a big
story. In Ban Luong, we saw a pangolin strapped on a
motorcycle to be carted across the border for sale, deer horns
exhorted as a cure for sexual impotency and porcupines
touted for dinner. We pushed a Landcruiser, driven by a
kindly French Unmo who feared his country's military in-
volvement with Cambodia would leave him stranded
('Ooooh, I am the loneliest Frenchman in Ratanakiri ... but
then, I am the *only* Frenchman in Ratanakiri'), through mud
and virgin forests to see the tribal burial grounds marked by
wooden, Easter Island-like funerary statues in Voensai, home
of the local CPP strongman and his private army, and
remarked on the endless straight rows of the rubber plantation Sihanouk's government had planted in the '6os. Streaks
of darkness and light striped the trees as the sunlight plunged

through the canopy. The rubber could only be processed with the help of Vietnamese technicians who had fled during the pre-election anti-Vietnamese attacks. Now raw rubber was smuggled across the border.

An afternoon had been spent interviewing a Jarai woman, supposedly deported to Vietnam by the local Cambodian police for helping some 30 Vietnamese Montagnards, yet another group of FULRO members, led by her former schoolteacher. The FULRO group had been working in the nearby gold mines and had missed the North Carolina call; they had disappeared into Pleiku prison, the woman claimed, from which only she had been released. Two other days were spent in an abortive search for a tribesman who had supposedly been Saloth Sar's butler; it should have been the good basis for a comic piece, even if we didn't find him, except nothing particularly funny happened. The FULRO story could run locally but, aside from Pol Pot's missing batman, we knew that none of these things would sell overseas. Andrea was up for the *Phnom Penh Post*, so the local market was gone. Shel's worry about too much competition on the trip had proven true.

We perused Lomphat, the former provincial capital which once boasted electric lights, sewage, and a teacher's college. All had been bombed to rubble. An old destroyed truck carcass still hung precariously over the side of the 15-metre-wide, water-filled B-52 crater where a college had once been. The only remains of Sihanouk's riverside palazzo on the leafy bank of the wide Sen river was a kidney-shaped dance floor, unused since the '60s. A lively city of 20,000 people 25 years ago now had only a few hundred squatting in its ruins. So while a UN policeman and the local children clapped in time among the trees, Louise and I improvised a waltz on Sihanouk's abandoned playground, trying to whirl life back into the old town. But Lomphat seemed destined for oblivion and, like the Jarai village to which we were offering cough medicine, aspirin, and tetracycline, the dance floor didn't made a newspaper or magazine story.

'Perhaps it was measles, but the spots didn't look that way in the book,' James muttered, trying to regain his rationality as he started the Landcruiser and we set off to find the Ho Chi

Minh Trail. The path out of the village was overgrown, branches and tree limbs whacked at the top of the Landcruiser, knocking off the radio antenna and making an open window a good idea only if you liked a face full of leaves. Route 19, the main cargo route into Vietnam, wasn't much better. With foot-deep ruts, the road was used only by smugglers' four-wheel drives, the heavy goods and rubber trucks which came across the Vietnamese border from Pleiku, and one work-elephant.

Despite the much ballyhoo'd wildness of Ratanakiri, and the declaration by Sihanouk of large swatches of Cambodia as national parks, even though part of that land was being farmed or logged, the large animals which once had made Cambodia a huntsman's paradise had mostly disappeared. There were still wild boar, lizards and deer, but elephants, tigers, *ko prey* – the forest cow last sighted in 1967 which was Cambodia's national animal; and leopards were scarce. The rare freshwater Irrawaddy dolphin, estimated to be barely 200 in number, swam in the upper reaches of the Mekong. To the consternation of their Laotian neighbours, Cambodian Mekong fishermen used explosives instead of nets, which indiscriminately killed any fish or dolphin nearby.

'Every time I try to make a report on smuggling one of my bosses keeps interrupting me to ask, "Have you seen a white rhino yet?" He's obsessed. If I don't find one I'll probably never get another job in the UN ...' James eased the Landcruiser into low gear as he bumped the truck over the remnants of a wooden bridge, which to the uninitiated might look like two logs thrown across a large hole.

'Bravo Charlie Ten, Bravo Charlie Ten can you read me?' Rajiv's voice crackled over the radio. 'We are having some trouble reading you, some trouble with our radio. I think we are in a depression.'

'I'll say,' James gritted his teeth, clicked on the radio handset and reported we were almost there, shoving the truck back into gear and sliding on the mud at the same time as we crashed through a rut.

James stopped the truck at a fallen tree along a road which had been one of the many Ho Chi Minh trails. This and the stream next to it, James said, actually marked Cambodia's border with Vietnam. The trees were part of Cambodia's hardwood forests which were being felled at the rate of 4–5 per cent a year. In 1989 Thailand had banned logging within its borders; the price of teak then shot up from $1,900 a metric tonne to $10,000. The Khmer Rouge had many lucrative logging agreements in which Thai contractors and workers cleared large swatches of forest between Trat and Pailin. Such was the devastation that the UN declared a ban on the export of raw logs from Cambodia. Instead, Thai and Japanese companies, among others, set up commercial saw mills which, along with innumerable two-man Khmer operations with large hand saws, worked to export milled timber.

The Ho Chi Minh Trail – no more than jungle paths and small roads across the border – had brought supplies, carried by porters, from North Vietnam, through Cambodia, to the Viet Cong forces in the South during the Vietnam War. When bombs closed the roads to trucks, the supplies came by bicycles. Now the trail was used to smuggle timber or cigarettes. A Cambodian cigarette seller, playing a hand-held Tetris game and waiting patiently for customers in an old Russian jeep in which he kept his Jet cigarettes dry with a tarp in the back, later told us that a carton of cigarettes which cost $180 in the market in Ban Loung fetched $220 underneath his tarp and $240 in Pleiku, tax-free. The Vietnamese smugglers walked in along the trails and carried the cigarettes out on foot.

Although Rajiv insisted the border was actually several kilometres further on, we invaded what we thought was Vietnam, took our pictures and drove away. At another Jarai village we stopped. An old Air France jeep, the perfect smuggler's transport, was parked next to a hut. Aside from the dirty teeshirts and trousers the villagers wore there were no other signs of modernity. The men standing near the Air France vehicle didn't seem pleased to see us, and disappeared through a round doorway when James brought out the medical kit.

Like everywhere in Cambodia, tourism was mooted as the way to improve Ratanakiri's future. But unlike tribespeople in much of Thailand, Laos or Vietnam, the hill-tribes in Cambodia no longer wore traditional gear. Potential tourist trekkers slogging across Ratanakiri would find villagers garbed in used cast-offs from street markets.

To return to the 'ethnicity' so beloved by tourists, the villagers would have to put on costumes, like actors. Tribespeople under 20 had never worn traditional clothing. It was not necessarily correct to assume the hill-tribes automatically missed the past. Playing Miss Concerned Liberal in one village of Lao brought down from hills near Lomphat, I asked the village leader if his people would like to return to the life they had been forced to leave two decades before. The leader looked a little startled by the question.

'Actually, what we need now is electricity and a school. What we really want is lights. I don't suppose we'll get them,' he replied.

The Jarai village next to the Ho Chi Minh Trail was riddled by a conjunctivitis epidemic. James's curative eye drops needed to be applied more than once. A middle-aged man with his arms folded across a torn teeshirt stepped forward from the crowd and offered in English to be in charge of subsequent doses. Behind him a grinning little boy held up an iridescent green beetle twirling slowly on the end of a string. In Thailand the beetle was called *malaeng thap*. Because of the beetle's sudden popularity as a fashionable item of jewellery, in Thailand the bug was faced with extinction.

Gil, the English speaker, had worked for the Americans during the war sorting out land claims. When nearby Pleiku fell, Gil saw the future and returned north. Now Gil lived in Vietnam, although his relatives lived in Cambodia. Like other Jarai, Gil wandered back and forth across the border at will, walking through the jungle for a day or two to visit friends and family, with no need of papers. He never wanted to return to the city.

By the way, Gil added when James finished explaining about the medicine, several months earlier a foreigner had stayed overnight in the village. Did we by any chance know a journalist named . . .

'Shel?' I had this funny feeling . . .

'Yes' Gil brightened. He asked when she was coming back.

'Oh, she's the one who stayed here and walked back to the camp. Is she your friend? We all thought she was nuts.' James had no urge to spend a night in the village.

Shel had arrived one day with the UN, Gil said, but when they left she had asked to stay. She had brought a hammock, water and food so she would not burden the villagers.

'Some of the bad men, they started drinking and saying they didn't like a foreigner in the village. I didn't tell her that but I had her stay in my house where they couldn't see her.' Gil still looked concerned. They had talked late into the night, Shel explaining about New Zealand, Gil about the Jarai. In the morning Shel had walked out the seven or eight kilometres to the main road after promising Gil she would be coming back. Gil was leaving soon and wanted to know when Shel might return.

A look of almost parental affection passed over Gil's face as I said Shel had almost accompanied us. I don't think Shel ever realized the effect she had on Cambodians in the countryside, showing up in a village even the mosquitos couldn't find and bunking down with her hammock and backpack full of MREs. She was either oblivious to or chose to ignore any possible danger, convinced by her own personal creed which combined the Catholicism learned in her childhood with the Buddhism she'd picked up on her travels that her time was not up. Shel represented a freedom and a confidence in personal safety which was almost impossible for the Cambodians to attain. But then Gil's own contentment with his jungle, wandering between villages and countries, with no goal except to be at peace with himself, was, if our mosquito-plagued, late-night conversations were anything to go by, something beyond both Louise and I, at least at the time.

James explained again about the medicine's timing and dosages. The Air France jeep boys had returned and were looking moody; the sky was growing dark and we needed to get back. We asked if Gil wanted to send greetings and let Shel know he was waiting. He said he had only one message.

'Tell her I will never forget her.'

The yellow house

Unlike Vietnamese, the colonial French had never successfully romanized curvy, Sanskrit-based Khmer script. Transliterations were haphazard. A Khmer word could be spelled several different ways in Roman script, with occasionally comic results.

'Welcome to Thmar Pork,' Louise read from a sign as we arrived at the edge of Thmar Puok, the 'Wild West' town where Suzie and Leon had hoped to make their photographic reputation and where The Animal had bought the Khmer Rouge running shoes during the election. Troops of all four factions wandered through Thmar Puok. A one-armed Khmer Rouge general named Pram Su lived near Thmar Puok market, yet Thmar Puok was a KPNLF stronghold. The now-closed refugee camps were once just across the Thai border. Several months earlier the Site 2 Cambodian refugee camp had been burnt, a message which said Cambodians should not even think about returning to Thailand if peace didn't last.

The soldier with an AK hung across his chest herding a gaggle of ducks, and the teenager who was trying to carry too many grenades at once and dropped a couple as our truck passed didn't inspire confidence, but Thmar Puok looked like it was going to be fun. The UN Human Rights Officer, a hard-working English solicitor called Adam, had spent his tour convincing the local bigwigs that human rights included building prison cells in which a person could stand up, rather than only squat, the way incarcerated miscreants had done in dark holes before the UN arrived. Adam liked a good time, missed his wife, and fought after-work boredom by dancing around his metal-hut office to '60s soul tapes dressed in a striped City shirt, a large orange straw hat and a sarong. He looked thrilled that someone new had arrived, talked the golf-playing Samoan administrator into cancelling his appointment with the Aranyprathet links, where much useful border information was to be found among prosperous, putting Thai businessmen, and put out a radio call in code to the NGOs saying there was an administrative meeting at 5:30 – which meant bring your favourite liquor – and could somebody bring some ice? Louise and I were an excuse for a party.

We wanted to clean up first. Thmar Puok had no hotel, only a bordello catering to by-the-hour guests, so we stayed in abandoned government offices which a Khmer NGO had taken over. The administrators, Sorn and Mrs Kim, lived and worked in four concrete rooms downstairs; each had one private cell and a wire strung between two walls to hold their clothing.

Sorn greeted us while sitting in his office, a desk in front of his bedroom. A squalling radio handset babbled Khmer in the background. Sorn had a high-pitched, reedy laugh and easy conversation. Before 1975 he had been a Phnom Penh lawyer. A strong nationalist, but believing that Cambodians were not yet ready for democracy, Sorn was very anti-Vietnamese. Rumour had it Sorn was corrupt but I didn't buy it. Even in Cambodia there were easier and safer ways to make a living than digging wells and building roads in the jungle, walking a diplomatic tightrope between four armed factions.

During the Khmer Rouge reign Sorn's wife and children had died. The Khmer Rouge did not respect Sorn's grief. Angka decided not only who should be torn asunder, but also who should be together. Widower Sorn had been forced to marry a widow he had not known. Sorn said he and his second wife could barely speak without arguing, 'We are completely unsuited.'

At present Sorn's unsuitable wife lived in Phnom Penh with their two children. The children Sorn loved, but the marriage meant nothing but pain to him. Sorn's unsuitable wife took his absence silently.

'They do not see or hear from him for months and then he comes with bicycles. She thinks he should not have another wife but she does not speak about love,' Pholla the Tuol Sleng guide, a friend of Sorn's unsuitable wife, told me later.

Sorn's co-worker, Mrs Kim, looked depressed even when she smiled. In another life in the 1960s she had been a successful, outgoing, fish merchant married to a Siem Reap schoolteacher. 'The Khmer Rouge would send propaganda via the teacher's organization. A friend of my husband's read it and said very seriously there might be a war. I laughed.'

Mrs Kim's husband had been murdered by the Khmer Rouge. 'He told me he thought they would take him. I came back one day and he was gone. I cried, I screamed, I did not want to live. I went to the Khmer Rouge leader and cried, "If you take him you must take me." The leader shook me and said be quiet, I had children I must live for. Who will take care of my children if I let them kill me? Do not let anyone hear me saying this. The leader said it was too late. They had already taken my husband to Phnom Penh. Later they took the leader, too.'

Mrs Kim's laughter disappeared. At night she would cry so no one could hear. After the Khmer Rouge's fall, Mrs Kim had removed her children to the Site 2 camp, where in the crowded refuge she started an organization to teach women hygiene and sewing. When her visa to the United States was granted, Mrs Kim found she couldn't leave Cambodia, even though Cambodia still lay beyond the camp's perimeter and across the border. She stayed in Site 2 and sent her sons to the States. When the Peace Agreement was signed Mrs Kim returned to Cambodia with Sorn.

Mrs Kim was eager to make sure she, too, had enough air time to explain life in Thmar Puok. She seemed compelled to talk, but Mrs Kim's eagerness was not just her ego competing with Sorn's: she wanted to bear witness to the many things she had seen. Unfortunately, she felt certain powers – soldiers and others – would not be pleased with all the stories she told.

'I can tell you these things but if you print them it will be bad for me,' Mrs Kim frowned, after regaling us with a dark tale of kidnapping. She worried that the villains might take revenge if we repeated her confidences. Mrs Kim's instinct for self-preservation was at odds with her righteous anger. Louise and I changed the subject and talked about Mrs Kim's work. When not supervising the women's NGO which ran an infant school and taught sewing, traditional weaving and catering, Mrs Kim helped the local monks trying to revive traditional Cambodian Buddhist culture. She wanted the townspeople of Thmar Puok to celebrate all the Buddhist festivals: for harvest, the New Year, and the two-week-long festival of the dead, *phcum ben*, when Cambodian families took food to the *wats* to offer the monks. Spirits whose families did not make the offering would not rest peacefully. Mrs Kim would take extra, for those ghosts who had no families left.

'It makes her happy,' Sorn shrugged after he mentioned Mrs Kim's religious fervour. Sorn said he did not share her ardent belief, but Sorn, at home with business plans and spread sheets, was not immune to Cambodian mysticism.

'I believe in the prophecy of Buddha now.' Sorn was serious and sober. Like Nostradamus' infamous visions, Buddha's prediction had several versions, but the one Sorn believed said that the supposed sighting of a black crow flying from a palace *stupa* during the election signified that 'blood will flow where the four faces meet when the waters turn.' Chatomuk, another name for the meeting of the Sap and Mekong rivers at Phnom Penh, translated as 'four faces'. Sorn feared the election would bring more bloodshed in the end and that Cambodia could not be a real democracy. 'If Cambodia were a democracy people would be in jail for what they have done.'

A road crew in a white pick-up sped into the work-yard. Sorn walked out to confer. Louise and I climbed the stairs to the second floor, divided into four aged-turquoise, wood-walled rooms, unpainted for 30 years. A bored American Unmo passed his evening hours writing spy thrillers on his laptop in the furthest chamber. Louise and I parked our bags in the nearest one. It was shutterless and open to the sky, with two camp beds and mosquito nets.

Mrs Kim had transformed one of the middle rooms into a Buddhist shrine to console the spirits of dead Vietnamese soldiers. Their bodies had been stored on the upper floor during the 1990 fighting. Each night monks' chants echoed through the splintered wood wall. One evening the door to the second room was ajar and I glimpsed Mrs Kim kneeling on the floor with the *bonzes*, hands pressed tight before her face in prayer. Fruit and flowers sat on silver platters before the shrine, illuminated among the shadows by rows of flickering candles. The scent of fresh-cut lotus blossoms, *mles* and other flowers mingled with the smouldering incense, as Mrs Kim and the monks prayed for the souls of the hated invaders who had possibly saved their lives.

Over the next few days Louise and I explored the surrounding border countryside. We were given lunch in Thailand and had to shake awake the ever-vigilant Cambodian border guard sleeping in his hammock to tell him we were leaving the country and would be back after dessert. The Thai town of Tapra could not have been more unlike Thmar Puok, with neat, clean streets, a concrete market, bank buildings and no guns. Even the dogs were different: the Thai mutts were lazy, tame and friendly, while Cambodian hounds yipped and bared teeth when a stranger came near. At the unkempt ruins of Banteay Chhmar temple, built by Jayavarman VII at the same time as the Bayon and as large as Angkor Wat, we clambered over fallen lintels. Banteay Chhmar was far off the tourist trail. No archaeologists had ever tried to restore the temple's demolished splendour. Trees grew up between walls and doorways; the collapsed stone walls were covered in hanging vines like an Indiana Jones set. In the one-room museum at Ampil, a neatly laid out USAID paid-for town which had served as Funcinpec headquarters, a clutch of baby pigs ran through the exhibit carefully chosen from the artifacts soldiers and thieves would ordinarily sell to antiquities dealers in Thailand. We stopped to see a general in his new house with roses, statues and a child's swing set on the front lawn, only several hundred yards away from a minefield, but he wasn't home. An interview with a *khmer kru*, a traditional Cambodian doctor, went nowhere. Traditional Cambodian medicine involved heated cups placed on the skin, coins which rubbed the flesh bright red to draw the blood and disease to the surface, potions and poultices of herbs and barks, toad soup as a cure for syphilis, and hot coals placed under the bed of a newly delivered mother to shrink the womb back to size. But conversation was stilted as we sat on hand-hewn stools in front of the *khmer kru*'s house, and the neighbours crowded around the giant water jars. The *khmer kru* was usually talkative, said Adam. The week before the *khmer kru* had been called out to treat a sick child. The child, however, did not exist: the *khmer kru* was met by Khmer Rouge and walked ten more kilometres to treat a wounded guerilla. Adam speculated the *khmer kru's* silence may have been caused by someone in the crowd who would report what the *khmer kru* told us. *Chhlops* may have been at work again.

On a sunset trip through the villages we pulled up behind a Khmer Rouge patrol. A group of green-clad teenagers stood in a pick-up bed, weapons clattering on the floor. The soldiers made fun of Louise and I, imitating our attempts to shoot pictures through the windscreen. Since no one had sold photos of the Khmer Rouge for several months, Louise and I jumped out when we came to a checkpoint. She flirted with the boys in the back. I ran to the cab thinking I would try to charm the front seat – hopefully one of us would get some shots. The Khmer Rouge driver, with his Chinese cap and rip-off Ray-Bans, smiled, leaned through the window and grabbed my wrist.

'Enchanté Madame,' the driver sighed melodramatically in French and kissed my hand. Then the Khmer Rouge Charles Boyer hit the gas and careened away, the hollering patrol in the back hanging onto any part of the cab they could. Louise and I stood at the red and white barrier pole, disappointed cameras in hand, and watched them disappear into the dust.

We turned to leave. The checkpoint guard in a Khmer Rouge puffy green cap and a Funcinpec teeshirt showing Ranariddh in supplication before Sihanouk cried, 'Wait! I'm Khmer Rouge! I'm Khmer Rouge! Take a picture of me!' and then ran off to bring back two friends so they could grin in the snaps.

Neither Louise nor I got a vendible shot. We decided we were bad luck for each other. I had to cover for a wire so I left Louise in Thmar Puok. Maybe I should give up this freelance idea and see what it was like to have a job for a change, I had thought, so a friend had arranged I should cover for her while she was on holiday. I hadn't forgotten Jerry's initial advice about the trials of scraping together a freelance living. 'Some just don't get the breaks . . . That's tough, but that's the way it is.'

At Battambang airport the connecting plane never arrived.

My partying gasman friend Stef, with whom I had shot bows and arrows in the lobby of Siem Reap's Grand Hotel, and whose motorcycle occasionally bounced off stone walls late at night, had just offered me a ride when in walked a skinny, moustached, middle-aged Cambodian wearing full army camouflage. He sported South American dictator sunglasses and more gold teeth than should have fitted in one mouth.

'Papa!' Stef had his nodding, wide 'it's-strange-but-what-do-you-expect-it's-Cambodia-I-should-have-suspected-this-all-along' smile on as he pumped the man's hand.

With joy and total recognition, Phnom Penh's premier opium dealer pounded Stef on the back.

Stef introduced me as another valued customer. An expansive Papa was only too delighted to meet me. Papa quickly explained the camouflage was for his other job: he had been an army colonel since Lon Nol's time.

Back in Phnom Penh, I immersed myself in the work, learning about slugs and write-throughs and getting the story out before the other wires. If you don't have the whole story yet, send what you have and modem a rewrite later. Most stories revolved around ministerial quotes and press conferences. I quickly learned that for the international wires a quote from, say, a prime minister or a general always outranked a quote from the poor shlub on the corner who actually saw the fire. Play-sheets told you how many newspapers carried your stories and how many carried the other wires. Most importantly, you removed yourself from the writing and your prose style stayed within strict guidelines. I liked the countryside and taking notes for the book better – but then I also liked receiving a pay-cheque, pathetic though it was.

The big story that hot, wet August was the secret committee writing the new Cambodian constitution. Human rights activists wanted constitutional consultations to be public: the new government-to-be firmly held to their belief that a select few should write the document, unseen even by their fellow National Assembly colleagues.

The Lon Nol, Khmer Rouge, Sihanouk, United States, and French constitutions were all considered as models: Sihanouk's regime had featured a liberal 'socialist' constitution, and many of the new document's provisions – like promises of adequate health care and free education – dated from that time. 'Sangkum Reastr Niyum', the name of Sihanouk's political party in the 1950s and 1960s, became political shorthand: it meant 'Cambodia's glory days'. If something had been done a certain way in the Sangkum Reastr Niyum era, the unquestioning philosophy went, it had to be all right, and that's the way things should be done now.

A bootleg copy of the new constitution showed up in the office: the monarchy was to be restored, polygamy was officially out, respect for human rights was officially in. The emphasis on human rights was probably sharpened by many politicians' belief that further development funds would be linked to the new government's human rights stance. But many constitutional articles were shadowy: the press, nationality and immigration would be governed by 'organic' laws, i.e., laws to be passed at will by the new National Assembly.

The UN human rights training during the elections had made a big impact on the current national Cambodian psyche. Respect for women, freedom of information and speech, habeas corpus – few malcontents were willing to say publicly that these conflicted with the traditional thinking of some members of the Cambodian public and power structure, in all parties.

Half a dozen Cambodian human rights monitoring organizations had been founded, although where the funding to keep them going would come from was undetermined. Not everyone in the Cambodian human rights community had understood every aspect of human rights thinking. Adam told the story of the two young human rights activists with whom he had discussed rape.

'Of course rape is terrible,' the first of two young human rights workers nodded, 'it's a crime.'

'But not if she's over 14,' one added quickly.

'Well, no, if she's over 14 it's different,' the other nodded just as quickly.

'We have a lot to do.' Kek Galabru, the head of Lidcadho, a Phnom Penh human rights organization, shuddered when she heard the story. 'If it's true, you can see, we have a lot to do.'

There was no getting around the fact that many members of the Cambodian human rights community had studied or lived abroad. Many feared being accused of introducing a moral imperialism into Cambodia, promoting 'Western' ideals over 'Asian' ones. One female human rights advocate had acquired a draft of the new constitution. The human rights community worried that the National Assembly would be presented with a *fait accompli*, a constitution which had little input from any except the two dozen or so politicians who worked on it, many of whom had a stake in maintaining the status quo. She was arranging for an English translation to be made, and for Khmer copies to be given to the Assembly members who were not on the committee. But she did not want to be seen as a leader. For a woman who had lived abroad to be seen in a leading role might bring charges of foreign interference. Better that the monks, the traditional leaders in the community, be seen to lead the protest, demanding an open debate on the constitution. 'We have to wait for what the monks say, that way no one can accuse us of bowing to outside influence.'

Monks and lay people formed *Ponleu Khmer*, 'Khmer Light', a coalition of monks, Cambodian NGOs and human rights groups, to try to open the constitutional process. The reaction to *Ponleu Khmer* was not encouraging. When *Ponleu Khmer* demanded public debate on the new document, Ranariddh, who had begun to make almost all the public pronouncements while Second Prime Minister Hun Sen stayed quietly in the background, blithely called the organization a CIA front. Sadly, Ranariddh had pulled the politician's ploy of accusing any domestic opposition of being in the employ of foreign powers. Rumour had it that the ambassador of an important donor country quickly invited Ranariddh in for a reading of the riot act, but my activist friend's reticence had been shown to be correct.

I had only been back in Phnom Penh a week when the government attacked a Khmer Rouge base near Thmar Puok, Phum Chat, and several other villages. The offensive was greeted as a sign that the new government would easily defeat the guerillas. There had been no leaks, the three factions had worked together, the Khmer Rouge had been completely surprised and a major prize had been seized, said most

pundits who never went north. Louise was the only journalist in the area for the first few days and did well, earning
what I made that month in less than a week. I kicked myself
that I ever got on that helicopter.

About ten days after the fall, a UN leak said bank documents had been seized in Phum Chat. Between logging and
gem mining the guerillas were estimated to make over US $10
million a month. The source said the bank was Swiss. The
civil war was as much about money as anything else, and
with all the side deals going down the Khmer Rouge looked
more like the Mafia than an austere political organization.

Get the Swiss bank name, write about the Khmer Rouge
and guerilla economics and I could make a nice sale to
European papers. Sheltering Khmer Rouge money made
financiers as culpable as arms dealers. It would be a serious
story. I headed to Thmar Puok, which is how Ieng, a thirty-
six-year-old taxi driver, and I ended up bouncing together
on the road from Thmar Puok to Banteay Chhmar, discussing the ways the Khmer Rouge time still affected him 15
years later.

'My mind is not right,' Ieng frowned as he drove. He was
sometimes very depressed, and he thought things he didn't
even want to describe. His fists held the wheel steady as his
little green Toyota plunged into another kidney-crushing rut.
A Mercedes sat marooned halfway into the roadside brush,
defeated by the red dirt road. The Thai owner had raised the
hood and was staring into the engine's depths, probably
trying to remember the Khmer for 'tow-truck'. An ox cart
jolted past the Mercedes. The ox driver looked smug.

'It's not right,' Ieng repeated again, shaking his head. Ieng
would be the perfect staff sergeant – smart, reliable and steady
but not an intellectual. Destined to be a rice farmer before the
Khmer Rouge, Ieng had learned to read and write English in
the Thai camps. He had made reconnaissance trips into
Cambodia for interested foreigners during some of the worst
years of the border fighting, Ieng said with a trace of
bitterness.

'I work for them, I cross the border at night and risk my life,
and then the last month the man he disappear and the man he
don't even pay me!' Ieng scowled and hunched over the

wheel, as if he were driving with both his palms and his elbows. The border, Ieng said, had changed more than once during the time he made his secret trips. Ieng wasn't the only one who felt the Thai–Cambodian border was amorphous.

'I was flying up to a UN checkpoint just like I did twice a week,' said a helicopter pilot I met in the immigration queue at Don Muang airport. He was finished in Cambodia and on his way to the next assignment. 'I landed in the same spot, just like I usually did, when out comes this Indian Unmo waving his hands, screaming at me to go back, and the blades hadn't even stopped yet. "You've landed in Thailand!" he was shouting. So I shouted back, "Well, this was Cambodia last week!" And he shouted, "You're right – but they moved the border markers." ' Thailand was not the only supposed culprit. Farmers in Svey Reing, on the other side of the country, had tales of ponds which had disappeared into Vietnam.

'I know the Khmer Rouge. I was a KP soldier. Everybody knows everybody else here. We fought together for ten years,' Ieng said, shaking his head again at the idea that anyone would be naive enough to believe one side did not know the other's plans. Contrary to the government's press releases, the Khmer Rouge had known well in advance of the government's Phum Chat attack. Most of the people and anything valuable had been moved out. After all, brothers, cousins, fathers and sons frequently fought on opposing sides, voluntarily or otherwise. Information freely flowed back and forth. Businessmen dealing with the Khmer Rouge would want to protect their investment. They included entrepreneurs from the military, both Thai and Cambodian.

After the Cambodian government's Phum Chat offensive the Thai government, which suffered from its own military/political schisms, proclaimed innocence: the Khmer Rouge had not fled into its territory. Bangkok politicians put out the press statements but some independently minded Thai military along Cambodia's border had their own agenda. Cambodia's conflict had been lucrative for these soldiers; Burma's troubles provided similar income-enhancing opportunities in the west. Two Cambodian generals and several Cambodians living on the border told me the Khmer Rouge paid corrupt Thai officers 3,000 *baht* every time a Khmer Rouge soldier crossed into Thailand.

Ieng drove toward the Khmer Rouge town of Ko Krabas which had been overrun at the same time as Phum Chat. He stopped the car to pick up three young soldiers. They had come to Thmar Puok to be paid by the UN, which was providing three months of military salaries to the practically bankrupt government in an attempt to keep the country stable and to stop more soldiers from becoming bandits. Unpaid ministry workers had already sold government office furniture in lieu of wages.

The three rode silently, as if they were on their best behaviour. Ieng stopped again in Banteay Chhmar to let the soldiers clamber out by the wooden school across from the ruins. Refugees from the offensive had parked ox carts and mats in the muddy school-yard ground. Kids were kicking a makeshift soccer ball around. The ball was a large wad of plastic bags tied with twine into a tight, uneven sphere.

North of the town we were the only car. After about ten kilometres one ox cart clopped past. I was nervous, since the day before Ieng would not drive to Ko Krabas because Khmer Rouge were nearby and during a Phum Chat military excursion we had missed two soldiers had stepped on a mine. An empty road was exactly where you shouldn't drive, according to the oracles.

Ieng and I agreed not to think about it.

Finally we came to a government checkpoint – two soldiers asleep beneath a pick-up truck. The soldiers said the road was clear until the Ko Krabas turning. At the fork a woman and her children were feeding wood to a fire under a home-made still which slowly produced cloudy white drops of rice wine. In the house behind, a colonel and several soldiers lounged on mats spread across the floor.

There had been documents in Krabas, the colonel agreed, but the stack had gone to the Funcinpec headquarters at Ampil. Yes, there were more, but, no, we couldn't go get them. The road was mined and Khmer Rouge patrols were still in the area. He would not sanction us driving or walking on now, nor could he envision Ieng and I visiting Krabas anytime soon.

The colonel was quiet for a moment. Now it was time for 'horse-trading'. I hesitated. Maybe it was because two 'Médecin sans Frontières' doctors had been late for dinner the night before that I felt I couldn't bribe the colonel to bring me the remaining papers. The doctors had apologized with the excuse that they had been ministering to the two young soldiers who had stepped on a Phum Chat mine. If I wasn't willing to go myself – and neither walking through minefields nor meeting Khmer Rouge patrols was on my list of things to do – I shouldn't ask anyone else to risk an extra trip through the booby traps. What if some poor sod who made $13 a month stepped on a mine simply because I wanted a story? Ieng and I thanked the colonel and said goodbye.

God, was I depressed as Ieng and I drove back to Thmar Puok. I was running around like an agitated crack-head but had found nothing. Maybe I should have tried to bribe the soldiers to bring out papers, but they wouldn't have known what I wanted, I thought, and I still couldn't justify sending someone through a minefield so I might have a story. It's not like this was Watergate: after years of the guerillas doing business on the border, lots of people had to know which bank kept the Khmer Rouge checking account. The information just hadn't made the papers.

We stopped in Banteay Chhmar and I interviewed the displaced villagers living under plastic sheets in the schoolyard opposite the ruins. For a second time I heard that Pram Su, the Khmer Rouge general, had decamped to a yellow house in the Thai town of Tapra, just across the border. My adrenaline shot up at the idea of finding a Khmer Rouge general sipping his G-and-Ts in Thailand, but then reality set in. What would I do, sneak across the border? And I wouldn't want the Khmer Rouge to find me sneaking an unauthorized happy snap.

That evening I sat on the steps of Sorn's office, watching the sun drift down as I tossed a ball to Mrs Kim's two-year-old granddaughter, and mentally consigned the yellow house to the 'Yet Another Interesting Cambodian Rumour You Can't Check' bin. Later I mentioned the yellow house to two journalists at the FCCC bar, but they showed a dismissive lack of belief. The two men hadn't been on the border much; I was too inexperienced to realize that some insecure correspondents, no matter how good their job, automatically dismissed anything potential rivals said. But even later I learned from a camp worker that a yellow house in Tapra had been a Khmer Rouge radio link. 'Of course he'd be there. Don't you know anything? Everybody knew that yellow house belonged to the Khmer Rouge. It had all the antennas.'

With no bank papers in my hand, my Thmar Puok adventure felt like a flop. I had stayed with Sorn again, back in the room I had shared with Louise. Sorn was not as forthcoming on this visit; a wire correspondent had quoted Sorn during the offensive when Sorn had thought he was speaking off the record. With the diplomatic balancing act Sorn wove between all four factions, quotes were dangerous. Sorn was now leery of writers.

The top floor's resident American Unmo and the other UN workers had gone. All the rooms except mine were shut tight with small padlocks. The shutters were still off the windows in my room and I could watch the stars in the dark, a comforting sight in the spooky silence of the top floor.

I'd been so busy chasing the papers I didn't notice until that last night at Sorn's, when I peeked first through the cracks in the wall of the Unno's deserted and padlocked chamber, and then the other one, why the top floor felt so eerily calm: every room except mine was now a shrine.

The Poipet road

UN helicopters no longer flew from Thmar Puok; I bounced back toward Phnom Penh in a shockless Toyota, stopping in the dusty railhead town of Sisophon to visit Candy, my friend who had ingested too much soup at Tim Page's birthday party. Ieng brought along a friend of his we had met in the street. The friend had worked with UNTAC but the job was finished; Ieng wanted me to ask Candy about getting his friend a new job at her NGO.

'You don't have a job, either, Ieng,' I couldn't help mentioning.

'He has many children, speaks French, no English. I have English,' Ieng replied. He was not sanguine about his friend's job prospects in Sisophon: there weren't many, but Ieng would do whatever he could to help the man. They had been through a lot together, Ieng said.

And, being a lowly freelancer, I had to rely on friends, too.

'I don't think I really like most journalists. It just seems they use you a lot,' Candy said as I settled onto her floor cushions. Sisophon had one scuzzy hotel; Candy's spare room had attracted more than one reporter's attention. Candy sometimes amused herself by throwing out aggressive statements just to see if you'd bite. As an NGO worker, Candy was wary. NGOers were well-informed, but if they were quoted it might upset local leaders and affect their ability to do their job. And the NGO's head office, worried about image in a country far away, might decide the NGOer was too involved personally in the life of the community and cancel their contract.

The UN was packing up, but Australian *bonhomie* still ruled on Friday night. At an Ozzie barbecue in a shack nicknamed

The Woolshed, a moustached English deminer loudly complained that a shell had almost landed on him at Poipet market earlier that day.

'Bloody disgusting,' the deminer shook his head. 'And the traders say it's the local military who's shelling them because they want the traders to move to the new market even though the government's saying it's the DK who're doing it. You should write a story. What a country.'

Well, at least I could sell the article to the *Phnom Penh Post* for $50, I reasoned as I waited at a roadside cigarette stand for Veng the next morning. An ex-UNTAC translator, Veng had puttered off with a friend to retrieve his bike from a mechanic's shop. He had barely disappeared when other motorcycle drivers descended. They were disappointed when I said I'd wait for Veng, especially an old man who said in French he was sorry he had never learned English. He'd like to be my translator.

The old moto driver sat down on the weathered wooden bench next to me, ready for a chat. I just wanted to read the three-day-old copy of the *Bangkok Post* which the resident British Unmo, known locally as the Lord of Sisophon, had lent me. I had hoped to talk the Lord into giving me a glimpse of the UN's Khmer Rouge bank letter in exchange for some papers Ieng had found for me, provided by helpful soldiers who had been using Khmer Rouge diplomatic archives as kindling. I had learned nothing from the UN worker I knew who had seen the bank letter. Although he spoke a dozen languages, he couldn't quite remember the name of the Swiss bank the Khmer Rouge financial correspondence had come from, or what was in it.

I knew I was onto a loser again when the Lord greeted me with 'Ahhhhh, my favourite journalist.'

Alas, said the Lord, there was no chance of seeing the UN's haul; the UN was not happy with my Swiss bank quest. 'But I told the general I couldn't stop you, you weren't doing anything illegal,' the Lord continued. To keep things nice, I chose not to ask why anyone except the Khmer Rouge and the banks would care if I learned which financial institutions handled Khmer Rouge deposits. Maybe a little information I couldn't do anything with would sweeten things. I told the

Lord that there were still papers in Ko Krabas.

'No there's not, we looked for them.'

'Oh, yes there are.'

'Oh, no there's not.'

'Well, how come the soldiers told me there were? The road's mined, or I'd have them. I just don't fancy being blown up for a by-line.'

At first light, the Lord had helicoptered over the Krabas mines and Khmer Rouge patrols and collected two more trunks of documents. As the Lord later read me selected translated passages of the new papers I wasn't allowed to see, I lay my head on his desk, banged my fist and cried fake crocodile tears: although the Lord said there were no financial records in Krabas, the Lord had enough to make me feel I had missed a good story.

The Lord's *Bangkok Post* was a consolation prize, but I needed something to file to pay for this trip. I couldn't sell a four-day-old copy of a Bangkok newspaper. Now I just wanted to quietly sit in my post-unsuccessful-story-chasing-snit and read it.

But the French-speaking moto driver, the type of story-teller who acts as if he knows you will be riveted by what he has to say, even if you're not too sure, already had his cigarettes out and was launching into his tale. The moto driver took his first drag and said he had met many, many Americans in South Vietnam, where he had gone in the 1960s to join the Kampuchea Krom units the Americans had trained there. He knew the roman alphabet because he had learned French in school in Phnom Penh, so the Americans taught him the radio and Morse code via a translator. He and the Americans had made dumb jokes together, without words, but they had never really spoken properly.

At first the moto driver had thought himself unlucky when he had been captured by the North Vietnamese in the early 1970s and imprisoned in Hanoi, but since he was held for seven years his curse turned into a blessing. If he had gone home he would probably have been killed by the Khmer Rouge.

'Oh, God,' I just wanted to go back to my newspaper, 'here we go.' Mindful of the MIA officer's comments at my first

Australian booze-up that most MIA stories were delights fashioned by con artists, I waited for the sting.

'There were no windows,' in his Hanoi cell, the moto driver said, but a pipe ran along the wall. The slow tapping he heard on the pipe, which he at first thought was merely the metal contracting, turned into Morse code. It came from an American, whose tappings said there were other Americans in the jail.

'Okay,' I thought, time to look official. I pulled out a little pocket notebook I didn't use much and a pen. 'What was his name?' I asked, expecting something like 'John Wayne'. The moto driver paused and spelled out the American's name clearly.

'So, what happened to him?'

'One day the tapping stopped. They told me later the Americans were taken to Laos.'

Wouldn't they just. 'If you didn't speak English,' I continued in my best Sherlock Holmes manner, thinking I would trip him up on this one, 'how could you understand the American's tapping?'

'He was an officer and he had learned French at university. He tapped to me on the pipe in French,' the moto driver replied.

'Did you tell this story to anyone?'

'No.'

'Why not?'

'Because no one ever asked me. Bonjour, Madame,' the moto driver nodded and sped away without asking for a penny.

I suddenly wished he had. When I thought the moto driver was a scam artist, what I was going to do with his MIA information was easy – nothing. But he hadn't asked me for money, which made my 'am I being too cynical or am I being conned' dilemma worse. On one hand, the old man simply seemed an old man wanting to talk with a foreigner. On the other hand maybe the reason he wanted to be my translator was to float his scam, but maybe he had thought better of it at the last moment. Whatever the truth was, the last thing I wanted to do was add even a little fuel to the MIA fire. The moto driver's story was 20 years old, whether it had or hadn't happened wouldn't change anything.

The repairs on Veng's moto were not successful; we drove 60 kilometres of flat asphalt between Sisophon and the border in a shuddering second gear. Only a few tiny bamboo villages hugged the road side. Mine signs dotted the bleak, treeless rice fields. By kilometre 45 I was in serious danger of expiring from boredom and a bruised behind, but a young officer added excitement by motioning us to the roadside, demanding my papers and informing me I couldn't go to Poipet. Veng looked edgy and kept his distance as I argued: I wasn't in the mood to be shaken down, thanks. A French UN Civpol officer stopped; he gruffly told the officer he was way, way out of line.

'Do not be angry with me, Madame, I am just doing as I was told to do,' the young officer smiled nervously as he handed back my passes.

Veng dropped me at the old market's edge and went to park his bike. Even if the old moto driver's story wasn't true, he had given a name so I should probably tell the MIA office, I thought as I headed into the market ground mud, but they would probably just pat me on the head.

My moral problem solved itself when I returned to Phnom Penh ten days later. Sorting my notes, I found I had an MIA problem myself. Shaking my backpack and turning out all my shirt pockets didn't uncover what I was missing.

There wasn't much in the little book, but the only notes I lost in Cambodia – probably shaken out of my pocket as I slowly sputtered along the Poipet road – were the ones containing the name of the moto driver and his American officer, Morse-code-tapping friend.

Poipet

Forty years ago when he had been growing up, a roly-poly, bridge-building Cambodian NGO worker from Sisophon later told me, Poipet had been small and surrounded by trees. Even then it had been a market town which served the travellers crossing the border with Thailand. Poipet was still relatively small, maybe 30,000 people who worked in the many small shops, but trees were scarce on the Cambodian side of the border. Although the crossing was technically closed to any nationality except Cambodians and Thais, once the frontier opened Poipet would be right in the middle of the eight-hour tourist drive between Bangkok and Angkor Wat. The grungy border town would become a truck-stop goldmine.

Which was exactly the cause of the traders' problems. Two Vietnamese women, conical-hatted food-sellers, threw their arms around me when I said I wanted to write about the shelling. They pulled me through the mud and debris to a group of men tearing down their stalls. Everyone tried to talk at once, but eventually one of the merchants from the clump of used clothing and plasticware salespeople who crowded around put the problem succinctly. According to the traders, a local army officer commander and friends wanted to replace the shabby old tin-roofed market stalls with new concrete lock-up buildings. The traders were told to move to the new market, half a kilometre further from the border, where rents were 50 per cent higher.

The commander had given the traders a deadline to move. The traders refused. The day before the deadline soldiers came through the market, threatening the traders and pushing goods off their tables and into the mud. The traders didn't budge. On the first morning after the deadline shells fell on the market. The shelling continued every morning, eventually killing 16 people, until the traders admitted defeat. On the morning they began dismantling their stands the shelling miraculously stopped.

The old market, they all agreed, was finished. Some traders were decamping to Battambang. The luckier ones would find another border market, like O'smach in the north, where the commerce could be as lucrative as Poipet. No one could go to Thailand, the traders grumbled, since the commander had told the border police not to let them pass. The government said the shelling was courtesy of the DK, paying the new Cambodian government back for its Phum Chat success, but as far as the traders were concerned the culprit was a local commander-cum-businessman using the B-40 as a business tool.

In the interest of impartiality – which I grew to believe frequently meant trying to give credit to an unbelievable, but official, story – I asked if by any chance the shells had come from the Khmer Rouge. The traders looked at me like I had lost my mind. Maybe the commander had paid the Khmer Rouge to shell, one offered, but the attack started on the day the traders refused to move and ended when they agreed to. What did it look like?

I had to agree circumstance supported the traders. Two soldiers appeared at the crowd's edge. The traders stopped talking. I played La Turista and began snapping pictures. Smiling cheesily, I even lined up the two soldier heavies for a shot. They leaned close to each other and grinned back broadly. While I was photographing traders pulling off a tin roof, a soldier pulled Veng behind a wall.

'You're the translator. Tell her the Khmer Rouge did this,' the soldier ordered.

Veng had barely reappeared when several stall-holders pulled him into another stall and huddled around him. 'You're the translator, make sure she knows the soldiers did this,' the traders demanded angrily.

'Because you are the translator sometimes the soldiers think you are a bad person. It is very difficult,' Veng shouted over his shoulder as we slowly sputtered back to Sisophon. Passing the shake-down checkpoint the young officer and another soldier gave a friendly wave: no hard feelings.

Veng and I talk-shouted at each other in the wind to break the second gear boredom. Veng thought the rules had been badly bent when Sihanouk declared the new government. He explained why. My moto driver, who needed a shave, knew far more about jurisprudence than I did.

'My father taught law in Phnom Penh,' Veng explained. In 1973 Veng had left his wife and child to study law in Lyon, France. At the end of his second year Phnom Penh fell. The remittance from Veng's father abruptly ended; his parents, wife and child disappeared.

'I took a job packing boxes in a factory. I didn't want to think.' For 16 years Veng packed styrofoam pellets into boxes over electronic equipment and then taped the cardboard box flaps shut. After work, sometimes Veng rode Lyon's metro system. Silent and electric, the clean, spare metro had been tunnelled through the Roman ruins which lay beneath the city. Glass cases exhibited the antiquities which had been found while digging each stop. Veng was as cut off from his former life, and the life of the content Lyonnais who bustled around him, as he was from the life of the Romans whose pottery and jewellery lay behind the glass.

'I didn't want to feel a thing. I knew they were all gone but I hoped they were alive.' When the Peace Agreement was signed, Veng returned to his boyhood village near Sisophon. He learned his father had been killed. Veng's wife had starved. No one knew what had happened to his son.

Veng had spent his savings coming back, so now he was a moto driver. There didn't seem to be much for Veng in Sisophon. I asked him if he ever thought of returning to France. I couldn't answer his next question, though.

'And what's in France?'

In an effort to look impartial, even though I knew emotionally I wasn't, I interviewed a regional military commander. A covey of Japanese journalists trailed out as Veng piloted the moto into the compound. At five o'clock in the afternoon the baby-faced, dimpled CPP general greeted me in his blue and white striped pyjamas. Dusty red plastic flowers sat on the table between us.

The general started the interview with, 'I just want you to know I think all journalists are scum.'

In my best Scarlett O'Hara voice, I said that, funnily enough, that's what I usually thought of generals.

'Lady,' Veng squirmed uncomfortably, 'I do not think I can say that.'

Veng was absolutely right; I was grandstanding and he had to live there. Translating my unnecessary sarcasm just because I was in a bad mood wouldn't make Veng's life any easier if the general took offence – but the general laughed. The general understood some English but refused to speak it. He didn't seem overly concerned about the refugees created by the attacks on the Khmer Rouge villages. He hoped the international agencies would provide food and sanitation and take care of the problem the army had caused. I knew the agencies were loathe to step in because of this very reasoning.

The Poipet shelling was, according to the general, of course caused by the Khmer Rouge. I asked if he wanted his sons to be soldiers. The general said he hoped when his sons were grown there would be other jobs in Cambodia.

I didn't find the real ending to the Poipet story until a month later. The Khmer Rouge had unsuccessfully attacked the northern market town of O'smach, on the Thai border, and were expected to try again. O'smach was about a six- hour drive from Siem Reap. To beat the competition, who had opted to drive, Anne and I hopped on a plane to Angkor. Neither of us wanted to head to a potential battle field on our own.

I was just picking up a day rate from Agence France Presse, but Anne was on a short lead. Because she had to file, we ditched our plan to drive immediately to O'smach. Instead, we talked our way onto the regional military headquarters sitting in the shadow of Angkor Wat. The presiding general, who kept a squawking aviary in the middle of the base, was in Phnom Penh where his wife was having a baby, said the army information officer. The information officer said he had been seconded to Siem Reap because of his excellent English, which Anne and I could barely understand. He insisted there was no one there who could tell us anything about O'smach.

'I am the journalist, yes,' he repeated, as if to convince himself, and insisted on acting as translator in the military hospital, which seemed the place to go to find out if fighting was going on. There were no new O'smach casualties there, only several mine victims laying on mats stretched across bed-springs. A pulley lifted the bandaged leg stump of one man high into the air. Skinny, scraped tree branches had been tied to the four corners of the steel bed frames, awaiting mosquito nets which the hospital lacked.

'I don't have enough drugs, look at the patients.' The hospital director was embarrassed by the way the soldiers were treated. Maybe if foreigners saw how little the hospital had they would get some help.

The hospital was interesting but not fileworthy: it was like all the others. Sleazily, I kept working on 'the journalist' – who wasn't a bad sort, just worried about his job. I asked about his children, complimented him on his English, listened to his woes, until at the end of the hospital visit he suddenly remembered there was another general on the base we could talk to.

'The neat brown house has flowers around the door' was chalked across the general's blackboard. He was an English student, shy but eager to converse, and had a field map to show us exact Khmer Rouge positions. This general had just walked for three days along a flooded, mined road from a second front at Srei Noi, 60 kilometres beyond Banteay Srei and south of Anlong Veng. The general jokingly asked whether Anne and I would like to walk with him the next time. He looked terrified when we said yes. I asked if the government would attack the big Khmer Rouge base at Anlong Veng soon, the way Phnom Penh military were bragging they would. '*Mien Khmer Rouge cheran,*' the general shook his head: 'Too many Khmer Rouge, mate.'

Anne and I filed the interview. The next day the presiding general returned from Phnom Penh and contradicted our general. Of course the government would capture Anlong Veng soon, *ot panyaha*, the big general said. But the government didn't attack until six months later, took the camp, and then lost it two weeks later. Too few supplies and too many Khmer Rouge, mate.

It was too late to drive safely to Samrong by the time Anne and I finished, so we stopped the car at a school on the airport road which housed Khmer Rouge defectors. They had responded to the government's offer of amnesty and a job in the new Cambodian army. Anne was anxious to catch everything. When we later finally visited the usually out of bounds Banteay Srei temple, where one of the delicately carved, pink sandstone heads had chisel marks around the neck – the sign of an unsuccessful art theft – and I stopped to make a note about a white-haired, goatee'd, German man delightedly explaining the lintel carvings to three giggling young girls he was training to be Angkor tourism guides – 'Und der munkees reprezint der junkle. All der animules reprezint der junkle' – Anne immediately rushed over to see what I was writing, although she quickly swore she was not the least bit worried about missing something. The rhyme the German taught the girls at the lesson's end would probably be the one thing they remembered: 'My first name is Tip, my last name is Dollar. When you leave Angkor Wat, don't forget Tip Dollar.'

The Khmer Rouge defectors were standing by the roadside watching the cars, motos, bicycles and horse carts go by, a bored bunch of teenage boys with nothing to do. One was drunk, dancing alone, a little apart from the others. The defectors backed up as we left the car. They looked wary, in teeshirts with printed slogans like 'Lucky Boy' and 'California', round Chinese soldiers' caps and rubber sandals recycled from used tyre treads. I started boogying with the drunken, dancing DKer to try to break the ice. If in doubt, act stupid. Anne didn't look sure that this was professional behaviour, but since the dancer laughed, and several other defectors started joking with each other, she pulled out '555' cigarettes and handed them round. Soldiers and checkpoint keepers always noticed the brand you gave them. As a more experienced cameraman, who told a hilarious story about being kidnapped at a Lebanese checkpoint by a splinter fundamentalist group who mistook him for the British ambassador ('... and I bet they're *still* waiting for that hydro-electric dam I promised ...') put it, 'Why do you give them cigarettes? Because they all have guns. And give them good brands, not the cheapest. Everybody knows what the cheap cigarettes are. You're thinking, "Hey, I'm giving them a freebie." They're thinking, "Hey, I haven't shot you yet..."'

The defectors were 16, 17, 18 years old. They had joined the Khmer Rouge because they'd been promised rice and guns. 'Yeah, a gun, yeah kill the enemy!' shouted the drunk, punching his fist in the air. Some of the other soldiers agreed. Join the Khmer Rouge, get a gun, kill the enemy, be a man, get fed. But the Khmer Rouge had given them little rice and, well, no, none of the boys had actually been in a fight yet. A few of their friends had already sloped off to find relatives. The Cambodian war was what it had been for 20 years – teenagers dragooned or tempted by illusions into killing other teen-agers. None of the defectors could read or write. One man was older, and the only one who had joined the Khmer Rouge for political reasons. He had volunteered from a border camp in 1982 to help defeat the Vietnamese. But now he no longer believed what the Khmer Rouge hierarchy told him. He said he saw no sign of the hundreds of thousands of Vietnamese troops his leaders insisted were hiding in Cambodia. 'The only Vietnamese I see in Cambodia now are the ones building houses.'

The next morning Anne and I drove to O'smach, waiting until eight o'clock to take the road, the way the local NGOs did, so that someone else would drive across any mines laid during the night. Our driver, Sokorn, was waiting to enter university. He announced proudly he would become a journalist. Sokorn had driven several journalists during the election; did we by any chance know his good friend from *Time*, the photographer Mr Greg Davis? Any disagreement we had, Sokorn cited the precedence of Mr Greg Davis. The innocent Greg became a running joke for Anne and I for days, the absent final arbiter of all discussions. Whether or not Greg had actually said or done what Sokorn professed was up for question.

Sokorn had lied to his father about where he was taking the car so he could drive us to Samrong, but he insisted Mr Greg Davis would have paid him more, as we suddenly had to or we wouldn't get on the road in time. Journalism had sounded like a nice job to Sokorn, until he realized he was wrecking his father's car by driving over a pot-holed unpaved road headed toward the fighting, which suddenly didn't seem such a good idea. Hoping for a way out, Sokorn checked road conditions with his uncle, the police chief in a commune halfway to Samrong. The uncle said the road had been clear so far that morning – no mines. About 30 kilometres further on, in the midst of scrubland, a drunken government soldier carrying a Frisbee-sized anti-tank mine wandered out of his sentinel shack beside an almost collapsed bridge. The car just scraped across the two planks. The soldier shouted drunkenly. Anne and I stared straight ahead – we were both in bouncing-over- a-Cambodian-road limbo. The soldier then threw the mine in a huge, slow arc over the car and into the brush ten yards away.

The mine didn't go off. Neither Anne nor I said anything. We were both still quiet, both still staring straight ahead. Several minutes passed.

'How did we know that wasn't going to explode?' I asked without turning my head.

'We just did,' Anne replied firmly, knowing that we didn't.

'My father's going to kill me, my father's going to kill me,' the driver moaned as the new Toyota hit a rut.

'Blame Mr Greg Davis,' Anne and I said simultaneously. At the *wat* in Samrong we found refugees from O'smach. The attack had come just before dawn. The government was winning, according to a man who had just listened to a field radio at the military hospital.

At the hospital, an old wooden school with several bombed-out buildings surrounding it, a helicopter was rising from the dust. A medic was cleaning a soldier's bullet wound. The bullet had carved a two-inch long, neat, half- moon shaped ditch into the soldier's arm. The wounded soldier looked dazed. Another soldier fanned the heat away from his wounded friend with a bright red death-head mine warning sign while a medic daubed the gash with white cotton gauze soaked in antiseptic. Behind them a third soldier, one leg bandaged, sat on bedsprings with his family. The uniformed husband, his saronged wife, and small baby chewing on a rusk, all sat stone still. They stared into the distance in different directions. Against the square-tiled floor they looked like an updated Cambodian version of a sixteenth-century Flemish or Dutch portrait, good burghers sitting peacefully while their pictures were being painted. We both took a snap of the family and the medic as he worked. Anne and I argued over whether to use a flash on the dazed man. Finally Anne's lightgun popped. The wounded man started slightly.

'Okay,' Anne concluded confidently, looking around the room for something else to photograph, 'now I feel really awful for doing that.'

A second medic said he had just put the seriously wounded on a chopper for Phnom Penh. He explained what had happened. The Khmer Rouge had come from Thailand and invaded O'smach and several villages around. Thais in cross-marked ambulances had driven the guerillas from the border near the Khmer Rouge base at Anlong Veng. But the Thais involved must have been feeling a little guilty about helping the Khmer Rouge, he continued, because after the O'smach attack they had also used their ambulances to carry some government soldiers to hospitals in Thailand.

Aside from the military casualties, altogether ten civilians had been killed, the medic said as he watched his co-worker finish dressing the wound. Two had been Vietnamese, traders who had just moved to O'smach from Poipet.

Their luck hadn't held.

*   *   *   *

'No, the wounded ones don't get me,' the AFP photographer said back in Phnom Penh, 'it's their families. I can't take the families when they're crying and upset. Sometimes I just have to walk out. It really breaks me up.'

Farewells were in order. The UN was leaving; the blue berets were a less common sight. I saw the end of several stories. James and Rajiv had emerged from the Ratanakiri jungle the best of friends. The Unnos at Kep, who had spent the last six months trying to control contraband, had departed Club Kep one bright Saturday at noon. The local smuggling baron had asked if he could start using their jetty early, as he had boats and trucks coming in. The Unnos left on time.

Emotions ran high. Alain was drunk in the Gecko one night and started in on me. 'You journalists, you don't like us, you only use us because we can get you rides.' We had drinks several times afterwards, but the relationship was never the same.

I sold a couple of local stories from the Thmar Puok trip, then did my accounts. After expenses I had made $75. The bank papers which I knew existed, along with six trunks of other Khmer Rouge documents, were given by the UN to the new government and disappeared. Shel's living-with-the-Khmer-Rouge story hadn't happened either. I wasn't the only freelancer in town chasing the scoop that got away.

Four months after the election, Sihanouk lit candles and incense, brushed his face with perfumed water, placed a banyan leaf behind his left ear, and regained the throne nearly 40 years after he first renounced it. The communist State of Cambodia was replaced by the royalist Kingdom of Cambodia. The new constitution was promulgated, full of promises for education and health and welfare services the government didn't have the money to keep. Ranariddh and Hun Sen, the first and second prime ministers, were sworn in. Cambodia had a new government. It was time for the UN to leave and let the country face the future alone.

I left before the turning of the waters in November, when the rivers in front of Sihanouk's palace began to flow backwards and Phnom Penh celebrated with three days of boat races and a beauty contest. The parks had been replanted and the homeless squatter families kicked off the banks of the river so a formal garden could be installed. The beauty pageant's contestants were required to read and write Khmer, know how to cook Cambodian dishes, and have 'no scarring'. Not only did the waters flow backwards, but the new regime wanted to turn time around, to restore Cambodia quickly, at least on the surface, to the supposed paradise it had been in the '50s and '60s. The government wanted a country that showed no scarring.

Living in Cambodia had changed me more than I expected. Landing in San Francisco after Phnom Penh, I couldn't imagine a more self-centred city. I hated it. 'Maybe now I can't live anywhere except Cambodia,' confided another restless friend from Phnom Penh, who had been anxious to leave Cambodia and was even more anxious to return. The country didn't seem to let you go.

The Cambodian community in San Francisco supported a

chapter of COERKR, the Campaign to End the Return of the Khmer Rouge. The members were primarily students, academics and young Khmer who couldn't really remember Cambodia before the Khmer Rouge. Not all Cambodian immigrants did well in the new surroundings. Depression, family violence and illness plagued many refugees who gained visas to other countries. Doctors found several score Cambodian women who had gone blind, their blindness having no physical cause, but perhaps brought on by the horrors they had seen.

Many of the younger Cambodians in the group were '80s émigrés who had spent their childhoods governed by the guerillas. Sochua was a University of California student who had come to the United States when she was ten. She had only learned to read and write then, but was still destined to take her Bachelor's degree, with honours, at 20. Her father was a social worker among the Cambodian community in Stockton, where Cambodian youth gangs were filled with drop-outs who had not achieved his daughter's success. At six, Sochua had seen people executed by the Khmer Rouge and applauded. 'I was young and I believed what they said. I thought it was good because these persons weren't working as hard as my parents were.'

One night at a COERKR meeting in Nob Hill community centre a Cambodia expert spoke. The gathering was small. Sochua was there. With seven or eight other young Cambodians she was putting together a cultural day, with dances and *bonzes* and Cambodian food, trying to reaffirm an identity and a past they had long since left and many could not remember.

The expert began to speak. I knew him from Phnom Penh. He was affable and I had been impressed by him when I first arrived in Cambodia, but when he started talking with authority about the great Cambodian army success at Phum Chat, how a 300-kilometre front had been opened and not once did information leak to the Khmer Rouge, I found myself disagreeing loudly. The Khmer Rouge had already taken back several villages. The expert, who flew to Cambodia several times a year, met with key figures and flew off again, was merely parroting the government line, part truth but a large part public relations fantasy. What a surprise to find out that I knew as much, and sometimes more, now.

Later that month I was sitting beneath the ornate Victorian ceiling of New York Public Library reading room while the first flakes of a bitter winter blizzard swirled outside, trying to convince myself that I didn't need to, lacked the time, and certainly didn't have the money to return to Cambodia again. The setting could not have been further away from Chang Aeu, where the A3 troops had fought Khmer Rouge intent on robbing the Sihanoukville train. Reading an academic article about the 1970 demonstrations in Kampot demanding Sihanouk's return in the weeks after Lon Nol's coup, a précis of a stringer's report caught my eye. The stringer had watched the army fight Viet Cong and Khmer Rouge trying to capture a train under those same coconut palms.

Since the 1930s, Kampot had been a troubled province. On the other side of the country, the Khmer Rouge stronghold of Pailin had been a 1940s stronghold for Issarak fighters. The same areas had been continuous centres of discontent for 50 years.

The new government and some analysts said the government's forces would clean up the Khmer Rouge quickly, but there was no sign this would happen. To the young monks at the Kep wat the Khmer Rouge had been their protectors; to the mother of the 12-year-old girl killed in the grenade attack on the train, the Khmer Rouge must have been nothing more than murdering bandits.

If only the Khmer Rouge were the sole problem. In Phnom Penh one could forget how ingrained dissent, arms and banditry were in Cambodian life. The countryside had almost never been truly secure, even in Sihanouk's time, and especially at night. On my last drive back from Thmar Puok to Battambang government checkpoints littered the road. Forty years earlier Norman Lewis had hidden under a bus seat to avoid bandits on this route. My taxi driver insisted on stopping the car far back from the checkpoint and paying the tolls himself. By then I had become accustomed, in Battambang at least, to throwing my weight around as a UNprotected *barang*, sticking my European face out the window and giving a little wave and smile like the Queen, to be let through without hassle or charge. This driver would not chance it.

Back on the road the taxi driver had asked me how much the checkpoints cost in America. I told him there were no checkpoints. He was stunned.

'No checkpoints ...' the driver kept muttering in disbelief, 'they don't have any checkpoints ...' He was impressed to hear there weren't as many bandits in America, either.

Reading about the coconut grove, and thinking about several generations fighting different wars under the same banner, I couldn't see how the political and military conflicts would end soon. Not that fighting in Cambodia resembled the slaughter in Yugoslavia or Rwanda. Usually the Khmer Rouge walked into a village, occupied it for several hours, stole a few motorcycles and disappeared. The death toll was usually low. At other times the Khmer Rouge sent shells or the government returned them. Shelling was a weapon which fighters could pretend didn't contravene the Buddhist admonition not to kill: if you couldn't see your target, you weren't responsible for what happened when the shell fell. People died in ones and twos, rarely more than 20. Certain towns were attacked again and again. Poipet and its Thai-border market was frequently mortared. Monkel Borei and Bavel, less than a day's drive from the skyscrapers, chain stores, designer clothes and tourist hot-spots of Bangkok, were often visited by Khmer Rouge foot soldiers; the towns were rarely held longer than overnight. If either side mounted a big offensive enough warning was usually given so that valuable goods were moved away.

But the guerillas only made part of the country insecure. Some people were convinced that deadly trouble lay ahead in the next few years between factions of CPP or between CPP and Funcinpec, but what was more insidious was living in a military state rife with banditry. Guns were ever-present. The military included nearly 100,000 men, maybe more – no one knew exactly. The continuing skirmishes of guerilla war created a Cambodian society where local, individual wrongs continued because bigger national issues were unresolved.

Bad things did not happen everyday or to everyone. But the fear that they might was always there.

What tourists, diplomats and aid administrators saw was usually Phnom Penh. The countryside was something you travelled through to reach Battambang, Kompong Som, Siem Reap, or Saigon – places with faxes and mobile phones, even if they worked infrequently. Most Cambodians still lived in rural villages, planting rice, just growing enough food to live. Any electric light came from a jerry-rigged system attached to a car battery. Clean drinking water was a luxury. Sanitation was several boards nailed together over a ditch to preserve modesty. Malaria was endemic.

Farmers had to cross the checkpoints to sell their rice, never travelled after dusk and hoped that bandits – either demobilized soldiers without jobs and without support, Khmer Rouge, unpaid military or just plain bad guys – didn't decide they had had too much. They prayed they didn't step on a mine, hoped their sons weren't pulled off the road and conscripted into the army if there was fighting or that their daughter wasn't one of the unfortunates kidnapped and sold to a brothel. As long as the Cambodian countryside remained poor while the cities and the military grew wealthy, the countryside would always be a fertile ground for dissent, Khmer Rouge led or not.

The UN peace had brought hope, but it hadn't changed the rules of the game or allegiances. A government structure had been put in place, but the lives of most Cambodians had changed only to the extent that the soldiers' uniforms had. A year later the medicines and protection the villagers needed had not appeared and people were disgruntled, even though expecting them so soon was unrealistic. The elections had been national, not provincial or local. Aside from the members of parliament, all state offices were filled by appointment. The input most people had into governing or changing their daily lives was non-existent.

When I returned, the checkpoints were still there.

Returning

Ten months after the election there were no UNTAC Land-cruisers left in Phnom Penh. Less than 200 foreigners from various UN agencies remained from the once mighty and overwhelming United Nations presence. The Western bars were no longer packed. Cambodia was coming into its own, again.

While I had been gone Chhoun's six-year-old daughter had grown tall; another ancient auntie had joined the family.

'And I'm a colonel now!' my landlord's nephew Chea announced cheerfully as he carried my suitcase back into my old flat. Chea's officer's uniform was crisp and new; his rapid promotion not unusual. Six months after the election the royal army boasted over 2,000 generals and around 10,000 colonels. Some had been created to repay political loyalty. Others had been ANKI or KP officers whose rank transferred to the New Cambodian Royal Armed Forces. Still others simply bought their position. General's stars cost $2,000 apiece and were considered a sound investment.

I slipped back into routines and checked out people I knew. Cyclo drivers, always looking for a customer, shouted 'Madam, I remember you!' The names of the streets were different – gone were the communist Achar Mean and Tou Samouth, the royalist Morivong and Norodom had replaced them. Monita's English had improved dramatically – we could now discuss her brother's love life, and what Monita should do since she had been asked to act as messenger between Chea and the object of his affection, because the usually loquacious Chea couldn't quite get the words out, although Monita swore she herself would not be interested in such things until she finished university.

The bubble that had been the UNTAC economy had burst. In Phnom Penh rents had fallen and hotels were empty. The UN's departure had left many of its Cambodian staff jobless. The traditional Cambodian way to find employment was through connections and patronage. Like other friends, Ieng, my Thmar Puok driver who had worked so hard on my behalf, wanted me to help him find work. 'I see you as a sister,' Ieng said, sitting on my couch. 'I know you will try to help,' which made me feel bad because I had no jobs to give.

A Sunday afternoon trip to Gin Svay; a collection of riverside restaurants and small picnicking huts where Phnom Penh inhabitants lazed on the weekends, with an Appeals Court judge who clutched his hands to his heart and melodramatically sighed 'Ahhhh, le Bateau d'Amour' at the sight of a young couple dressed in their best, looking stiff and unhappy together in a sinking boat; and Heng, who was sputtering, laughing and trying not to drown after he had plunged straight down into the Mekong because he was too busy talking to look where he was going and completely missed the edge of our rented skiff, made me remember how giggly Cambodians could be after so many people at home had asked about how awful the place was.

Many people had changed their livelihoods. Heng scraped by teaching English, Eddie had given up the Stockton. Sorn's Thmar Puok road-building had ended. Puth had abandoned his cyclo to plant rice in Prey Veng. 'Sok Sin's guest-house is a lot better since he got rid of all that wood,' a resident said, but Sok Sin was still struggling to make his tin-roofed hotel pay.

The new coalition government was eagerly trying to build a new state apparatus. A Herculean effort had been made to distribute text books; child immunization was now strongly promoted. While many lower-level civil servants – who remained on $20 a month salaries set when the State of Cambodia communist government rigidly controlled the economy's prices – signed the attendance book each morning and left their offices to work as moto drivers or English teachers, other government employees toiled long hours planning Cambodia's future.

Upper-level positions in Cambodia's new government had

been carefully apportioned. If a minister belonged to Funcinpec, his vice minister would be a CPP member; if a governor was CPP his first deputy governor would support Funcinpec. Funcinpec had done well in the cabinet: Sihanouk's half-brother had become Foreign Minister; Ranariddh's political colleague and friend from his French exile, Sam Rainsy, had been made Finance Minister. But below the top tiers of government the state administration remained resolutely CPP. Funcinpec didn't have enough qualified people to fill the positions and the Funcinpec party structure was virtually non-existent in the provinces after the election.

'We intend to deal with banditry by passing a very strict gun control law,' an optimistic, some might say deluded, official had told me just before I left. It was true that in Phnom Penh there were now virtually no night-time gunshots. The coalition legislature, however, was stalemated, unable to pass any law, partly because the question of whether to seat the seditious Chakrapong and Sin Song in the assembly lay unresolved. In the countryside, illegal road-blocks by government soldiers and bandits were as feared as Khmer Rouge attacks, although the road-blocks happened more often. Several thousand ethnic Vietnamese, who had fled Khmer Rouge attacks before the election, still floated in a no man's water at the Vietnamese border waiting to return. Some had sold their boats at bargain prices and taxied back to the Tonle Sap lake, others had sold their vessels simply to stay alive. After Cambodian police gathered identity cards and issued papers stating that ethnic Vietnamese born in Cambodia had been born in Vietnam, many worried that they would never be allowed to return. Fortunately for the fishing families, nearly two years later most finally would be allowed to go home.

A new problem had been thrown into Cambodia's political future: Sihanouk had cancer, bad enough to warrant multiple chemotherapy sessions in. Beijing. Talk about succession became serious. Any male from one of three branches of the royal family could be chosen. The obvious choice was Ranariddh, but not everyone felt he would abandon politics for the throne. Doubters included Ranariddh himself. Another frequently mentioned candidate was Monique's son Sihamoni, a ballet teacher in Paris. His brother Narindrapong, who had supported the Khmer Rouge, was not a contestant. After Narindrapong saw what the Khmer Rouge had done he had become 'psychologically ill', Sihamoni later told the *Phnom Penh Post*, and was 'psychologically ill' to this day.

Many spreadsheet romances were written in ministries, but the government still had little money. Half the nation's budget came from foreign aid. The International Committeee for the Rehabilitation and Reconstruction of Cambodia (ICORC), a group of donor countries which met every two years, and the International Monetary Fund still controlled new, democratic Cambodia's fiscal destiny. But Finance Minister Sam Rainsy had done a good job in keeping inflation down and collecting import duties, one of the few sure sources of revenue. Foreign companies, alas, were not rushing in to invest. Laundering money through Cambodia's loosely controlled banks seemed Cambodia's only true growth industry, Sam Rainsy noted.

New statutes were being pencilled in the ministries to regulate the press, immigration, the rights of women, and to define who exactly was Cambodian. In these draft laws, Cambodia's future political soul was being cast. New allegiances were made, old alliances discarded. Hun Sen and Ranariddh, who was now referred to occasionally with 'Varman' inserted into his name, worked well together, to much surprise. But Sam Rainsy, Ranariddh's Funcinpec friend from his days in exile, railed against corruption and found himself more and more at odds with his First Prime Minister and old companion. And some felt that certain foreign powers now favoured Sar Kheng, a CPP minister, as an acceptable future prime ministerial candidate, should Cambodia turn into a 'strongman democracy' like Singapore or Indonesia. Sar Kheng was seen as carrying a less uncomfortable Khmer Rouge and communist personal history than Hun Sen, and easier to work with than Ranariddh. Being related to Chea Sim, an ex-Khmer Rouge commander with strong military support who was the National Assembly's chairman, and who was considered Hun Sen's strongest opposition in CPP, didn't hurt Sar Kheng's profile as a possible future leader either. For Cambodia to develop, to put behind the economic devastation of a quarter century of war, there needed to be stability and peace. Some voices whispered that perhaps true democracy, with the hurly burly that political discussions and multiple parties entailed, would not provide the cohesion the country needed right now. This attitude seemed to most affect the legislature, which had few assembly members who dissented from government proposals.

In the countryside guerilla skirmishes continued. Maha Gosananda announced a new peace march, this time to the Khmer Rouge financial headquarters of Pailin. The government temporarily overran the Khmer Rouge military stronghold at Anlong Veng, north of Siem Reap, to much rejoicing. They lost it quickly. Ranariddh, among others, suggested that journalists who strongly criticized the new government's performance should be considered Khmer Rouge sympathizers. Several Khmer language newspapers and the *Phnom Penh Post* were singled out. The Khmer newspapers were accused of being secretly financed by the outspoken Rainsy.

Several ghosts from UNTAC's time appeared in town, back for love, or a business opportunity, or simply because they missed the place. There were more tourists, especially backpackers drawn by Cambodia's cachet as an exotic destination, and because they could save 50 bucks off the Bangkok-Ho Chi Minh route by flying to Phnom Penh and catching a bus to Vietnam. Some travellers came because of Phnom Penh's reputation as an easy place to score drugs. Aside from marijuana, there weren't many recreational substances around. Drug couriers, however, especially those who worked the Bangkok-Lagos connection, were rumoured to be using Phnom Penh as a cut-out stop. Soon post-communist, free-market Phnom Penh had its first large-scale heroin bust.

On the square around Psar Thmei, expensive watch, jewellery and clothing shops had opened. It took one stop at the Foreign Correspondents' Club, which now had a much more equal Cambodian-foreigner mix, to see that the resident barang community was smaller and bored with itself. The foreign population had fallen from 30,000 to under 3,000. Many *barang* evenings were spent watching pirated videos.

The tapes were either copied distributors' versions or illegal cassettes entrepreneurs made by taking a video camera into a Bangkok cinema and simply filming the screen – and the heads of the people in the row in front.

Trips to Sihanoukville provided pleasure and escape. Fester, who had been nicknamed Fester the Molester by another wicked-tongued newsman because of Fester's penchant for women half his age, scoffed when I wanted our beach-bound car to leave early. Fester, a bit of a control freak, had been going through a moody teenage-like phase but refused to admit to any worries. Fester's female friends, including me, took this to be mid-life crisis: perhaps Fester was more traditional than he thought. Shel's many public and sometimes fictive pronouncements that she desired only Asian lovers had been a desperate attempt to disinterest Fester, who now employed her.

Shel's ruse didn't work. Fester had already confidently announced to me that Shel was simply going through a 'slut' phase and that she would eventually see that he was right. But when Fester later learned that Shel had been secretly seeing a quiet, self-effacing Italian photographer and that, even when the photographer left to cover Mozambique, Fester was not on Shel's list, Fester promptly fired her.

I wanted to leave for Sihanoukville long before noon, hating the road and drunken soldiers and the dried-out no man's land with the scrub brush and the pepper plants. Fester, who rarely went outside of Phnom Penh for longer than one night, pooh-poohed this, saying the road had changed and security was better. Cambodia was settling down.

Although security seemed to have improved, my relationship with Fester hadn't by the time we reached the sea. The water was still clear, the beach still pretty and relatively empty. Fester was unsuccessfully courting another passenger, a laid-back, mid-twenties NGO worker with a nose ring. Someone had told Fester he resembled the main character in *The Bridges of Madison County*, which Fester subsequently declared one of the best books he had ever read, so Fester sat alone, staring at the shore as if the waves were washing deep thoughts in his direction, while he tried to lure his prey.

'It looks peaceful but you have to remember it's still

dangerous here,' said Kellie Wilkinson that night. Fester was still angling hard for the NGO worker, who didn't seem to be taking the bait. Kellie and I sat talking, ignoring Fester who was anyway rivetted by the NGO worker's conversation, as her Sihanoukville restaurant closed for the night. Despite the safety admonishment, Kellie and her boyfriend Dom loved Cambodia. The restaurant was hard work, but the two felt they had found a home. Kellie and Dom fed the street kids who sometimes slept on the restaurant's sidewalk and paid when the children needed medical treatment. Kellie's caution, however, was well-founded: the week before, a jilted lover had grenaded a woman who ran a soup stall across the road from the restaurant.

On the return trip I didn't even bother trying to talk to Fester much; hopefully he would snap out of his bad mood eventually. Phnom Penh was a small town, Fester probably just needed a vacation. Back in my flat, logistical problems consumed me: I wanted to revisit places I had been before, but without the UN travel wasn't as easy or as cheap. I had braced myself for another spate of Shockless Toyota Syndrome when, standing in a friend's office, a fax whizzed off the machine offering my friend a World Food Programme (WFP) press tour.

Instead I signed up. WFP wanted publicity for its development work, which it deserved, so we visited the Battambang IDP (internally displaced person)/returnee camps in Ratanak Mondul, where returnees still waited for unmined farmland. The 370,000 refugees living in the camps along the Thai border had all been returned in time for the election. Some camp inhabitants had spent more that 13 years living in cramped huts surrounded by barbed wire. During that time the refugees held no control over their fate. Each faction fighting the Phnom Penh government, including the Khmer Rouge, governed separate camps and their populations. After the one non-aligned refuge monitored by the UN closed, attempts to create camps without political affiliation went nowhere: all the factions used the settlements as forced recruitment grounds.

At one time the Site 2 camp, which held around 170,000 people, was Cambodia's second largest city – except it had been in Thailand. Khmer Rouge-controlled settlements were frequently closed to humanitarian aid, but refugees in other factions' camps had daytime access to medicine, food and relative-tracing through UN and non-governmental organizations. Hospitals, prosthetic workshops for mine victims, schools and a college, rudimentary at best, were established. However, by five in the afternoon the voluntary agency workers, known as volags, all left. At night the camps became home to violence and rough justice. Occasional shelling also brought inside the compounds the war which the refugees had fled.

After the signing of the Peace Agreement, the UN oversaw the camps' closing and the exiles' repatriation by train and truck. Some refugees returned reluctantly, but were offered a small amount of cash, tools or land to help resettlement. WFP provided rice, fish and salt for their first 400 days. Camp residents, other than those in Khmer Rouge camps, chose their destination; many went where they had families and friends. Others had no relatives left. Battambang province, near the border, was frequently favoured. 'A lot of people settled in areas where they were moved to in Pol Pot's time,' explained a United Nations High Commission for Refugees (UNHCR) representative.

Cambodians who had stayed in the country sometimes resented the help the returnees received. Returnees with camp-learned skills and languages were favoured by NGOs, but they were effectively locked out of the provincial patronage systems controlled by Cambodians who had stayed and fought the Thailand-based factions for the last decade. Jobs were scarce.

In Battambang province especially, there was not enough secure, unmined, unfarmed land to be distributed. In some areas, the land given to returnees was under Khmer Rouge control. IDP villages, the bright blue plastic sheets printed with 'UNHCR' serving as temporary roofs, replaced border camps for some. The largest IDP village was Ratanak Mondul, 25 kilometres outside Battambang city and home to 20,000 people. The surrounding, potentially rich rice fields were among the most heavily mined in Cambodia.

'There are two problems – insecurity and the politics of land ownership. About a year before the returnees came back rich people in all the provinces grabbed land. Ownership was decided through connections, influence, you name it. Then when land is demined the army sometimes wants it. They say, "We kicked the Khmer Rouge out, it's ours." You can say it's all the generals taking the land and you can say it's all soldiers with nothing,' said a border veteran who had spent years working with displaced Cambodians.

In Ratanak Mondul, the deminers would mark the next section of earth to be cleared with red tape. Sometimes the deminers returned the next day to find that anxious claim-jumpers had staked out plots on the wrong side of the tape, before the mines were cleared. On WFP's food-for-work projects, rural villagers built roads and dikes, excavated ponds or cleared canals in exchange for rice, repairing the shattered secondary infrastructure. This was important in a country where most people worked the land, away from the business deals, mobile phones and Mercedes of Phnom Penh. WFP had more applications for food-for-work projects than it could support.

We pulled up for dinner at the doughnut restaurant in Battambang. Eager members of the Phnom Penh press corps had been waiting several days in Battambang to enter Pailin, the Khmer Rouge financial centre which the government had captured.

'Come on, Carol, it'll be fun,' urged a Cambodian *Phnom Penh Post* reporter. I wasn't so sure; besides I didn't have a news string and the story was three days old already. In the end the hacks had to hike 40 kilometres. Those who demurred and stayed in Battambang predicted a journalistic *Lord of the Flies*, but most walkers shouldered their backpacks and were on best behaviour, except for Fester – several people told me later – whose aching feet led him to try to bluster and push the army for a helicopter, citing the extreme eminence of all these journalists. The army had not been impressed. His requests for a Coke instead of water didn't even make it through translation. The first night in Pailin a nervous sentry shot at a reporter, a public school Englishman. The reporter was saved by tinned pâté in his rucksack which deflected the bullet. In the scuffle to board a helicopter out, the life-saving liver was lost, but the story quickly made the rounds.

I didn't get a Pailin Scout badge. Instead I stayed with WFP
and stopped in Bavel. There the local police laughed about
running away, dressed only in *kramas*, during a surprise
Khmer Rouge attack that morning. When we reached Poipet,
the market town which jutted into Thailand, a local official
told us guerillas had attacked the day before. Maybe Fester
was correct that Cambodia was settling down in that government structures were in place, but the low-level violence and
hit-and-run forays in the north-west had not stopped. Development couldn't take off with this kind of insecurity.

'Khmer Rouge cut through Thailand to fight in Poipet and
went back the same way,' the Poipet commune chief said,
smoking a cigarette on a rough wooden bench parked
sideways in front of the decrepit government offices. 'They
fired at the people as they ran. The ones who couldn't run
were shot.

'Fifty Khmer Rouge came back yesterday in the daytime to
try to take their dead back and took three,' the leader
continued, watching the border crossing close for the night.
'In the afternoon, Thai officials came to ask for the other dead
Khmer Rouge back. The provincial governor knew them. We
didn't give them. The governor asked them to make an official
request from the Thai government.'

The provincial governor, a friendly, fiftyish French-Khmer
with deep black dyed hair, confirmed the commune chief's
account. A Khmer Rouge leader who owned a hotel in
Aranyaprathet had been killed during the first raid, said the
governor. The guerilla commander's wife wanted her husband's body returned. She had sent the Thai officials. 'It was
only private business,' the governor shrugged.

'The Thais don't see the problem,' explained a Bangkok
businessman later. 'When they have their uniform on then
they work for the government. But when they change into
civilian clothes after hours they're private businessmen, and
their dealings with the Khmer Rouge are business. It's okay in
their minds because they're out of uniform.'

The border was shut tight as we drove away from Poipet,
trying to make it to Sisophon before dark. Eight or nine large
trucks, all carrying huge, uncut logs, moved in convoy toward
the Thai border. Someone was merrily breaking the logging

ban, making money off Cambodia by stripping its natural wealth. Away from the trading in Phnom Penh, Poipet and Sihanoukville, the little projects building local wells or dikes, or developing acquaculture, excavating family ponds to raise fish to eat or sell locally, and growing different kinds of crops (which didn't make for exciting writing – there were no heroes or villains, Khmer Rouge guerillas, glittering dancers, distraught mine victims or government pronouncements) were the things Cambodia needed for the next decade. The development projects were cheap, but cost more than villagers could afford to invest. It was doubtful that the thousands of dollars each of those truckloads would bring would come anywhere near the countryside, or people, which needed them.

Our Landcruisers bounced on to a Pursat hamlet where a local rice bank loaned rice to be repaid in kind at harvest. Traditionally farmers borrowed money or rice at high interest rates, sometimes as much as 500 per cent. Rural debt was a major drawback to development beyond subsistence agriculture; without capital villagers could not buy animals or produce market goods.

The truck barely made it across a deep stream into the ricebank village. Almost 75 per cent of the village's population were widows and their families. The WFP press liaison, a large man who paced around the village snapping pictures rapidly, joked he was taking his photos to Phnom Penh to find the women husbands. The WFP press liaison was a big hit.

In retrospect, the peaceful village beside the river surrounded by trees was one of my favourites. *Kramas* wrapped around their heads, red beetlenut juice staining some mouths, the village women patiently squatted on the ground or stood with their arms folded while the rice payments were weighed on an old iron scale. The project worked well. No family had borrowed from moneylenders; every family had managed to pay back the rice seed they had borrowed, plus more to increase the rice bank's stores. As we left the village children followed us across the single pole bridge which was the village's only connection with the main road, a half moon spanning the river. The kids jumped on and rode the truck bumper as we drove away, dropping off one by one, until only a feisty little boy remained. Eventually he leaped down and ran behind us, appearing like a wraith as the clouds of red dust swirled around him, until he tired and we couldn't see him anymore.

Back in Phnom Penh, I sat down to start the book again. Going through my notes, I kept looking at all the incidents which weren't anything in themselves but telling nonetheless. What about 'Sam, Sam, the cyclo man', a handsome white-haired driver who always bowed slightly as I got into his cyclo and at night always waited at the gate to see I was inside safely? Some *barangs* romantically thought Sam had possessed a previous occupation which he had lost in '75, like several other cyclo drivers who had been government clerks or merchants, but Sam swore he had never been anything but a cyclo driver. One clear moonlit night Sam pedalled me home along the palace road, the spires stretching toward a panoply of black-backed white stars, and recited all the words for the heavens he knew in Khmer, English and French. 'Thnai, the sun, le soliel; lok kai, the moon, la lune; pkay, the stars, l'étoile.'

Sam's vocabulary lesson didn't end a story, didn't fit anywhere else, and I never thought I would be able to use it, but the novelist in me, who wanted to paint with people rather than issues and statistics, quotes and press briefings, could not give Sam up. And how to fit in Sam's friend, another cyclo driver who had been hired full time for an entire year by an UNTAC worker to cycle her around Phnom Penh? Sam's friend would occasionally stop you outside the Foreign Correspondents' Club and ask when you were going abroad – he wanted to send another letter to his former employer. He had written her several already, and was disappointed she had not responded. Quite possibly she had meant to write, but slowly it dawned on the old man that what he had seen as a life-time friendship had been only a timely convenience.

Suddenly I was aware of the tremendous power of print. It seemed unfair to immortalize on a page people who might be embarrassed, or suffer repercussions because of what they had told me if I left their lives sitting on Phnom Penh bookshelves long after I was gone. And what about the newly returned government minister, studying contracts made in the old communist government's last days, who declared 'This entire country was for sale!' What about the resentment of the Cambodian maid whose *barang* employer had forgotten her name and called her by the wrong one? What about the royalist supporter who had left on Sihanouk's downfall to study in Moscow? His mother had convinced him not to return when the Khmer Rouge told students abroad that they should come home and help build the new Kampuchea. Later, he found his friends who had returned from Russia had been taken straight from Pochentong airport to Tuol Sleng prison. His name, too, was on the list of those to be murdered. Then there was the middle-aged *barang* television cameraman, a renowned drinker, who had lived in Phnom Penh before 1975. He had married a Khmer girl. Waiting until the last plane out, his wife, who had gone to see her family, had missed their embassy rendezvous. The cameraman left, thinking his wife was with her relatives and that surely she would be safe. Because her father had been a banker, his wife, her parents and all her siblings were murdered three days after the Khmer Rouge entered the city. None of his younger colleagues, now Cambodia's 'old hands', knew his history. In the Foreign Correspondents' Club the cameraman and his beer can were considered a bit of a joke by some who didn't know him well.

This was the cameraman's third post-'79 trip to Cambodia. On his first trip back he had learned that his father-in-law had been killed on the local tennis courts, along with Sirik Matak, the Prime Minister who was Sihanouk's cousin, the FULRO leader who had left his hill tribe guerillas in search of aid to their cause in Phnom Penh, one of Sihanouk's wives and some Lon Nol officers. On his second trip the cameraman had left the past alone.

This visit, walking around the town to kill time because the story he was working on had gone cold, the cameraman found himself staring through a wrought-iron fence at the house he had shared with his wife. One day he started talking to the children playing in front, then went inside to meet their parents. The furniture was different, of course, but the tiles and the way the light fell through the wire screens were the same. He explained to the family he had lived there. The family were Chinese traders, and very polite and respectful on his subsequent visits. Sometimes he just sat on the porch, watching the street.

Of course things had changed, the cameraman thought, but some things had stayed the same. The tree at the front of the house still blossomed, caterpillars still fell on his shirt if he lingered beneath its branches for too long. Maybe, the cameraman told me later, this place would be all right.

Monks

A friend and I had just spent a silly, goofy, drunken dinner unsuccessfully planning an Ulan Bator vacation when we ran into Tim Page, in a foul mood, at the Déjà Vu restaurant. Tim had returned to photograph a hunt for the elusive *ko prey*, the wild cow that was Cambodia's national animal, unseen for almost 30 years.

There were actually two *ko prey* expeditions in town. An aerial survey was being conducted by several environmental and wildlife professionals. The other search, the one Tim joined, consisted of Tim and his co-conspirator Nate Thayer, the slightly deaf editor of *Soldier of Fortune* magazine who introduced himself with 'HI! I'M THE EDITOR OF *SOLDIER OF FORTUNE MAGAZINE*! I'M HERE TO SHOOT IT!' a former professional mercenary, the *Phnom Penh Post*'s publisher, a reluctant Thai TV cameraman and an Italian camel expert. No girls were allowed, which gave an added ego boost to the boys by making several independent females desperate to go.

The second expedition's provisions included masks of Margaret Thatcher, Richard Nixon and Mickey Mouse, a healthy stash of pre-rolled joints and a tiger gun. The trip's weapon collection had not been all it should be, some people felt. According to a current bar-room story, six months before a friend of the team's leader had tested an AK-47 and other assorted toys from the leader's rooftop one midnight, shooting across the spires of the wat next door. The police promptly arrived. Instead of raiding the house, the police invaded the wat and found guns, grenades and, if rumours were correct, a B-40 rocket launcher. The next day *bonzes* visited. If the *wat* had to get rid of their weapons, the expedition's leader did, too.

Further security on the trip had been arranged via the liberal sprinkling of cash at provincial authorities. The local Khmer Rouge commander, who supposedly ruled his jungle while wearing a Harley Davidson leather motorcycle jacket, had been warned the wild cow-hunters were coming.

'With a group as gonzo as this how could I not get good pictures?' Tim had asked before they left, envisioning a Rolling Stone double-spread.

Neither expedition had turned out as planned. The aerial survey team, dipping and weaving in a small plane over the jungle, was promptly airsick and chucked up from 1,000 feet across Ratanakiri. Several sorties were curtailed due to motion sickness.

The land team didn't do much better. Promised high-tech helicopter support never materialized; the intrepid *ko prey* hunters ended up travelling by low-tech elephant. Water ran short. A forward tracker met a lone Khmer Rouge in the jungle; each scared the other so badly they ran in opposite directions. Page returned early, cut down by a seeming heart attack which turned out to be heat exhaustion. The remaining members of the expedition saw no wild cow, although they claimed to have found *ko prey* spores.

'If they haven't seen a *ko prey* in thirty years,' asked one keen observer of the *ko prey* scene, 'how do they know what *ko prey* crap looks like?'

Tim's six weeks of Cambodian cow-hunting effort had been a bust, and freelance Tim had made virtually nothing for his efforts. The final ignominy had occurred when an airport thief had lifted the bag containing Tim's pictures of his new son.

A backpacker and her friend, Tina, came up to compliment Tim on his autobiography. They were young, maybe 21 or 22 and doing the Malaysian/Thai party circuit, celebrating the full moon with other travellers in numerous all night parties on beach-ringed islands. Tina hadn't been out of England before, everything in Asia was new and exciting. She said she was having a blast. Mutual friends in England had given her Dom and Kellie's names; she planned to visit them in Sihanoukville next week.

The two backpackers quizzed Tim about taking and selling pictures and what it was like to be a photographer. A little attention cheered Page up enormously. He offered the women a joint and like a patient uncle explained the hassles and income-generation problems of freelance life, then the talk drifted. I was tired. The restaurant was now closed; the stereo turned up. I only halfheard the conversation, but I could hear the subtext. Didn't many travellers at one time or another speculate whether they might make some extra money selling freelance articles, maybe a photo? Hadn't several foreign journalists in Phnom Penh started the same way?

Two days later, Dom and Kellie came to Phnom Penh to collect Tina, lunched with friends at Déjà Vu, and left. The only firm facts afterwards were these: an hour outside of Sihanoukville, they came upon a truck hijack. Their car stopped. Tina, Dom and Kellie were pulled from the line and marched away. The village near where they were taken, like many villages, contained some people who sided with the Khmer Rouge, some whose allegiance lay with the government, and others who wanted to avoid politics and trouble altogether.

A fortnight earlier an American Christian NGO worker, Melissa Himes, later safely released, had been kidnapped in a Khmer Rouge village which wanted a new well like the ones NGOs built in government-controlled areas.

'It's become Khmer Rouge policy to kidnap foreigners,' said You Hockrey, the government Minister of the Interior. An ambassador quickly echoed his sentiment.

'Great. If the Khmer Rouge hadn't thought of kidnapping foreigners before, they sure will now,' sighed a disgusted Phnom Penh resident.

Many Cambodians, however, weren't sure the kidnappers had been guerillas, even after villagers testified they were. Government soldiers controlled many shakedowns along the road, and there had been nasty murders by soldiers cum bandits along that route.

'The Khmer Rouge have it together, but the government operation is a mess,' said a businessman about the security payments companies made along the Sihanoukville road. The government shakedowns weren't by the government per se, rather they were run by renegades. Kellie and Dom's friends were sure the three would return – Cambodians were kidnapped all the time, explained a woman with a close schoolfriend whose father had just been released by kidnappers in Kampot. $10,000 was the usual ransom for a wealthy Cambodian.

Foreign wires and TV stations at first were desperate for news; this was not easy on the journalists who knew the three. The Reuter's correspondent told friends he wouldn't press the story; Nate didn't want to get involved. Even Kevin's Irish articulacy faded and he mumbled with embarrassment when the Hong Kong desk rang him on his mobile and pushed him to push friends he shared with Dom and Kellie for information, as he sat at the dinner table with them.

On the other hand, Fester and Shel made themselves deeply unpopular with Kellie and Dom's friends by chasing Kellie's worried father and brother for interviews and pictures when they arrived. One night Fester claimed he had been authorized by a news organization to offer cash immediately for the abductees' story when they were released. Whoever signed the three would have a scoop on several continents. Fester professed surprise at the large amount of money involved, which surprised me. As far as I was concerned, when Dom, Kellie and Tina returned they would need a drink first, then an agent.

My book's contractual delivery date was looming larger and larger and I was trying to write it. I'd stopped penning local articles since the *Phnom Penh Post*'s new editor, a vertically challenged Fleet Street man who wanted it kept quiet that he had formerly worked for Rupert Murdoch's *Sun*, spiced up two of my stories without permission. After alienating many of the staff, the secret Sunworshipper exhibited the cultural sensitivity associated with his kind when I suggested he, who had not left Phnom Penh, see the countryside. The tiny tabloid terror aggressively replied, 'Why would I want to go to a pit like Battambang?', making not a few people feel that Murdoch's Midget, as one disgruntled staffer called him, was wary of any part of Cambodia not bounded by *Phnom Penh Post*'s offices, the Martini dancing restaurant and the bar of the Foreign Correspondents' Club.

Not really able to believe I was working on the book, people kept dropping by to see if it was true, thus ensuring that it wasn't, and a friend was distraught that her NGO, the only one teaching Cambodians how to organize political local parties, was being defunded because the powers that be at best didn't think it was necessary and at worst possibly thought encouraging too much democratic expression of alternative opinions potentially destabilizing; and I listened to Shel, soon to be fired by Fester, when she burst into my living room in total anger at his lordly behaviour; and the electricity kept going off, and the closed hotel next door opened up again, this time as a bordello with a beer garden, video games and an all-night kitchen underneath my bedroom window, and, really, I complained to Candy, who was returning to Sisophon the next day, I just needed some peace and quiet for a couple weeks.

Candy suggested I sequester myself at her Sisophon office and work on the book where there was absolutely nothing, and I mean nothing, else to do. I reserved the last seat on the Battambang plane – I could take a shockless Toyota north from there.

That night I went upstairs to visit my neighbours. The president of the Khmer Journalists' Association, Pin Samkhon, stood on the porch trying to improve his mobile phone's reception. The government had taken Pailin the month before, but whoever called Samkhon said that morning the Khmer Rouge had grabbed it back. They were rapidly pushing the government troops toward Battambang.

So much for my peace and quiet.

*   *   *   *

'Are you for the Khmer Rouge?' the angry soldiers who sat on the outskirts of Battambang asked me. They obviously believed the government charge that journalists were Khmer Rouge sympathizers. It didn't make me feel welcome. Several colonels at the Battambang army camp said not to go any further out of town – I was sure to be robbed by the retreating soldiers, who were in a nasty mood. Their men, of course, would not do such a thing, but they couldn't vouch for other troops. Many soldiers, Buddhist verses tattooed in Pali across their chests, necks or arms to protect them from bullets, carried booty. One limped into the compound wearing a tea kettle on his head and holding a ceiling fan. Wires trailed in the dust; bunches of plastic flowers sprouted from his uniform.

A colonel testified that the night before the attack he had been at the hillside wat in Pailin. In the dark he had seen the headlights of Khmer Rouge trucks coming down the road which led from the Thai border. Wounded comrades had been abandoned on the landing pad, waiting for helicopters which would never come. All the soldiers standing in front of the field hospital were visibly upset by that.

The government had ordered a retreat, the soldiers complained. They were angry that people thought they had fled – they weren't afraid to fight. Some had walked 30 or 40 kilometres along the mine-strewn Route 10 before trucks picked them up. Others had traipsed the entire 80 kilometres back to Battambang.

The one thing which did frighten the troops, however, were the *khmer loeu* the Khmer Rouge had recruited. The soldiers couldn't place the exact tribe, but the highlanders had worn hooped gold earrings, seemed fearless and kept coming forward despite the bullets, like zombies. They were drugged, perhaps. 'Opium or maybe speed,' a Bangkok-based observer later suggested. Troops had taken pre-fight drugs in the Vietnam War, and throughout history, for that matter. Why not now?

In the morning soldiers still straggled in, but the angry feeling of the day before had subsided a bit. I sent my translator, Channo, to the station to see if anything had happened to the train which I could file on, and had a rice breakfast surrounded by silent moto-drivers riveted to a blaring 'Let's Learn Lambada!' video at a ten-stool hole-in-the-wall café. As I left I ran into an NGO worker who told me her secretary had seen a vegetable seller being arrested by military police. The military was forcibly conscripting new soldiers.

The nervous secretary wouldn't let me quote her, but she named a man who worked along the river who'd seen the same thing. He told me where to find the vegetable seller's house. When I arrived a relative said the frightened wife had fled.

'I could tell you many things but I'm afraid,' whispered a taxi driver. He walked away quickly, quite possibly because of a certain lack of subtlety in my approach. I was impatiently watching my life slip by as I waited for the radio phone to connect that night when Channo came in with a man whose brother had escaped the soldiers' drag-net.

'I should tell this to the human rights people. Who should I go to?' the man asked after we had talked for a while.

Troop transports continued to whizz through the town. Drunken military revving 100cc motorcycles careened around street corners, laughing when pedestrians jumped back onto broken pavements. But while Battambang was teeming with soldiers, it was also filled with orange-robed *bonzes*, most in flip-flops but some in trainers, striding through the streets every morning as the green trucks carrying soldiers sped past them toward the front.

Despite the Khmer Rouge recapture of Pailin, Maha Gosananda's peace marchers strode off each day to the sound of a drumbeat for 'get-in-shape' walks. They were going, no matter what. From Wat Bo Vel on the river's edge, a long arc of several hundred monks crossed the Sangke in single file over a high wooden bridge, their orange robes in contrast with the green and brown of the water and the banks and the brilliant blue of the sky beyond.

The organizers, mainly women who kept the respectful distance from the monks that Buddhism dictated, were worried. 'We kept calling the Khmer Rouge to talk about safe passage,' confided a harried organizer, 'but they would either shout abuse or hang up. The morning Pailin fell to the Khmer Rouge we called and all they did was laugh.'

Logistics were a nightmare. The roads were mined. There was no space for latrines and support vehicles couldn't follow the marchers. Walkers were mostly very old or the young. Buddhist monks were joined not only by Cambodians, but also by Japanese, Americans, Australians and Thais; Methodists, Catholics and Muslims. The organizers wanted publicity and several journalists, up for the Pailin story, wandered out to the wat. The calmness the monks exhibited was a complete contrast to a wire stringer's frantic charging around, always worrying slightly that you had missed a story which was more important than the one you filed and that the competition had found it.

I tried to remember all my Buddhist manners for these interviews – don't get agitated, never sit with the soles of your feet pointed toward someone, don't accidentally touch a monk because you're a woman. Channo, who had spent his adolescence in a monastery, was immensely pleased. It was peaceful to sit in the shade of the temple and interview the marchers: old women and men, young boys and cripples who all said 'I want peace for Cambodia,' and 'I am not afraid.' One of the old women, who for some reason reminded me of my grandmother, scoffed at the guerillas. 'I'm 72 years old. I'm not scared of the Khmer Rouge. What can they do to me at this age?'

The only disagreeable part of the afternoon came when I ran into Fester. Fester had driven from Phnom Penh that morning and, after a short spell with the soldiers, dismissed me when I said I had been told the fearsome fighters with the earrings were *khmer loeu*. Fester had been told that the earring-wearers were Burmese gem miners, and, of course, Fester's information was always superior. The fact that neither of us had seen the fighters but were simply repeating what others had told us, which didn't actually prove anything, didn't seem to faze him.

'How could *khmer loeu* have gotten to Pailin from Preah Vihear?' Fester's condescending, don't-be-silly tone lingered in my ears as he walked away.

Only the presence of several hundred monks and nuns kept me from loudly screaming out transport possibilities, punctuated by appropriate obscenities. One minute with Fester almost blew my attempt at Buddhist rectitude. Why Fester thought *khmer loeu* wouldn't be able to travel overland along the border, or through Thailand, like other Khmer Rouge, he did not deign to explain. Of course in Fester's eyes I had to be wrong – the unthinkable alternative was that perhaps he was. I decided I'd gone off Fester and the always-more-knowledgeable-than-thou-even-if-he-wasn't ego he'd developed lately in a big way.

It was so much more pleasant to rest beneath the trees and interview Yos Hut, the monk second in command to Maha Gosananda. Yos Hut was chubby for a monk, wore round, gold-rimmed glasses and had a dry sense of humour. He gave short, pithy quotes, while Maha Gosananda veered onto longer, more philosophical tangents or, as Kevin put it when I filed, 'Maha Gosananda's a bit of a space cadet, isn't he?'

The next day Channo and I found a village where the press gang had invaded a video showing in the local wat. We stopped at a cigarette stand, said we wanted to talk, and promised not to name individuals or the village.

The cigarette seller had been in the wat when the 'recruiters' came. So had one of his customers. The soldiers nabbed the customer, who pleaded that he'd already been a soldier for ten years. They let him go. Both said the village men now slept in the fields or the jungle in case the press gang returned. 'It was like this during Heng Samrin,' the ex-soldier complained, invoking the name of the SOC prime minister before Hun Sen.

By moto the customer led me to a student the soldiers had taken. The student would only talk to me behind his father's house where we couldn't be seen. The student's mother brought out tea in small cracked china cups. His grandfather was drunk and kept asking if I wanted some of his special tea. The whole family smiled at grandpa.

The student and his brothers had been watching the video when the soldiers came. They fired shots outside the darkened room. People screamed. The soldiers put the student onto a remorque with two other men. They were taken to the military camp, shoved in a room, given a cigarette, and asked their names. The soldiers went away and didn't return. After an hour, the three conscripts took a chance and ran.

'There won't be any more videos. The owner is closing his business,' the student said. 'He's afraid this might happen again. I want to talk to the human rights people, but I'm scared.'

Channo and I drove back along the river. The bank was green and the mango trees heavy with fruit. This was the way Eden should look. We stopped at a school. Students had stayed there overnight to avoid the recruiting squads. One student had an 18-year-old soldier friend who had fought at Pailin. Now the friend belonged to a conscription team which set up roadblocks and grabbed men to send to the front. The student had not seen his soldier friend in a year – they had gone separate ways – but the friend had appeared at the student's house the day before and warned the student not to stay there. The friend had already taken several truckloads of conscripts to the army base. From there the shanghaied men were driven to the front, where they would be given a gun. There was no training. The soldier did not like what he was doing and did not want the student to be sent to the front.

I was going to write the conscription story that night, but I knew the wire would want a government rebuttal to the charges included. Channo and I agreed that the army at the moment might not take kindly to questions about kidnapping students out of video halls. Perhaps the governor, I suggested.

'Please don't make me ask the governor about conscription,' Channo meekly asked. The governor of Battambang had an evil reputation; the translator was a gentle man. Until the Khmer Rouge took over Channo had been a monk. He had married in Site 2 and worked in the camp hospital. Back in Battambang Channo could not find a job. Now Channo worried how he would feed his children when his returnee rations ended.

Channo had to live in Battambang and I didn't. Another NGO worker had told me that the UN human rights office was investigating stories of secret prisons and murders by some members of the army in Battambang. If the stories were true I could see why Channo would not want his face associated with the conscription article. When I dictated what I had over the radio phone I could hear Kevin's disappointment, and disbelief, that the story contained no government rebuttal. The Hong Kong desk would give him hell if he filed it that way. He was already having enough trouble because my prose kept slipping out of wire style.

Three months later a UN report on Battambang's secret prisons came out. The UN human rights centre found evidence of kidnapping, torture and at least 53 murders by members of the Battambang military, either in retribution or as part of extortion scams. I understood even better now why Channo had been afraid. People disappeared in Battambang.

Cambodian human rights groups bravely documented and publicized the rights abuses they found, but they could not protect anyone. Publicity and the threat that aid might be withdrawn if human rights were not observed were the two weapons the Cambodian human rights community had. When America granted Peking the Most Favoured Nation trading status, despite little improvement in the Chinese human rights record, Cambodian human rights activists despaired.

'Forget it now. They'll think they can do what they want,' grimaced a Phnom Penh rights advocate.

The Cambodian government later denied that Battambang's secret prisons had ever existed.

*   *   *   *

Early the next morning the march's drums and loudspeakers woke me an hour before Maha Gosananda led the walkers through the temple gates. The streets of Battambang were lined with well-wishers. As they left I waved to the 23-year-old one-legged nun, whom I'd met on the peace march the year before and interviewed again this year, to the shrivelled, 72-year-old woman in the big black glasses who looked like my grandmother, and to the boy monks walking under red and white sun umbrellas advertising cigarettes. All carried small backpacks loaded with water, hammocks and mosquito nets. The old women at the back had to run to catch the young monks confidently striding away at the front.

In the afternoon I hopped an NGO convoy lift to Candy's place in Sisophon, but down the road the Khmer Rouge had begun to pound Poipet with shells. The market was abandoned; only porters too poor to pay for a remorque ride to Sisophon stayed in Poipet. At Kohn Domrei, a little town graced with a huge statue of a baby elephant, the general commanding the government troops pointed on the map to a small reservoir in Thailand just south of Poipet. The lake was where the Khmer Rouge had positioned their guns, the general said, so he couldn't really shell them back across the border.

By the end of the week the foreigners evacuated Sisophon. Neither Candy nor I would admit we were stressed, but we took an inordinately long time to pick a hotel in Battambang. Candy had left most of her belongings behind; she kept remembering things she'd forgotten, and she felt guilty about 'abandoning', as she called it, the Cambodians she worked with. Along Route 10, the government forces continued to lose five or six kilometres a day to a small number of Khmer Rouge. The government defences crumbled. My quiet time disappeared.

I started out to the front. As the car jolted along, sometimes pulling aside to make way for a hurtling army vehicle, the driver, my translator and I all took turns muttering, 'Oh, this is terrible . . .'

A seemingly endless number of people were fleeing toward Battambang, the line winding back to the horizon. They rode ox carts or bicycles, or walked. Cattle and pigs were herded along the road; chickens were tied to bicycle handles or held by children. Pork buyers, paying half the normal price for slow-moving swine, sped along the track with huge hogs tied in wicker baskets to their back seats. The elderly and cripples who couldn't travel had been left behind in villages which were now being shelled. The refugees weren't sure how those who remained would feed themselves or survive.

'We don't know where we're going. We just keep moving forward, until it's secure,' one elderly man said, shaking his head as he talked and watched the line snake past him down the dirt road.

The car stopped where some families had camped in the open under trees. At breakfast that morning an NGOer with an experienced eye had estimated there were as many as 30,000 people displaced by the fighting. I wondered how many old people or small children wouldn't survive this move. One mother, suckling the youngest of her five children, could talk only of the roof of her house. It was a tin roof, 'the best', she said, and she worried it would be stolen. One man's children were so upset that their dog had run back to the family house that he had braved the shelling to retrieve the pet. The look on the father's face as the dog peeked from beneath his shirt said he couldn't really believe he had done that.

The villagers with market stalls along the road were doing a roaring trade, selling water, coconut-flavoured ices, rice and anything else they could.

'But the prices are high. It's always like that when new people arrive,' complained an old woman who'd been displaced since 1970 more times than she could remember when I asked her to count.

The car crept forward. The line of people walking along the road didn't seem to end. At each stop, people crowded around, asking where they could get help, could we get milk for their baby, what would they do if it started to rain – they'd die in the wet without roofs. At the wat beneath Phnom Krapov, Turtle Mountain, the peace marchers' supply trucks were leaving. The one-legged young nun was riding on top a truck cab. The marchers waved as they passed. The Khmer Rouge had not granted them safe passage, claiming that if the government soldiers violated the guarantee the guerillas would be blamed instead. Disappointed, the marchers had changed their route to avoid the fighting. No one wanted to be a martyr.

Dusk was falling as the dust swirled around the car on the road back into Battambang. Cooking fires were lit. Families were settling for the night under ox carts, trees, tarps, or under other people's houses, where animals usually stayed.

Back in our room, Candy poured drinks. The red dirt was just beginning to wash off me and down the shower drain when more bad news crackled across Candy's hand-held radio: the peace marchers had been attacked.

I begged Candy to drive me to Battambang hospital. Inside the hospital's front room, two achars and two monks were lying bandaged on stretchers. Other *bonzes* hovered nearby, looking lost. The peace marchers had been attacked near Bavel, they said: one monk and one nun had been killed. Some said the foreigners had been kidnapped by the Khmer Rouge, others said the foreigners were all right.

That night shelling boomed in the distance, just loud enough to disturb sleep. In the morning smoke billowed above Treng and Ratanak Mondol.

The Hong Kong desk wanted me to drive to Bavel and find the marchers; I wasn't crazy about going alone. Some deminers and two UNHCR workers were driving in convoy to Bavel, if it was safe. Ostensibly the trip was to retrieve a stolen truck, but one man also had friends among the peace marchers and was visibly worried. I prayed the UN group would go, because I really didn't want to drive to Bavel by myself . . . and on the other hand I really didn't want to miss the story. Every hour we waited meant I had less time to file. An ambitious little voice inside said why not go alone: the peace marchers' kidnapping would have international play; the other journalists had left and for the moment the story was all mine.

We sipped coffee and waited for news to filter in. By eleven there seemed to be no trouble on the Bavel road so we left. At Bavel we found that the Khmer Rouge had attacked the town that morning. A dead guerilla still lay behind some houses. I was suddenly very glad I hadn't come earlier, on my own.

At a nearby *wat*, the chants of a memorial service for the murdered monk and nun were just finishing. What had happened was this: the government's front line had fallen back 20 kilometres overnight. The marchers did not know that. Young monks had asked soldiers to head the column and look for mines. A Khmer Rouge patrol appeared. The Khmer Rouge and the soldiers began to shoot. Several monks stood upright among the fighting, trying to stop the soldiers. Fighters for both sides shouted for the monks to get down, for the marchers to take cover, but the firing continued. The monk who died had hidden behind a military backpack in which he had been carrying his hammock and mosquito net. The guerillas had fired at the backpack thinking it sheltered a government soldier. The monk was killed.

The firing stopped. Guerillas had moved through the marchers, taking belongings. The Khmer Rouge soldiers were very young. They marched the foreigners away, asking, 'Are you afraid? Are you afraid?' The Thai marcher was roughed up because he had a camera. The Khmer Rouge soldiers thought that the Thai was a journalist and, worse, Japanese. When the soldiers realized the marcher was Thai he was suddenly their long lost buddy.

'The Thais are our only friends!' the soldiers repeated while apologizing – but they still kept his cameras, along with the other foreigners' valuables. When the foreigners met the Khmer Rouge commander, the commander apologized for the monk's death and said they should tell the world that the Khmer Rouge only wanted peace, too. He let them go.

'Look how many have joined us!' exulted a sunburnt walker stepping away. The march was beginning again. I stood aside and watched the procession stretch through the gate. The number of marchers had indeed grown; flags waved, drums sounded. Holding up buckets of water, people lined the roads waiting to be sprinkled and blessed by the monks. Maha Gosananda got a big laugh by dousing me several times with a dripping lotus stem; I didn't care. The marchers were on a high – they had been tested and their resolve had remained. The old woman who looked like my grandmother, the young crippled nun, the boy monks I had talked to were all safe. I ran to the front of the line to ask Yos Hut for a quote.

You wanted to believe that all that hope for peace – marching down the dirt road in the shape of old people, children, the disabled and just pure believers – would make a difference. Cambodians were fed up with 20 years of fighting and war. Tired of watching people lose their livelihoods, property and futures, families erecting makeshift camps under the stars, not knowing what came next, thrilled that the people on the march I knew were safe, and caught in the waves of belief and adrenalin and euphoria that the walkers were travelling on, I truly lost it, in front of the entire peace march. Out of sheer relief I unthinkingly did absolutely the worst thing a woman in Cambodia could do.

Even now I wince to think about it. I threw my arm around a monk.

The taxi driver

'You're going to take this seriously, yes? This is serious. You cannot laugh.' Ung, a well-connected friend who was escorting us to the fortune teller several cabinet ministers used, looked up into his rear-view mirror at Louise and I, sitting in the back seat.

'Ung, why ever do you think we wouldn't take this seriously?' Louise asked innocently.

'Because I know you two – and I saw that!' Ung admonished the mirror, as he caught me making a face to Louise.

Alas, Louise and I were serious about having our fortunes told, but after Ung turned left at the television transmitter and right at the paint plant, we saw that the step into the fortune teller's waiting room was covered with two dozen pairs of plastic flip-flops which a couple of red chickens merrily danced across. The hot airless waiting room, decorated with oils painted from photographs of someone's grandparents, was packed. Next door the fortune teller, a sweating, middle-aged woman, sat in front of her shrine to Buddha, with burning candles, smouldering incense, fruit and flowers and her cat walking across it, advising a young couple on their upcoming wedding. The couple had diplomatically planted a healthy stack of dollars on the offering tray to the spirits. The crowded waiting room sighed collective relief when the fortune teller announced that tomorrow was still an auspicious day for their ceremony.

But that day hadn't been an auspicious one for Louise and I to have our luck foretold; the room was stifling, the fortune teller was going slowly. Seeing Ung she smiled, and advised us to come back another day, when she was not so tired. *Barangs* and officials were good business.

Inside two months I had been offered a couple of wire jobs and the editorship of the *Phnom Penh Post*. Running around Battambang had briefly turned me into the local journalist flavour of the week. A year before I would have leaped at any of these spots, but now I declined. Ostensibly I turned them all down because of my book, but I knew that wasn't really the reason. Louise was feeling at loose ends too; we might as well see what the fortune teller had to say.

Sunday morning we rose early to beat the crowd. Heng, who had volunteered to translate, led the way on his bright red Honda Dream. We saw the trucks filled with military police outside a hotel on the other side of Monivong. We considered stopping, but decided the commotion was probably just some soldier who'd gotten too drunk and fired his gun once too often, so we didn't brave a U-turn in the amazingly heavy early morning traffic.

There were only two people ahead of us at the fortune teller's; the chickens were still in bed. The fortune teller gave me better luck than Louise because Louise went first and kept saying 'Actually, I disagree . . .' to the woman's analysis, which annoyed the fortune teller no end. But the fortune teller neglected to mention to us, even though she told Louise she would find love in Phnom Penh, and that I would not leave the country until I had learned to read and write Khmer ('Ahhh, work for life!' Heng cheered), that if we had stopped to see what the military in those trucks were doing, instead of coming to see her, we would have been there before anybody else and wouldn't have missed the chance for a scoop interview with Chakrapong. At that moment the wayward prince was hiding in the hotel and negotiating to leave the country with his life, because supposedly he had attempted another coup the night before.

By the time we left the fortune teller and stopped behind the crowd gathered before the hotel, two Khmer journalists were already on the scene; others began to filter in. Nate, who had interviewed Chakrapong the week before, was upstairs in Chakrapong's room; he had arrived to find the supposedly seditious prince trying to hide in a hole above some ceiling tiles.

I couldn't help noticing that Fester wasn't there, nor was

anyone who worked for him. Fester had come off my 'avoid' list even after he fired Shel because she had spurned him sexually. People often did uncharacteristic things when hurt in love, I reasoned. Fester climbed onto the list permanently, however, when he cut Heng's day rate as a translator from $25 to $15 – after Heng had finished working the two weeks for which Fester needed him. Heng, who struggled to make the $200 a month he said he and his wife needed to buy fresh water for the children and charcoal for the fire, didn't want Shel or I to raise the problem or our voices with Fester. There was so little work around that Heng, needing any potential employer, swallowed his pride and his anger.

'Fuck it, I'll be a cow,' I thought, looking at two photographers and one reporter, all with mobile phones, standing near me. 'Let someone else call Fester. He wouldn't call *me* . . .'

No one else did, it turned out later, because the other three also felt the same way: everyone was tired of Fester's attitude. Chakrapong was whisked away in a blaring convoy. The American ambassador came out looking relieved; he announced he had only been present because an American citizen, Nate, was upstairs, and to ensure that Chakrapong's human rights were not violated.

The pack hopped on motos and headed to the airport. Fester, looking grim, arrived on the tarmac as the flight carrying Chakrapong flew off, and only caught a picture of the plane's tail wafting away.

The bar-room analysis of the coup went on for weeks. Most pundits considered the coup members' plan to disable Phnom Penh by disrupting the power station a complete mistake; the power was out half the time anyway and everyone would have simply flipped on their generators. People remembered stories, or rumours if you will, from the months before, about a politician who had supposedly returned from a trip abroad with a pair of high-powered rifles, considered 'assassination' tools by people who considered that sort of thing, and about shadowy soldier types practising calisthenics at night outside a house near the palace. Others concentrated on the fact that some politicians had been looked on with favour by powerful foreign countries, still others noted the allegiances that the supposed conspirators supposedly had to various members of CPP. A number of Thais, who had vague connections with the Shinawatra telephone company, were detained, but the government quickly cleared the company and its owner of any wrongdoing in connection with the supposed coup. Just as well – the next month the owner was appointed foreign minister of Thailand. And everyone swore it was only a matter a protocol, several months later, which made Ranariddh decline a meeting with Shinawatra when he paid an official visit to Phnom Penh. All this didn't make Cambodia feel any more stable. Insiders said that when one of the prime ministers left the country he made sure that troops loyal to him were on full alert. The only person without a theory, it seemed, was a recently arrived, peroxide blonde Russian, a bubbly girl who had just come to Phnom Penh from Macau. She hoped there would be less competition here than in Macau for her services. Macau was evidently crawling with Russian blondes.

At least Chakrapong's coup rid the stalemated Assembly of the problem over seating the rebel prince and his supposed co-conspirator, Sin Song. The government quickly got down to business. A business investment law was passed, which allowed companies investing in Cambodia tax-free status for several years, with no import duties on goods to be used in the business, and low company tax rates after the new business exemption ended. Malaysia led the charge, small though it was, to take advantage of the new investment code. Malaysian prime minister Mahathir headed a 100-strong delegation of influential Malaysian businessmen to visit Phnom Penh. Malaysians were a little over an hour away by air, had money to invest from their own booming economy and yet had no common border with Cambodia. The territorial, political and economic disputes, historical and present day, which shadowed Cambodia's relationships with Thailand and Vietnam were notably absent from its Malaysian association.

Things were hard for the government during the summer. The government still desperately wanted foreign aid; donors still demanded stringent reporting requirements. The Khmer Rouge were formally outlawed, and tales of MPs being threatened into voting for that law were legion. But the Khmer

Rouge were the glue that held the coalition together. Once the Khmer Rouge were defeated, power struggles within the government were sure to intensify.

The government also addressed other nagging issues. A potentially repressive press law was prepared for the legislature; Cambodia's neighbours wanted Cambodia to conform to the 'little news is good news' press laws which govern most of South-east Asia. Two French journalists were told they would not be given visas to Cambodia because of their negative reporting, which had appeared in Paris. Two Khmer newspaper editors, critical of the government, died in what could best be called 'mysterious' circumstances.

'What are they complaining about? We only killed one . . .', a well-connected government official supposedly said in a rumour that went round Phnom Penh for weeks afterwards. If the rumour didn't accurately portray the government's position, it accurately portrayed the common perception of its stance. What gave the rumour extra spice was that the speaker had supposedly been a member of Funcinpec, not CPP. When the government announced a perpetrator had been arrested for one murder, a judge threw out the suspect's confession. In the meantime, the report of secret prisons and deaths in Battambang set the government at odds with the human rights community.

While the Khmer Rouge no longer pretended that they had changed, the coalition government proved no bastion of free thinking. Those expecting a Western-style democracy were disappointed. Most legislation was decided in the Council of Ministers. The parliament was little more than a rubber stamp assembly. An immigration law unfavourable to the waiting ethnic Vietnamese was passed. Politicians of all persuasions encouraged anti-Vietnamese sentiment. The lone dissenting vote was cast by the Muslim Cham representative, afraid of repercussions against his people. One journalist reported that UNHCR had been approached to help the government plan and build holding camps for Vietnamese who were to be deported. His report said UNHCR refused. Brothels were closed in Phnom Penh, but they simply moved elsewhere and gave the police an excuse to ask for an even higher kickback from the pimps and madams.

Despite the pronouncements several months earlier that the Khmer Rouge were targeting foreigners, more North American, Australian and European tourists arrived. But still no one had heard from Dom, Kellie and Tina.

There was much dissatisfaction with the embassies and the Scotland Yard detectives who had come out to help. 'There's going to be some red faces when this is over, I can tell you,' said tall, shaven-headed Paul, a travelling contractor who had built Dom and Kellie's brick pizza oven. The year before, Paul had founded the Phnom Penh Surfers' Club, mainly as an excuse to walk around the capital wearing a woman's bathing cap on his head to confuse uptight members of the UNTAC military. Dom and Kellie's friends, including Paul, put all their efforts into finding information. They may have been conned occasionally, but any chance to release the three was worth the risk.

Phnom Penh's favourite pastime – gossip – was in high gear. Wild rumours quickly spread about Dom, Kellie and Tina. The unspoken logic said that if Dom, Kellie and Tina were kidnapped for something they had or hadn't done, something that was personal, then the rest of the foreign community were safe, but the *barangs* were only learning to live with the anxiety about their own safety that many Cambodians lived with. One fantastical yarn speculated that Dom had been involved in illegal logging, a more frequently heard tale was that the couple were drug dealers. It turned out that a Scotland Yard detective had found a kilo of grass in their bungalow. Extrapolating the British street price for that much dope, the detective assumed the two had been professionals. The new-to-Cambodian Scotland Yarder had to be gently informed that a kilo of Cambodian grass only cost 4,000 *riels* – one quid, a dollar and a half – and nobody cared much if you smoked it. The new arrivals didn't understand how things – or people – worked in Cambodia.

At the beginning of June, the government said it had 14 communications with the kidnappers. The three were basically well, evidently, although Kellie was poorly. Woodcutters said that Dom and Kellie lived in one room, Tina had another. A mine victim said that on 5 May he had been nursed by a very tall Western woman – the description fitted Kellie's frame, the action her personality. Investigators, however, were not sure the stories were true.

By the time I heard the taxi driver's story three months had passed since the kidnapping. The taxi owner who had driven Dom, Tina and Kellie the day they were taken had ferried a barang from Sihanoukville to Phnom Penh at the beginning of July. The taxi driver, my informant said, told the *barang* the reason Dom, Kellie and Tina were taken was that one of them had jumped from the car to grab a picture of the men stealing the truck.

A cold shiver ran through me. I remembered the A3 captain trying to get into the truck after he saw my camera. The friend who told me the taxi driver's story had a similar experience. I remembered the talk Tina had with Tim Page about photography two nights before the kidnapping, and how exhilarating things were when you were new to Cambodia. The hijacking could have looked like an exciting picture to her. All of us had done something stupid when we first arrived. Maybe Tina, to whom Cambodia and armed robbery was all fresh and new, had wanted to take a picture. This was all conjecture, mind you, although when presented with the scenario a high government official went white and asked, 'How do you know this?' – off the record, of course.

On Tina's birthday, the parents of the three went to the village near where the three had been marched. The parents gave out rice and flyers which said that today was Tina's birthday. They asked for the release of their children.

For days after hearing the taxi driver's tale, I couldn't sit down to write. I started to chase the taxi driver story, but the fear of being involved on some *barang* faces was obvious. I put the story aside. Part of me wanted to follow what I had heard; the other part of me didn't want to be classed as another journalist profiting off a friend's misfortune. On Saturday night I met Kevin and his girlfriend for dinner at Déjà Vu. As I climbed the front steps I glanced up and saw that Kellie's father had returned from Sihanoukville to Phnom Penh; he stood on the private upstairs balcony, dejectedly smoking a cigarette and watching the crowds come in. Kellie's dad, a white-faced friend of Kellie's said knowingly, was leaving in the morning.

Later in the upstairs bar Fester, who had assigned Anne to cover the story, dismissed the idea that their bodies had been found if he didn't know about it. 'They haven't found anything. Anne has the best sources on this and if the bodies had been found she'd know,' Fester frowned, but he immediately took his mobile phone to the other side of the room to make a private call. Fester played everything close, and represented several different high-powered news organizations on the story; professionally, the kidnapping had been a lucky break for Fester. He would often be seen standing next to Dom's father at the bar, whenever Dom Senior was in town. Fester seemed to have a father-to-father relationship with the elder Dominic Chapell, providing moral support.

Despite the rumours, people were stunned the next day when the news came from London, courtesy of BBC World Service Television, that when the parents had returned to Phnom Penh the embassies announced that bodies had been retrieved. The remains had been flown to London for identification. It was hard to believe that the Cambodian police and the embassies didn't know that Kellie, Dom and Tina had been found before their parents went through that little piece of village theatre. It was also hard to believe, in the small town that Cambodia is, that someone in the government had not known exactly what had happened for a very long time. Heng, however, felt he had his worst fears confirmed. As translator, the always discreet Heng had accompanied Anne. Now he just said, 'When the villagers asked me, "What will happen to us if they are dead and if we bring the bodies? Will the foreigners be mad at us?" Then I knew they were dead.'

Shel's wire had faxed her a preliminary autopsy report and she needed to fax an article back. She came to use my computer printer and suddenly burst into tears as she called her story to the screen. 'It just wasn't real before. And then I'm writing about what was found and it's all so horrible. I feel so bad for them all.' Shel had made herself persona non grata with many of Dom and Kellie's friends by aggressively chasing Kellie's father for an interview, as if the kidnapping was a story in which she knew none of the participants; now she couldn't keep away sorrowful reality.

But, in some ways, the discovery of the bodies released the other foreigners in Phnom Penh. The drama had ended, no other foreigners had been kidnapped. Dom, Kellie and Tina's deaths, it looked like, were an unfortunate one-off event. The out-of-town journalists departed. An ex-NGO worker at loose ends, who had just been fired by an NGO which he claimed was riddled with bad management and malfeasance and wanted me to do a story about it, kept encouraging me to take the train down to Sihanoukville with him in a group he wanted to put together. I was locked in a hotel, desperately trying to finish my last chapter, and the guy would arrive with beers at absolutely the worst time, trying to tear me away from the Toshiba. If I wasn't typing I wouldn't answer the door in order to avoid him, but when I heard three backpackers had been kidnapped by the Khmer Rouge during a train attack in a coconut grove near Kep, I rushed around trying to find him. Thankfully he'd gone to Bangkok instead.

Mark Slater, David Wilson and Jean Michel Braquet, riding on the train roof to get a better view, were taken in the same spot where exactly a year earlier Shel and I had seen the A3 try to stop the Khmer Rouge from attacking another train. A cabinet minister publicly admitted that the Kep local government military, who had not helped the A3 when Shel and I had been there, had assisted the Khmer Rouge in the later, successful train robbery. The out of town journalists returned, one making a bad, bad joke in the bar, saying that whenever Fester's business started to slow down he just radioed the Khmer Rouge to take another tourist.

'It makes me very angry that this happens in my country. It is very bad for Cambodia.' Heng shook his head over the kidnapping. To ordinary Cambodians, the kidnappings were the fault of the Khmer Rouge and Cambodia's instability.

'Oh, we don't want tourists like that. We want tourist with money,' an overseas Khmer woman from the tourism ministry said one night at a party. The other government officials sitting around her looked embarrassed. More than one official, though, privately denigrated the foreigners for taking the train, as if the kidnapped men were more to blame than the Khmer Rouge. They seemed not to grasp the dichotomy of their position: the government was encouraging tourists to come. By this very fact many travellers were bound to think the place was pretty safe.

With the second kidnapping the government's official reaction was different. There was communication. The big guns, both in personnel and artillery terms, had been called in immediately. The government was willing to pay a ransom – murdered travellers were not good for business. It made the lackadaisical effort to pursue Dom, Kellie and Tina's kidnappers all the stranger.

While most Cambodians taken off the train were released, the three *barang* men and several Vietnamese stayed in Khmer Rouge hands. The effort to get the three Western men released became a circus. The Vietnamese, alas, didn't figure.

More reporters descended on Phnom Penh. I rarely saw Anne: she was in her glory, chasing a story and hanging out with the more experienced male journalists who'd descended on the town; besides, we couldn't talk about much. The Fester News Empire, Inc. revelled in, and was terrified of, competition, ergo Anne couldn't discuss the stories she worked on.

Rumours of payments for details flourished. If the embassies and journalists weren't paying, many people still hoped to make money from the hostages' plight – even members of the Cambodian government tried to sell information. While the foreign embassies maintained they would not pay ransom, the Cambodian government was ready to part with $150,000. New self-proclaimed and self-promoting 'negotiators' appeared. Demands now arrived from the central Khmer Rouge command, rather than from the local kidnappers. The ransom soared to $1 million and included the cessation of military assistance to the government by foreign powers. 'I am too young to die,' Braquet pleaded hauntingly in a letter smuggled off the mountain. He begged that the ransom be paid.

The longer the three men remained in Khmer Rouge hands, however, the more frustrated and strange the entire scenario became. The government said the foreign diplomats and journalists were obstructing negotiations and that press attention was causing the demands to escalate. Embassy personnel and journalists were then banned from the area.

'Too many cooks spoil the cuisine,' the francophone Ranariddh declared.

The politicians wanted to negotiate, the army wanted to
attack. As usual in Cambodia, the army won. The best
estimate is that the day a massive shelling offensive started,
the three Westerners were murdered. The Vietnamese and
two Cambodians also were killed.

Although privately I had given up hope of seeing Dom,
Kellie and Tina again early on, because there had been so
much negotiation I had believed the three men would survive.
One man's girlfriend was in town, pretending to be simply a
traveller, and she was so convinced they would live you
wanted to be convinced, too. Thanks to a video camera
smuggled onto the mountain – without payment, the television company loudly declared – we saw the three in front of
their prison hut, regular guys whose down-at-the-mouth
demeanour would have hinted at a hangover in other circumstances. They looked like they needed a shave and an
afternoon on the beach only a few miles away, where they
should have been had they not taken the train on the wrong
day. All six hostages had only been pawns in Cambodia's
political game, as many Cambodians had been before them.

But the government wasn't the only group who knew more
than they let on. I rarely saw Anne, but she strolled over to
visit one afternoon when I wasn't feeling well. The visit was
welcome, but one of the things we talked about didn't make
me feel better.

Three weeks after Dom, Kelly and Tina had been kidnapped, Anne told me, she had the first of several conversations with the head of the village near where the remains had
been discovered. The conversations concerned what body
parts the parents would have to see to know Dom, Kellie and
Tina were dead.

Although Anne said the conversations were theoretical in
content, I couldn't imagine Cambodians making small talk
about death. I was startled by the date Anne mentioned and
honed in on her first dialogue with the morbid village chief,
when Anne really wanted to talk about a later conversation:
that first conversation had supposedly happened the day after
the last 'confirmed' sighting of the hostages when Kellie had

supposedly nursed the mine victim. At that point, with no inquest yet held, it seemed to me that Anne and Fester might have information which indicated when the three had been killed.

Anne said she and Fester hadn't told the embassies that the village head had talked, albeit theoretically, about bodies because the embassies 'won't play ball'. The diplomats didn't give information to journalists. She hadn't filed a story because any suspicions the village head's conversation raised hadn't been 'confirmed'. When I asked directly, Anne said she and Fester hadn't told the Cambodian police, again 'because nothing was confirmed'. Ergo, they hadn't told anyone. Of course, only a cynic would have pointed out that the only true confirmation there could have been was to see the bodies and, if Anne saw the bodies, she had a very important, potentially lucrative story.

Several days later, Anne wrote an article for a local newspaper. In it she said that the embassies should help the journalists more, as if the embassies bore a burden to provide information so the journalists had something to file. The gist of the article was that the 'world's press' could provide the embassies with what they found if the embassies gave them more – quid pro quo, if you scratch our backs, we'll scratch yours.

You know, I was really tired, at that point, of the non-journalists in town, many of whom had heard the stories of journalists chasing down friends and relatives of all six hostages, looking at me like I was pond scum whenever I said what I did for a living. Reading Anne's article, I could only see Paul and the ashen face on Kellie and Dom's friends in Déjà Vu the night the story broke. News was a business: the embassies bore no burden to provide reporters with a story. If an embassy refused to provide a talking head to give reporters a quote that day, the intrepid journos should find another story to write about. Indeed, if the embassies accepted any responsibility at all, and I wasn't particularly sure they had, it was to protect the families and find out what happened. I didn't believe one could truly be uninvolved, especially where friends were concerned. On a simple human basis, journalist or not, we had a moral duty to try to help. Who knew if telling someone that Anne had discussed retrieving body parts, two and a half months before the remains were returned, might have helped the families and friends – people Anne and I knew – learn what had happened and end their anguished waiting sooner?

I wrote about Anne's conversations with the village chief in a reply piece of my own. How much had the journalists' behaviour affected the outcome of the two kidnappings, and how much 'right to know' was involved when people's lives were at stake? The article was faxed to Fester for comment.

Anne quickly appeared at my house, saying I had the story all wrong. They were just trying to protect their source. There had only been one discussion. She had tried to tell the embassies, Anne insisted, but the door to the investigators' and diplomats' Sihanoukville quarters had always been resolutely closed to journalists. And she had been working closely with the Cambodian police the entire time. The reason they had not told anyone else, Anne suggested, and the reason they wanted no one to know the story now was to protect the relatives and friends.

As she sat on my couch, fervently denying most of what I'd heard on her last visit, Anne looked like her job with Fester was on the line. Anyone can misunderstand one part of a conversation, but I couldn't believe I had been mistaken on every single pertinent point. If I had been mainlining LSD I couldn't have gotten that many details wrong. And Anne's original story had explained Fester's firm assertion in the Déjà Vu bar that Anne would know first if the bodies had been found; it also explained why Heng had been sure the three were dead after translating for Anne.

As for protecting sources, if Anne had worked with the Cambodian police then the embassies, the investigators, the army and their third cousins twice removed probably already knew with whom she had spoken. It was unlikely the local Khmer Rouge would not hear when police – or a young barang reporter – visited the village. Another friend said later that, before Anne spoke to me, Anne had boasted that she had been within ten minutes of retrieving the bodies, although the friend said Anne had never explained what she meant by that. Later it turned out that if the Cambodian police knew about

the villager's morbid queries, they had not told at least some of
the foreign investigators in Sihanoukville.

In Phnom Penh you saw embassy people socially every day.
The foreign investigators and embassy personnel were not
difficult to contact or speak with, as long as you didn't want an
interview and as long as they trusted that you wouldn't quote
them. Dom and Kellie's close friends, and sometimes their
fathers, were in Phnom Penh. It should have been simple to
say, 'Hey, this may not mean much, but we had this
conversation . . .' I firmly believed in protecting those who
provided information at risk to themselves, but Anne did not
need to identify her informant. Besides, Anne herself was
writing another article, destined, she hoped, for the prestig-
ious *Columbia Journalism Review*, about the ethics of her
response to the chief. Who she told about the conversation,
however, had not seemed a problem.

Anne had always looked on Fester as her teacher. As she sat
there, rolling back her story, or at least the one I had heard
before, I thought she had chosen the wrong master. Neither
Anne nor I any longer were innocents in Cambodia. We were
not new in town, we now understood how things worked,
how Cambodia worked. The more people I interviewed, the
more stories I filed, the more I realized that simply digging for
information, even if I never wrote an article, carried with it a
large responsibility. Now I thought I had been irresponsible
not to guard more carefully that little, difficult-to-use
notebook with the scribbled names of the supposed MIA
soldier and his supposed Cambodian prison-mate. I may not
have totally believed the story, but there was a chance that
what had seemed like a tall tale to me may have been real life to
some missing serviceman's family. Our actions were as much
a part of the story as the events we reported on, and indeed
could change those stories. Anne and I differed about what
those actions should be: she had developed more ability than I
had to remain uninvolved, detached. More and more, I had
trouble keeping a safe emotional distance from what I saw and
learned.

Even then I didn't believe Anne's new story but I cancelled
the article and tried to square things for her with Fester. Anne
looked like she was in such trouble already – and, as a friend of

Dom and Kellie's said when I had tested how friends and families would react if I followed the taxi driver story, publishing wouldn't bring Dom and Kellie back. Anne's job meant more to her than anything – being a journalist defined who she wanted to be, who she thought she was. Fester had fired Shel, why wouldn't he fire Anne? Despite Fester's much touted experience, his *éminence grise* routine was an act, as far as I could see; he was another fantasist come to Cambodia to live a life in which he hoped no one would question him. He stood next to Dom and Kellie's friends and relatives every night for almost three months and neglected to tell them that the village chief was talking about retrieving bodies, making cautious offers.

But better now, I thought, when almost everything was known, that I should protect my friend Anne than pursue what was, in the great scheme of things, an unimportant piece. Publishing the piece now wouldn't help the families and friends. The only thing it would do would make Fester look bad, and I figured he was capable of doing that himself. Thinking about it later, though, I knew I had made the wrong decision.

Of course, after Anne had taken so much trouble to tell me I was wrong, I checked around with various other people on various parts of her two stories; the first version still rang true. Several weeks later while having a drink with someone else who worked for Fester, I heard more. The other employee said Anne had returned to their Phnom Penh office after the first conversation and asked Fester whom – and if – she should tell; Fester, according to this person, had said that since Anne had no confirmation she should not tell anyone, but that if Anne retrieved the bodies, she should bring them to Phnom Penh. Why Fester chose Phnom Penh and not the closer Sihanoukville, where the Cambodian police handling the murder investigation, the foreign police and Scotland Yard detectives who had come to help, and sometimes Kellie and Dom's fathers, were located, was anybody's guess. Extremely cynical individuals posited that this would have been one way to ensure exclusivity.

When reports of the inquest into the deaths of Dom, Kellie and Tina came out, the statement of the taxi driver said he had tried to help by telling the kidnappers Dom, Kellie and Tina were newspeople. According to a report in London in *The Times*, they spent the first night in a Khmer Rouge farmhouse. When the Khmer Rouge leader asked them why they were in Cambodia, Kellie had replied she was a restaurateur, but Tina and Dom had claimed they were journalists. This had enraged the leader so much, the report said, that he ordered their murders. The report added that – in traditional Khmer Rouge fashion – Dom, Kellie and Tina had been clubbed to death, as Braquet, Wilson and Slater were two months later. A Scotland Yard detective testified that he had been informed the bodies had been found after one of the murderers had turned away from the Khmer Rouge and taken an 'undercover agent' to the bodies. The undercover agent had been instructed to ask for $150,000 for the remains. After all the fake stories of parlays with the kidnappers and reports of Dom, Tina and Kellie's good health after they were dead, one couldn't help thinking that the government's undercover agents either hadn't done a very good job, or they had known more than they were telling for a very long time.

Later, as Christmas neared, the embassy grapevine in Phnom Penh was saying that the government now knew that four men had killed Dom, Kellie and Tina – two Khmer Rouge and two villagers. But one of the locals had helped police to find the bodies, said the grapevine, so the government felt it would be hard to prosecute. Other diplomatic sources, however, said privately the kidnappers had been soldiers. Who knew if anyone knew? Several weeks before the bodies were recovered, two high-ranking Cambodian government officials and a Cambodian intelligence source, from three different parties, had sworn to three different reporters – off the record, of course – that the government had known all along who had kidnapped the three: it had not been the Khmer Rouge. Of course, who knew what these officials really knew?

Nearly a year after Dom, Kellie and Tina had been kidnapped, two Cambodians claimed they were promised money by the embassies to recover the bodies. The money had not been paid. Embassies denied the story. Several months after that, a Khmer Rouge defector admitted responsibility for shooting Dom, Kellie and Tina. In the end, another sort of story emerged from the kidnapping and murders, the story of so many lies told, by so many different people, for so many different reasons – all, in the end, merely self-serving. No one really had been helped, as far as I could see, by any of them.

From then on, Fester and I avoided each other. Not suprisingly, it seemed the only people Fester mentioned the story to was Kevin, for whom I worked, and another mutual friend to whom Fester hurtfully mourned that I had the story totally wrong, even though I didn't.

Anne and I had lunch once or twice after that, but I always had the feeling that she thought she had gotten away with something; I don't think it ever occurred to her that I might have pulled the story for reasons other than feeling I had been mistaken. Perhaps, though, that perception was just me being angry at myself because I hadn't stuck with it. Others later admitted that I had the story right. But Anne, shades of Fester, believed that life was confidential, unless stated otherwise. The trouble was, Anne couldn't help but brag a bit about her big story that barely got away.

I thought I had been helping Anne but, in the end, I think I had done the opposite. Anne seemed to believe in Fester more and more, and in a way they fed each other's fantasies: she wanted an older man to believe in, he wanted to be believed. My view of the world was nothing like Fester's. In a way, Fester had made me realize that I didn't want to work as a journalist if I had to act like Fester to get the story, or at least the story business demanded on that day. Maybe Anne and I would retrieve our friendship some day, when she understood why I felt both she and I had made bad decisions, even if it was to save her job.

Despite all the talk of impartiality, there was judgment implicit in reporting any story. To be able to report objectively, we needed to look at ourselves first, and truly decide why we chased each story, and why we reported the way we did. Whether we were driven by the ego boost of seeing our names in print, or a need to prove something, or even a passion to tell a particular story, we needed to be sure we didn't kid ourselves about what was in it for us.

As for Fester, well, he truly didn't understand. He was just another part of the tale.

*　　*　　*　　*

In the interest of national reconciliation, Khmer Rouge defectors, even those involved in the murder, had been awarded a general amnesty. One defector known as Colonel Rin, a Khmer Rouge commander on the hill where Braquet, Wilson and Slater had been kept, transferred to the Cambodian army. His wife was brought to Phnom Penh and given a day at the hairdresser. It was a showpiece defection. Rin's new government command was the Kep shore, the same area he had covered for the Khmer Rouge, the same place where he had attacked the train carrying the three foreign men. Moral considerations, and foreign sensibilities, took a back seat to the search for peace. National reconciliation meant, if not forgetting, then at least legalistic forgiving. Like the Cambodians who lost people they loved to the killing fields, and in the violence before and after, however, the families and friends of the six murdered foreigners would never forget.

For the Cambodians life continued – jobs or rice planting, marriages, babies, and acquiring less important things like motorcycles. Sitting in the quiet Phnom Penh evening, listening to the crickets hum and watching children with tiny nets fish for tadpoles in the deep puddles, after talking to the neighbours standing out in the street at dusk, seeing what there was to see, you could remember that bad things did not happen all the time here, that they were the anomaly, not the rule, that most people just wanted peace and safety, to have a good time and to feed their kids. The yellow-orange sun setting across a golden wat rooftop, against the brilliant blue sky and green palms, reminded you that the beauty of the country remained, no matter what happened; the scaffolding for the new Phnom Penh climbing the side of an expensive half-built apartment block shooting up on Monivong Boulevard, the renamed Achar Mean, hinted that no matter how bad the past, the future eventually claimed its rightful place. Death for people I knew had been bad luck; if Buddha was right the murderers would have bad kharma in the next life.

The Buddhist next life was important, because there was little justice in this one.

After the party was over

My new Australian flatmate, Nicole, was spread-eagled flat on the linoleum floor of our kitchen. Nicole hadn't been in Phnom Penh long, liked a good time and kept a tailor busy running up new party frocks from the very affordable Cambodian silk, but the festivities next door were a little much. The boys at the volleyball net were celebrating victory with a completely different sort of volley.

'Jesus, Carol! Get down! They're shooting!' This sort of thing didn't go on in Melbourne.

'Nicole, they're not shooting at us.' I dismissed Nicole's concern with indifference and kept leaning against the fridge as I read a year-old issue of *Cosmopolitan*. Amanda's favourite comic trash reading had been *Cosmo*.

Then I thought about Amanda and I hiding in the Monorom bathroom the first time we heard shots in Phnom Penh. I looked up from the magazine and down at Nicole, now doing a duck walk on her haunches across the green and black linoleum, crouched so her head wouldn't appear above the window-sill. And Nicole was staring at me like I was nuts. Hmmm, she might have a point. Maybe it was time to leave Cambodia.

For some reason I was always walking around angry, angry at I don't know what. I loved running around the countryside, the adrenaline buzz of being the first one to find out what had happened, but Kellie, Dom and Tina's deaths had broken that sense of *barang* invulnerability I unwittingly carried.

Any of us could have been on that road and decided at the wrong time to take a picture that at best would sell to a wire for a whopping $50. It could have been Shel, it could have been Louise, it could have been me, it could have been Anne.

I didn't think the voyager fixation on that buzz was my most pleasant characteristic, either. The allure was hard to explain, but other Phnom Penh journalists had the same problem.

'When I go home my friends say, "Brian, you're so quiet." But they're all talking about mortgages and new washing machines, and what I've got to talk about is driving down a road and wondering if I'm going to meet the Khmer Rouge or drive over a mine. What do you say? How do you explain you like what you're doing? It's sad, isn't it?', mused the *Voice of America* correspondent, who happened to be Welsh.

Even the Battambang-hating *Phnom Penh Post* editor had caught the buzz, and ventured into the countryside to see the aftermath of the Route 10 fighting. Soon afterward a documentary maker arrived in town and featured the editor bravely showing the camera around the back of the Battambang front like an old hand.

There was a general consensus that backpackers who came to Phnom Penh looking for a close-to-the-action thrill, or those travellers who did stupid things in Cambodia like not stop for a police checkpoint, something they would never consider at home, were playing with fire, living out a fantasy and chasing an adrenalin high that could land them in serious trouble. Stringing and reporting, however, meant that you got to go for that adrenalin rush, call it work, and no one would question you. Unless, of course, they did. Besides, Cambodia articles had very little play. Celebrity sex scandals received far more column inches than real-life stories of small, relatively oil-less and strife-ridden countries. I wanted to write about what I saw myself; business demanded that many stories were built around politicians' quotes. And financially, writing was the wrong medium; the money was in video.

I made plans to leave when I finished the book. Maybe I was just tired of being considered rich when I wasn't. I had lost that expat ability to keep misery at a distance and poverty at bay. I was disgusted that the local police had hit my new landlady for $50 a month simply because foreigners had now moved into the house. The landlady felt she had no choice.

I couldn't explain to my conscience that giving the guard $60 a month was okay, simply because that's what everyone else paid; he couldn't even afford the most basic English lesson.

The expats in the house at the end of the block had fired a security man. Several thousand teeshirts had been stored in the expats' garage, accepted as payment for a bad debt. The guard's wife and children lived in a village 50 kilometres away; their house had been robbed the month before. Thieves had sawed through the bamboo wall while the guard's wife and new baby slept. The wife had pretended to stay asleep. The thieves took everything. A month later the guard was caught stealing some green cotton teeshirts from the expats' garage and was promptly fired.

Shel had no sympathy for the guard. 'They had a TV in their hut. Eighty bucks a month is enough for them to live on. He's rich by Cambodian standards.' The guards at the other houses on the block were very upset. They didn't think the fired guard should have taken the teeshirts, but they sympathized with his problem. 'In Cambodia the most important thing is the family. You always take care of the family first, no matter what you have to do. Sometimes I don't think the foreigners understand how hard things are for Cambodians.'

*   *   *   *

I wanted an upbeat ending for this book and I couldn't write it. High on the hope with which UNTAC had infected almost everyone, both Cambodians and foreigners, I'd come to write an optimistic travel book but I'd become much more realistic.

Watching the refugees stream down Route 10 had made me realize that Cambodia was not going to settle down in a year or two. Heng and other friends were going to work just as hard as they always had, for little reward. But some things were better. Corruption in awarding exam grades and university places had been curtailed; Phnom Penh had more expensive shops to cater to the growing middle class. There was an entire new generation of children who had grown up without any memories of the Khmer Rouge years, children who wanted to play Khmer Rouge, the way other kids played cowboys and Indians, even though at school they were taught little about the Pol Pot days. And opinions were mixed, when government officials suggested closing the Tuol Sleng museum, over whether the government was trying to put away the grim reminders of the Khmer Rouge past in order to concentrate on the future, or whether they were simply pandering to the guerillas' requests.

Throughout that rainy season, the Khmer Rouge had made small gains. But then it seemed the Khmer Rouge helpers along the Thai border had begun to change their minds. New stories filtered back of Khmer Rouge soldiers being denied border crossings. If the guerillas were denied passage through Thailand, their days, though long yet, were surely numbered. A secure Cambodia now looked like a better money-making proposition. Think of all those tourists.

The Khmer Rouge, meanwhile, called for the 'total liquidation' of all civil servants who worked for the Cambodian government. The reported December 1994 massacre of 96 people, primarily teachers, village chiefs and government workers in Siem Reap, proved that the Khmer Rouge strategy hadn't changed at all; they could be just as vile as they had been in the 1970s. In the same month as the massacre, however, hundreds of disillusioned Khmer Rouge soldiers and villagers under the control of the guerillas defected to the government side, taking advantage of the soon-to-end amnesty. Many were disgusted by the new Khmer Rouge policy of total destruction – burn all the houses, kill the animals – when the guerillas took a village. Others were dismayed by Khmer Rouge corruption: before the guerillas' honesty had always been their virtue. 'We are not the force we once were,' a 30-year Khmer Rouge veteran told Kevin after many Kampot Khmer Rouge surrendered. 'The trucks which once carried ammunition now carry logs.' For some guerillas, almost their entire adult lives had been spent fighting for the Khmer Rouge cause; it now seemed a waste.

The defectors included a 17-year-old girl who had been sent as a 2 year old to a special Khmer Rouge children's camp in northern Ratanakiri. The Khmer Rouge held that children were the key to their success; children could be moulded. The Ratanakiri camp, the girl told a *Chicago Tribune* reporter, had been run by the Chinese. She did not know who her parents were, who her relatives really were, who she was. She could neither read nor write nor add. The Khmer Rouge had not taught her these things, but when she was eight they had taught her how to assemble a mine. The girl began portering for the Khmer Rouge troops at ten. Given a Khmer Rouge uniform to wear when she was 14, the defecting teenager thought the skirts worn on Phnom Penh streets were immoral.

The girl had a bad case of malaria and was transferred to a government military hospital from where she disappeared, alone and knowing no one in a city she had been taught to hate. The doctor taking care of her thought she had awakened, found herself surrounded by men in government uniforms, and run away. He had diagnosed her malaria as cerebral; without treatment she wouldn't live.

New faces continued to appear, longing to be amazed by Cambodia's past even if they could't decide about its present. The Angkor ruins still lure travellers, in the way they had first brought me to Cambodia, and although Banteay Srei was placed out of bounds, the tourists continued to be inexorably drawn to the jungle temples, even if the Khmer Rouge had supposedly put a large bounty on foreigners. A new wonder appeared when the government defeated the Khmer Rouge based in the Kulen mountains. They found the 'River of a Thousand Lingas' still rushing through the hills, its shallow, crystalline waters splashing over hundreds of apsaras, vishnus and lingas carved into the riverbed stones.

While the riverine lingas from Cambodia's past were visited by new pilgrims and tourists, business continued. Small 'rag traders' set up shop, using Cambodia's cheap labour force to produce dresses for richer markets. Sam Rainsy continued to rail against corruption in the awarding of big government contracts; the Malaysians continued to be the most successful bidders and investors.

The basic power structure in Cambodia had not changed. A small group, a mixture of Funcinpec and the CPP, ruled the country. Instead of the *devarajas' okya* each governing his own fiefdom, military commanders and governors held powers far above the call of duty in their own manors. Working democracy at the grass roots in Cambodia was still an illusion, despite the efforts of the many Cambodians who sought it, and those who had died for it in the run-up to the election.

More than one pundit said Cambodia now felt much the way it did in the early 1970s, but it would be unwise to think that history ever repeats itself exactly.

The 1998 election to come would be a true test of Cambodia's new democracy, although the omens were not the best. The outspoken Sam Rainsy was dismissed as Finance Minister, ejected from Funcinpec, and finally stripped of his seat in the Assembly. Reports on the wires, faxes from friends, and telephone calls all said that the dismissal had been another 'rubber stamp' affair. Almost no MPs voted to let Rainsy retain his seat; whispered tales of intimidation of legislators to ensure they cast their ballot against Rainsy circulated.

After the vote, Rainsy made his final speech in the Assembly hall to only five other MPs and a crowd of journalists. There were tears in the eyes of some politicians. In the next election, there would be no UNTAC to protect and encourage those who believed in democracy and accountability. Within six months of his ouster, however, Rainsy was busy forming a new party to fight the next election. His nationalist platform for the new party discouraged some observers, who felt he was pandering to Cambodians' xenophobic prejudices. Sihanouk, changed perhaps by the wisdom that age sometimes brings, was now seen as one of the leading voices supporting human rights and a second election. The coalition government, which to much surprise had held together, seemed headed toward a one-party state like Indonesia or Singapore, where any real opposition stood little chance of gaining power. CPP and Funcinpec announced they would fight the next election together, dividing the provinces between them.

Cambodia, like Sihanouk, had altered: not dramatically, just step by step. There were many, many problems but, despite the small Khmer Rouge presence, it was not the 'Pol Pot' time anymore. The foreign perception of the country, however, was still mainly the past, still the 'killing fields'. I turned in my manuscript and immediately lost the agent who was supposed to sell the book to New York publishers. The agent had never been to Cambodia; he couldn't imagine there was humour there. An article the agent had recently seen –

written by someone I knew had only made short post-UNTAC visits to Cambodia a few times – talked of the 'thousand-yard stare' one saw on 'so many people' on Phnom Penh's streets, and of how Cambodians had forgotten how to care for their children. The agent demanded to know why I hadn't written about that.

I hadn't written about that because, as far as I was concerned, it wasn't true. Thousand-yard stares were rare – you saw more on New York or London streets. Cambodians loved their children, like anyone else; there were good parents, and bad parents, many made so by circumstance as much as character, just like anywhere else. And, despite everything, Cambodians laughed a lot. The article's author had been selling stereotypes, selling Cambodians short to fit the article's preconceptions. He had probably been desperate for something to file.

By the time you read this, much of what I've written will be out of date. Cambodia will continue to change. Hardy tourists on the South-east Asian run will continue to visit. Phnom Penh won't be so very dangerous, the countryside will be so only if the traveller's unlucky. Skirmishes of guerilla war will go on for a while. The good guys and the bad guys will not be easily defined. The only thing you can rely on is that anyone who confidently assures you they really know what's happening in Cambodia, and why, is probably wrong.

UNTAC and the election absolved the rest of the world of guilt over Cambodia's future, at least in their own eyes, but whether that election was the answer to the country's enduring instability is still undecided. It may be that Cambodia is yet swallowed by the Tiger or the Crocodile, or both. Most likely, Cambodia will become a *de facto*, if not *de jure*, economic colony to its richer South-east Asian neighbours. Cambodia will continue to fascinate those who see in it a different Asia, one which is not yuppified and moving toward the twenty-first century, but one where the Wild West is a more applicable comparison than Wall Street.

The good things in Cambodia will stay. The gold-costumed apsaras will still dance, the rice fields will still burst into life-giving green each rainy season. Angkor will remain, and the hard work and hopefully Cambodians' good humour. They will continue to rebuild their country. But the bad will take some time to go.

It's Cambodia.

All Orion/Phoenix titles are available at your local bookshop or from the following address:

> Littlehampton Book Services
> Cash Sales Department L
> 14 Eldon Way, Lineside Industrial Estate
> Littlehampton
> West Sussex BN17 7HE
>
> *telephone* 01903 721596, *facsimile* 01903 730914

Payment can either be made by credit card (Visa and Mastercard accepted) or by sending a cheque or postal order made payable to *Littlehampton Book Services.*
DO NOT SEND CASH OR CURRENCY.

Please add the following to cover postage and packing

UK and BFPO:
£1.50 for the first book, and 50P for each additional book to a maximum of £3.50

Overseas and Eire:
£2.50 for the first book plus £1.00 for the second book and 50p for each additional book ordered

---

BLOCK CAPITALS PLEASE

name of cardholder ....
address of cardholder ....

delivery address
(if different from cardholder)
....
....
....
....

postcode ....

postcode ....

☐ I enclose my remittance for £............................

☐ please debit my Mastercard/Visa (delete as appropriate)

card number ☐☐☐☐ ☐☐☐☐ ☐☐☐☐ ☐☐☐☐

expiry date ☐☐☐☐

signature ....

prices and availability are subject to change without notice